P9-AQL-984

EX

MOUNT MARY COLLEGE

SAINT IGNATIUS

SAINT IGNATIUS

By CHRISTOPHER HOLLIS

HARPER & BROTHERS PUBLISHERS

NEW YORK AND LONDON

1931

THIS BOOK
is dedicated to
MY WIFE, AND ALSO MY SON,
in the unlikely event of its not being
' pulped ' long before he has learnt to read.

The author wishes to express his thanks to Mr. V. F. Revely for his kindness in reading the proofs.

BALLAD OF OUR LADY OF MANRESA

Queen of the skies, almerciable Queen,
  Queen of our world the wind will blow away,
Through whom Ignatius, like a sword, cut clean
  Across a startled, cankered age, oh, say,
  Shall we not love your lover, Mother of May,
    Who for love's sake turned love's iconoclast.
By the dear merits of Manresa pray
    That Jesus Christ receive this soul at last.

Your son was Xavier, gentle and serene;
  That other Francis, too, who puffed away
The empty, luscious fruits that might have been
  His with the great ones of a little day;
  Young Aloysius, too; Campion, the gay,
    Unquestioning soldier, sweet enthusiast.
By the dear merits of Manresa pray
    That Jesus Christ receive this soul at last.

Kind Mother, these, the heroic spirits, had seen
  The vision splendid and the fiend at bay.
Earth was a foolish toy, a jest obscene
  And death for them a boon for which to pray;
  He beckoned and they did not yearn to stay
    But glad to their triumphant rest they passed.
By the dear merits of Manresa pray
    That Jesus Christ receive this soul at last.

ENVOI

Mother, for us there waits the Judgement Day.
  The world we dared not turn from holds us fast.
By the dear merits of Manresa pray
    That Jesus Christ receive this soul at last.

CONTENTS

SAINT IGNATIUS

CHAPTER I

THE IMPORTANCE OF BEING HOLY

I BEGAN this book with the intention of quoting my authorities
and giving chapter-and-verse references for all its statements.
To do so, I soon came to see, would be to mislead the reader.
Except perhaps for a small detail to be elucidated or corrected
here or there, such, for instance, as that of the date of his birth,
whatever historical research had to be done on the life of St.
Ignatius has been done once and for all. Father Tacchi
Venturi's *Storia della Compagnia di Gesù in Italia* and the late
Father Astrain's *Historia de la Compania de Jesus en la Assistencia
de Espana* between them contain

" all
Ye know on earth and all ye need to know "

about St. Ignatius. All the evidence concerning the early
history of the Society is collected into the *Monumenta Societatis
Jesu*, published by the Spanish Jesuits. For lighter readers
Father Astrain, in the year 1921, the fourth centenary of St.
Ignatius' conversion, wrote a short, popular life of the saint
which has been translated into English by Father Hull. At
about the same time Father Pollen wrote his *St. Ignatius Loyola*,
a biographical essay rather than a full biography. The most
complete study of St. Ignatius in English came in 1923 from the
pen of an American non-Catholic, Mr. Sedgwick. This work
is particularly clear and good in its estimate of St. Ignatius'
relation to the general historical movements of his time. Another
American non-Catholic work, that of van Dyke, deserves
honourable mention.

There remain to mention the two works most familiar to the general English reader—Stewart Rose (Lady Buchan's) *Ignatius Loyola* and Francis Thompson's *St. Ignatius Loyola*—works which, though published before the results of the most recent research were made known, are yet perfectly reliable on everything but a few details of little importance.

It is clear then that the historian's work is already done. If it were not I should certainly not be writing this book, for I am no scholar, and the tasks of historical research are for more learned men than I. My interest is in a psychological rather than a historical problem. If it were true that St. Ignatius was a busy ecclesiastical politician who was canonised for being clever enough to found the Jesuits, in much the same way that Lord Northcliffe was made a peer for being clever enough to think of the *Daily Mail*, the historical problems would be the important problems of his life. But the political interpretation is, of course, fantastically false. The fundamental life of St. Ignatius was his spiritual life. It is true that the living of his spiritual life forced him into contact with the political problems of his day and that he there showed himself possessed of a capacity which places him in the very first rank of European statesmen, but those gifts which put him into the company of Richelieu and of Chatham were the least of his gifts. St. Ignatius' life was a spiritual life, and of a man's spiritual experiences there can in the long run be no authority but himself. Ever since he published his *Spiritual Exercises* and dictated to Nadal the account of his early life, ever since Ribadaneira and Polanco, Gonzalez and Laynez and the others who knew him in the flesh have told us what they had to tell us about him, we have really known everything that we can ever hope to know.

The question then that I asked myself before I began to write this book, and that I have asked myself again and again during the writing of it, is, " Granted that St. Ignatius was such a man, why did he behave as he did ? " Or, to generalise it, " What is the point of being a saint ? "

To many searchers after truth, one of the greatest obstacles to the Faith is that of popular Lives of the Saints. There are honourable exceptions, such as Father Martindale's *Vocation of St. Aloysius Gonzaga*—but nine out of ten of such biographies cannot but seem to the general reader intolerably dishonest. I do not refer to the biography of the sceptic who patronisingly condemns the saint's excesses of sanctity by some standard of Victorian suburban respectability or healthy Public-School heartiness. Such a writer is irritating but honest. I refer to the biography of the pious believer. The pious believer was only too often, I used to feel when I first came across Lives of the Saints, dishonest, and, as often as not, the more pious the hagiographer, the more dishonest the hagiography.

The dishonesty was this. We would read how the saint on a sudden impulse gave away all his wealth, how he submitted himself to incredible mortifications, how he starved himself, how he flogged himself. In such biographies as those that I have in mind all these feats would be recorded with pious approval but with no critical examination at all; those who tried to restrain the saint from them would be dismissed as blind children of the world, whom the saint, the reader, the writer and (for all I know) the publisher were united in thinking of as very miserable creatures. And yet I always used to wonder whether the writers of these biographies would have been so certainly delighted if some friend or relation of theirs had started to behave as their saint behaved. Was it an admirable thing for the saint to have gone his forty days without food, to have flogged himself till the blood ran, to have lived in a cave on the mountains or performed whatever other feat of austerity he may have performed ? If so, ought we to go and do likewise ? If not, why not ?

I do not wish to be misunderstood. When I say " If not, why not ? " I put it as a real and not as a rhetorical question. I did not then believe that the lesson that we ought to learn from the saints was to imitate their lives in every external detail, nor, as the reader of this book will find, do I believe that now. But I did believe, and do believe, that merely to record incredible feats of austerity and pass on without any explanation does more harm than good. The only result of it is that we come to feel, whatever we may continue to say with our lips, that a saint is of a quite different substance from ourselves, that his life is lived on a plane so fantastically different from ours that it is quite impossible for us to expect to learn any lesson from it at all.

The other day a young friend of mine found me reading a book about St. Ignatius. He asked me why I was reading it. I said, " Because I have to write about him." " Worse and worse," he answered. I asked him why he did not like St. Ignatius. He said that he found him a bore.

My friend was as pious as a person of his age ought to be, as intelligent as there is any sense in anyone being, and had good taste and an excellent sense of humour. I understood very well why he had said what he had said and I liked him the better for it.

I asked him if there were any saints whom he liked. He said that there were not. He found St. Aloysius particularly detestable, but he did not care for any of them. Yet after reflection he admitted that he quite liked St. Pancras.

I said, " So you do not want to be a saint then ? "

He said, " No, I want to be a policeman."

I admitted to him that, if there had not been authority to teach me better, I should probably consider the attitude towards life of a Chaucer to be saner than that of any of the saints—the attitude which admits the ultimate truths and their checks on conduct but applies itself to the extraction from life of all its permitted fun. For a measured contempt for the passing baubles of this world is a mark not of sanctity but of common sense. Yet there is a subtle difference between St. Paul, who used the world as though he used it not, and Shakespeare, or rather Antonio, who held the world but as the world, and my instinct is to side with Antonio. It is only the compulsion of authority which in the first place could ever have brought me to St. Paul. My friend said that he, too, liked Chaucer, but for the moment would I lend him *Alice Through the Looking Glass* ? I did and he went away.

I am a Catholic and therefore believe that one whom the Church calls saint deserves my honour. Indeed, I would not

be so foolish as to refuse honour to Ignatius of Loyola, even
had the Church not canonised him. Therefore, when I come
to his life, I come not to teach but to learn. At the same time
I am a normal member of the 20th-century English public,
writing for that normal public among which I live. Therefore
in writing of St. Ignatius I have tried to follow what seemed
to me to be the only intellectually honest policy. Private fads
I have endeavoured to spare you. But wherever in the record
of St. Ignatius' life I have come across him doing things which
we, normal people of England, not only do not do but even
do not think ourselves under obligation to do, I have tried to
discover and to explain why it was that St. Ignatius did this
thing. An essay in interpretative biography some might call
this book, but I shrink a little from such a title. To me it has
been a voyage of discovery rather than an essay in interpretation.
I have learnt from my study many things about St. Ignatius
which I had not understood before, and I shall think my trouble
well repaid if through this book any others should come to
understand him a little better than they did before.

Having said so much, I cannot but add in honesty that everything which I have set out to do was done once and for all,
finally and perfectly in the first life of St. Ignatius that was ever
written in English, in the fourth quarter of the 17th century.
The authorship of that book is not quite beyond dispute, but
there is reason to think that it was written—or at least translated from the French of Bouhours—by the first English writer
of his day and one of the grandest Englishmen of all time—the
great John Dryden. There is no kind of fault to be found
with it, except the one damning fault that nobody reads it.
Why a certain small proportion of the public should be willing
to read a life of St. Ignatius written by me, when no one at all
is willing to read one written by Dryden, I cannot imagine.
It seems to me insanity. For myself I would read Dryden
morning, noon and night and every day of the week, while
nothing on earth would induce me to read myself. But one
must take the mad world as one finds it. And the result of the
deluge with which the publishers submerge the poor reading

public of the 20th century, of the tumult and the shouting which never dies—which never even dies down—is that there has not been a time since letters began when people have fallen into so deep an ignorance of the great creative work of the score or so of men through the ages who should really be the leaders of the world's thought.   Again and again one comes across intelligent people, voracious readers, who yet never read a book by an author who wrote before the 20th century.   And therefore if the work of such a man as Dryden is to survive, it can only survive in a poor, sad, silly way by being done all over again by a modern hack.   In a way it is a piece of luck for the hack, but it is a little mad.   If you have a grain of sense, burn my book when you have got this far (the library from whom you have borrowed it will not much mind) and go and read Dryden instead.

There are some of St. Ignatius' opinions and actions which it is not at first hearing easy to understand.   It is but common sense and sensible humility that, instead of hastily condemning, one should expect that St. Ignatius had good reason for what he said or did.   Yet even before the teachings of such a man it is not permissible to abdicate intellectual independence.   As he himself commanded at the beginning of the *Spiritual Exercises*, you must " preserve always your liberty of mind ; see that you lose it not by anyone's authority nor by any event whatsoever." Where one cannot agree, it is but honest frankly to say so— the more frankly, the more honest.

The body of this book will be filled with the account of St. Ignatius' greatness.   To guard myself against the charge of dishonest and uncritical eulogy, it is only fair that I state what seem to me to be his two great deficiencies.   This I do, not because I think that I am wiser than he, but because I know that he was wiser than I, because I think it very probable that a man, whom I can see to have been right ninety-nine times out of a hundred, was also right the hundredth time, though I cannot see it.   Intellectual honesty forbids me from saying that he was right until I can understand the reason ; common sense teaches me that there probably is a reason if only I could understand it. So, though the confession is probably but a confession of my own stupidity, it is well to make it, if only in order that the reader who understands more than I may be put on his guard against my blindness.

The two deficiencies in St. Ignatius then seem to me to be, first, the lack of a capacity for intellectual pleasure ; second, the lack of delight in the share and contemplation of the pageant of vivid life.

Take the first point. I shall have occasion to discuss St. Ignatius' relation to Erasmus and to all the new learning of the Renaissance, and shall give my opinion that there was a great deal to be said in favour of his suspicion of much that passed for new learning. But in honesty, I think, it must be admitted that, while he condemned Erasmus, he never at all understood what is to such a man as Erasmus one of the keenest delights of life—the delight in knowing simply for the sake of knowing. As little did he understand the artist's delight in creating simply for the sake of creating, or that purest of all intellectual pleasures, the fun of doing geometry in one's head. It was not that he denied himself these pleasures through asceticism. In his asceticism he denied himself the pleasures of the flesh, but the pleasures of the intellect never came to him at all, whether as temptations to be rejected or as glories to be received.

As to the second charge, I do not criticise St. Ignatius because he restricted the intercourse of himself and his followers with the world. They had a special vocation, and for those of the vocation such restrictions are necessary. Indeed, he was criticised by such people as the hermit, Antonio, for not restricting it enough. I am for the moment concerned not with his policy but with his uncurbed likes and dislikes, and I cannot express what I mean better than by saying that I do not feel that it would ever have occurred to him that it was great fun to go to Blackpool. *Immenso hominum salutis desiderio exarsit.* Had he gone to Blackpool, he would have yearned and hungered for the souls of the people there. He was no Puritan ; he would not have condemned them for their innocent pleasures. But I cannot think of him revelling in the pageantry of vivid exist-

ence, feeling it grand to be alive in the m̶ ̶ of so much living,
as the gorgeous soul of Geoffrey Chauc̶ would have felt.
And this is not because St. Ignatius was a sai̶ ̶nd Chaucer was
not.   It is perhaps because St. Ignatius was ̶ ̶entleman, and,
to tell the truth, never quite got over it, but, wha̶ ̶er the reason,
he did quite lack the grand Herodotean, Chauceria̶ Villonesque,
Rabelaisian, Cellinian, Cervantesque, Fieldingian̶ ̶ohnsonian,
Dickensian spirit—lacked it as other saints have n̶ lacked it.
Imagine the great cry of joy with which St. Francis̶ ̶uld have
greeted the illuminations of Blackpool.   How good G̶ was to
permit so lovely a spectacle !   Was it not evidence of H̶ ̶ ̶ood-
ness that the world which He had given to us was so gl̶ ̶us ?
Do not Brother Penny-in-the-Slot and Sister Waterwhee̶ ̶ng
His praises ?   But to St. Ignatius the service of the greater g̶ ̶y
of God was a more dour, less poetical service—a service ̶ ̶
solitary places and for Manresa cave.

I cannot imagine St. Ignatius on a waterwheel.   It is not that
the General of the Jesuits would have shrunk from the scandal
that might have been caused by such a recreation, but that it
would never have occurred to Inigo of Loyola to behave thus.
Yet how grand a thing is the loud, crowded Chaucerian life,
that embracing zest for all created things, that interest in everything from the light in the eye of a frightened hare or the table
manners of a fussy woman up to the tremendous throne of the
" almighty and almerciable Queen of Heaven."

" How good is man's life, the mere living !   How fit to employ
All the heart and the soul and the senses for ever in joy."

In all the world there is not language enough to praise it as it
deserves.

Life is so good, there is so much goodness in man that there
are moods in which we are inclined to feel that the Chaucerian
life is enough, that the sterner Ignatian way is a savage way.
But it is the sad, and yet ultima ely merciful, truth that this is
not so.   For, lest we should love this world too much, God
ordains that sometimes the laughter and the fun should be on
the Devil's side.   Does the Chaucerian life breed men of a fibre

strong enough to stand up for the good things when the laughter and the fun is all on the other side? The sad answer of the 16th century was that it did not. The Chaucer of the 15th century was ready to " smell a Lollard in the wind " and laugh on, but, when worse men than the Lollards came to rule in England, the Chaucers of the 16th century were not of the type that was willing to lose all so that the Faith be saved. It was then that the world came to need its St. Ignatiuses.

CHAPTER II

IF you travel from Paris to Madrid the train takes you round the western end of the Pyrenees. You pass Biarritz, the Brighton of France, which glares across the bay at San Sebastian, the Brighton of Spain, and, travelling on, you come soon to the frontier town of Hendaye, whence come the evil rumours that the journalists make up. You continue on your journey in a Spanish train which winds through a country that has been famous in the wars of Europe for a millennium and a half from the days of Charlemagne to those of Wellington. A little to your left lies Pampeluna; a little beyond it the great pass of Roncesvalles, where

> " To the Haut King came at morn
> Dead Roland on a doubtful horn "

and where

> " *Par grand iror chevalchet Charlemaigne
> Desor sa broigne li gist sa barbe blanche,*"

whither " God sent down His cherubim and St. Michael of the Peril, and St. Gabriel joined them, and they bore the Count's soul to Paradise." It is a magic country, and the bus which takes you to it leaves St. Jean Pied-de-Port just after lunch. You are in the diocese of Vittoria, before which city, in 1813, the Duke of Wellington, reinforced for the first time in English history by a band of Army Chaplains, who had been sent out by special request in order to " restrain the enthusiasm " of the troops, drove helter-skelter from the field the wine-skin, Joseph Bonaparte. At San Sebastian, as I have said, the rich are bathing.

The diocese is the diocese of Vittoria, but you are in the

province of Guipizcoa. And in Guipizcoa, in the little town of Azpeytia, was born Ignatius of Loyola. His parents were Beltram Janez de Onaz y Loyola and Maria Saenz di Licona y Balda. His family was a good one. His father was not only a noble, but also one of the "*parientes mayores*," who had the privilege of a personal invitation from the sovereign whenever the nobility of Spain were summoned to do homage. There was only one other such noble in Guipizcoa.

St. Ignatius was, then, by birth a gentleman. The word is a confusing word, for people are apt to use it indiscriminately in either of two senses, meaning at one moment a person who enjoys from birth some wealth and a certain position in the State, at another one who has a keener sense of honour than his fellows. Whether this keener sense is more likely to be found in the rich than the poor is debatable. Certainly the authority of the Gospel would not make us inclined to expect it, and as we look round the world we are inclined to say that, whatever objections men may bring against the other teachings of the Christian religion, its teaching of the great danger of riches is one which is proved certainly true by the experience of every day. We expect to find in a gentleman certain valuable quali-ties, but those qualities are very different from the qualities of a saint. The battles of Manresa are not, as a rule, won on the playing fields of Eton. Yet, when we look through the history of the Church, we find that a surprisingly large proportion of her saints were gentlemen by birth. Take, in particular, the founders of religious orders. There were, I suppose, people in Florence who would have turned up their noses at the Ber-nardones, for they had made their money within recent memory instead of merely inheriting it. But St. Benedict, St. Dominic and St. Ignatius—so different from one another in so many other ways—were at least alike in these two respects, that all three of them were gentlemen and all three of them were saints.

It is not an irrelevancy or a flippancy to meditate on this. The pious are sometimes apt to say, " What does it matter what a man was in the world so long as he served God ? Are we not all equal in the sight of God ?" It is true enough that we are all equal in the sight of God. God does not love any of us the better for having been at a public school. As I once heard a politician very truly remark, " Several of the Apostles were working men." Yet language which refuses to inquire into a man's worldly position is not language of which St. Ignatius would have approved. It was his saying rather that the qualities which make for success in the world were also the qualities which make for success in the spiritual life. This was not, as is sometimes thought, a confession of *Realpolitik*. He did not say that the conduct which makes for success in the world makes also for success in the spiritual life. (A strange rewriting there would have to be of the ecclesiastical calendar if that were true—Blessed Frederick the Great; St. Talleyrand, pray for us.) St. Ignatius said " the qualities." Now there is no doubt that a man born to wealth and an assured position in the world, exposed, as he is, to a thousand terrible temptations of pride and greed, yet at the same time has a greater capacity for leadership than others. This capacity for leadership is not a virtue ; it is a quality. You may lead people right or you may lead them wrong. But it is a quality the possession of which it is clearly fatuous merely to neglect. For, used rightly, it can be used, as it has been used by the gentlemen-saints, for the greater glory of God. Saints have been gentlemen ; that is to say, saints have been brought up in conditions from which they could easily have acquired great riches had they wished to do so. I do not think that there has ever been a saint who did actually enjoy great riches during his mature years. For the love of riches is not compatible with the love of holiness. For " where the treasure is there will the heart be also." Nor, it is hardly necessary to add, though there have been saints who have been gentlemen, have there ever been saints who have been snobs. For snobbery is the most directly anti-Christian of all the vices.

The date of Ignatius' birth, as of that of so many of the notable people of the twilight time of the Middle Ages, is not absolutely certain. He himself says that his conversion took place in his twenty-sixth year, and the date of his conversion was certainly 1521—according to which he would be born in 1495 or 1496. However, there is a weight of counter-evidence, which has always been accepted by most of his biographers, that he was really born in 1491, though Mr. Sedgwick argues for 1494. It is a matter of small importance and one that can never be certainly settled. Whatever the exact date, what a time it was for a Spaniard to be born into ! In the 8th century the new vigour of the Mahommedan had swarmed across the African straits, had rapidly overrun all Spain, crossed the Pyrenees and looked for a time as if it might establish itself in the very heart of Christendom. By the grace of St. Martin, Charles Martel met and broke it in the fields of Touraine in the year 732. The tide was turned and receded back again behind the Pyrenees. But it was to be another seven hundred and fifty desperate years before Spain was to be united and wholly Christian. For three-quarters of a millennium she was to be the frontier battlefield of Christendom. At last, in 1469—twenty-two years before St. Ignatius' birth, if we date that birth 1491—Isabella, the daughter of John II. of Castille, married Ferdinand, the son of John II. of Aragon. In 1474 Isabella succeeded her brother as Queen of Castille. In 1479 Ferdinand succeeded his father as King of Aragon. In 1492 by the reduction of Granada the last Mahommedan power in Spain was destroyed. The long disunion and the long division were at last ended.

For eight hundred years Spain had been the desperate defender of Christian things. That long task was at last accomplished. What was the new task that lay before her ? To some it seemed that Providence itself had given a clear answer. For in the very year in which the conquest of Granada brought to an end Spain's old struggle Christopher Columbus made for her the first of his American discoveries. Were not the purposes of the Almighty most evident ? An old era was ended, the treachery had not yet been perpetrated, and Europe, it seemed, was saved. A new era was dawning, and the Cross, triumphant in the Old World, must be carried in triumph to the New. It was the task of Spain to give to the Americas that divine Faith which she had preserved for Europe.

Thus the romantic and the pious, but Beltram Janez de Lonaz y Loyola was not of them. We do not know much of St. Ignatius' parents. His mother died when he was but a child. His early years he lived under the influence of his father. Of Beltram a persistent tradition has left us a clear and probable picture. He was of a type common among well-to-do Catholics of the 16th, of the 20th, and of every century. Catholic by tradition, by environment and in the practice of all that was of obligation, he was, if a stern man, yet probably at bottom kind, certainly conscientious, what is known in the expressive slang phrase as " straight." He would have been honestly both angry and amazed had anyone suggested to him that he was not a good Catholic. Did he not every year make the pilgrimage to St. James of Compostella and take his sons with him—a very considerable journey—the length of the north coast of Spain? When the end came he doubtless received the Last Sacraments and God, let us pray, has accepted his soul. Yet he was of the world. Paying a lip service to the things of the spirit, yet in practice he taught his son in making the decisions of life to look always to worldly advantage. The object of life was to be what is known as " a success."

Of the details of St. Ignatius' life we do not know much. Like St. Augustine, he once robbed an orchard, as he himself afterwards confessed, and there is an incomplete record of an Eastcheap-taverny escapade in which Ignatius and an elder brother played a part of some violence—it is not clear exactly what.

When he was but a boy Ignatius left his father's house, perhaps because it was thought desirable that he should come under female influence, and went to live at Arevalo in Castille with Dona Maria de Guevara, his aunt. Dona Maria was a pious woman, but she was not allowed, even had she been able to do so, to exercise over her nephew sufficient influence to turn him from the path of success that Beltram had marked out for him. As soon as he was old enough he was taken into the household

of Juan Velasquez de Cuellar, contador mayor to Ferdinand
and Isabella. The post was one which would bring him from
time to time to the royal court. The career was launched.

Ignatius kept his post up to the death of Velasquez in 1517
—that is to say, in his twenty-sixth year, if we again accept
1491 as the year of his birth—and of these twenty-six years he
afterwards said, " Up to his twenty-sixth year he was entirely
given up to the vanities of the world; but that he especially
delighted in martial exercises, being led thereto by an ardent
and innate desire of military glory." As the corregidor of
Guipizcoa somewhat pompously expressed it, when Ignatius
was had up before him because of the brawl just referred to,
"He displayed the insignia not of celestial but of earthly
soldiery."

A dwarf of a man, he stood but five feet one and three-quarters, but, like so many little men, he made up in self-assertion
what he lacked in inches, and felt that he must assert that self
which Nature would not assert for him. He earned for himself
the reputation of a fop and a gallant, with a name for good
humour and for the love of hearty laughter. He was imagina-
tive in a strange way, possessed a quite extraordinary capacity
for visualising the object of his imagination in concrete form,
and, though his soul was emotional rather than poetic, yet he
gave much of his spare time to the scribbling of sonnets and
canzones. Even during these years his poetry was often of a
religious character, but more often it was addressed to the lady
of his ardent affections.

Who was this lady of Ignatius' sonnets? He has nowhere
told us her name. Some have thought that she was but a creature of the poet's imagination, but that has been said of every
poet's *inamorata* from the time of Horace to our own. I think
that poets are a coarser lot than commentators and prefer the
flesh and blood, and St. Ignatius' very definite statement about
her more than noble rank can hardly refer to a lady of the fancy.
In this tantalising phrase, before which the curiosity of his
biographers cannot fail to be aroused, he told Gonzales that she
was "not a countess nor a duchess but of a rank more exalted

than either "—that is to say, I suppose, she was of royal blood. According to Genelli, there were at that time only two princesses at the Spanish court to whom he can have been referring. The one was Princess Catherine, daughter of the Archduke Philip of Austria and mad Queen Joanna, and later to be the wife of that King John III. of Portugal whom we shall find playing a considerable part in the first years of the history of the Society of Jesus. The Archduke Philip, however, died about this time, Ferdinand, according to Ferreras, " receiving the news of his death with great resignation to the will of God " —which was hardly surprising, seeing that he had always loathed the sight of him—and Catherine was kept too busy looking after her mad mother to have much time to spare for romance.

Genelli's other candidate was Germaine de Foix, the young French princess, the second wife of King Ferdinand. Stewart Rose parades two more candidates for the honour of Ignatius' devotion. Ferdinand, King of Naples, had married Ferdinand of Aragon's sister, Joanna. Ferdinand of Naples was dead and his widow and daughter, also called Joanna, were given a home by the Spanish royal family at Valencia. It is this daughter whom Stewart Rose imagines to have been the object of Ignatius' devotion.

However that may be, it is certain that Ignatius ever afterwards referred to these years of his life as years during which he lived as a great sinner. Exactly of what small sins he was guilty we do not certainly know, but his was no theatrical character and he hated exaggerated talk. The pretence that he meant no more by his confessions than that during these careless years his thoughts were not continuously fixed on things above is not at all probable. There is no reasonable doubt that he was guilty of some of those sins of passion which are in a young man both the most pardonable and the most dangerous of all sins. " He was free in making love to women," Father Polanco says of him. He gave himself, says Maffei, to " *caecos errores et vitia*."

If it be so, it is but another illustration of the great Ignatian principle that the qualities which bring success in the world are also the qualities which bring success in the spiritual life.

Ignatius was, above all things else, a great lover. Now if a young man is guilty of sins of meanness or of treachery or of gross selfishness, these sins are not only evil of themselves but they are evidence of gross and deep blemishes in the character. But the sins of the flesh argue no such deep baseness. It is rather the attractive qualities which often lead youth to these sins—a love of beauty, a sensitiveness to the romance of life and, above all, a lovable capacity for affection. Those harsh souls who condemn most brutally have often only not fallen into the sinner's vices because they are quite incapable of his virtues. Yet, because such sins are not to be hardly blamed, that does not mean that, in the loose phrase, they "do not matter." They are indeed an expression of affection, which is attractive, but they are a misdirection of it. The expression is, to use the Ignatian phrase, inordinate.

In youth the will is weak and untrained, and the degree of moral responsibility difficult to assess, but the dangers are unfortunately not wholly dependent upon the immediate moral responsibility. For the danger of sex is that by its very nature it must either be controlled or it comes wholly to dominate. It is perhaps a generous, lovable, unselfish person who surrenders himself to these temptations, and it may be that this is his only fault and that in all else he is the superior of his neighbours. But, if his indulgence is allowed to go on unchecked, it soon happens that this indulgence, which is, as it were, the product of his attractive nature, begins to turn on and oust all his virtues. A gross and animal selfishness comes to dominate all his nature, and he is so tightly gripped by his vice that, except through especial mercy, escape is impossible, and he comes at length to that most pitiable condition of old age, where desire remains and power of satisfaction has perished.

The tradition, then, which looks on the sexual as among the most dangerous of the sins is a true tradition. A society that neglects it must perish or sink to impotence. And yet it is only an uncomprehending and stunted mind which shrinks back from those whom a somewhat crude phraseology describes as "strongly sexed," but whom I should rather prefer to call "great lovers." The saints have all, I think, been great lovers, men and women of strong passions, and a fair proportion of them—from St. Mary Magdalene and St. Augustine onwards— have been men and women whose strong passions led them sadly astray before they came to the love of God. A certain type of mind is always anxious to explain of the visions of a mystic, such as, say, St. Catherine of Siena, that they are but sublimations of sex. The believer is apt angrily to repudiate such theories, but to me it always seems that they are not so much falsehoods as topsy-turvy truths. It is, of course, a gross begging of the question indiscriminately to insert the adjective "sexual" every time that you use the word "love." Sexual love is a particular sort of love ; mystical love is another sort of love. But it is true that the forms of love have this relation— that both the one and the other presuppose a strong capacity for affection, which may be directed either into the one channel or the other, presuppose a strongly "conative" nature, as the psychologist Jung calls it. Every Don Juan was once a poten- tial saint ; every saint was once a potential debauchee or harlot.

Even among the Don Juans who are far from saints, among those sinners who do not so very notoriously repent, I have a sneaking feeling—I do not know—that perhaps a François Villon or two may creep into heaven before some respectable citizens who left several of the commandments unbroken. For to love is a very great thing, and even to those *deteriora sequentes* it will surely avail much if they can claim *meliora vidisse et probasse.*

As I have already said, and as I shall insist again and again— for it is the key to his character—St. Ignatius was a great lover. The whole demand of his spirit was a demand to love.

> "Love, thou art absolute, sole lord
> Of life and death,"

he would have cried with Crashaw, or, as he himself put it in a quaint and delicious phrase in one of his letters, " it is always very profitable to live in love." If he was a soldier, it was the romance and not the discipline of soldiering which appealed to him. His intelligence, indeed, taught him the necessity for discipline and obedience and subordination, but anyone who imagines that, like some horrible ecclesiastical drill-sergeant, he loved ordering people about simply for the fun of ordering them understands little of his character. The discipline was a means; the end was love, and every act of his life can only be understood if we look at it as an expression of this imperious demand to love—every act of his life, and not least that in which he bound himself by a vow of chastity. For in the vow of chastity the priest does, certainly, deny himself a good thing—the love of the creature. But he denies it only that he may enjoy more certainly a better—the love of the Creator, in Whose image the creature was made.

For a time Ignatius of the world thought that his demand for love might find satisfaction in a creature—thought perhaps that he, like most of us, could only come to the love of the Creator through the love of the creature. After Manresa all that was changed. He had seen his God face to face, and thenceforward nothing but the direct love of God could suffice.

In the early days of 1516 the great bell of Villila, in the metal of which, as the story went, was melted one of the thirty pieces of silver which were given to Judas, tolled out of itself. It was the presage that some great man was about to die. Sure enough, a few days later, Ferdinand of Aragon died at Madrigalejo, and Velasquez, Ignatius' master, followed him in 1517. Ignatius took the opportunity to break with the futilities of court life, of which he was beginning to grow weary, and to seek for better fortune in the wars.

Before Ferdinand could claim that he had achieved the grand task of the unification of Spain beneath his sceptre, it was necessary not only that the Moors should be expelled from Granada, but also that the little kingdom of Navarre up in the north should be brought under the central power and the Spanish frontier thus carried to its natural boundary of the Pyrenees. Ferdinand's father, John II., had married as his first wife Blanche, the Queen of Navarre, and for a short time the kingdom of Aragon and Navarre had thus been under a single rule. But, while Aragon had descended to Ferdinand, Navarre had gone to his half-sister, Eleanor, and had passed after her death to her grandchildren. Francis Phœbus held the throne from 1479 to 1483, and Catherine, his sister, wife of Jean d'Albret, a wealthy neighbour of Navarre on the French side, from 1483 to 1514. The dynasty was foreign in sympathy and policy, and the people were but little attached to it. Local politics were little more than a running feud between the two powerful family factions of the Beaumonts and the Grammonts, the Spaniards always supporting the Beaumonts and the French the Grammonts.

In 1511 the Pope, the Emperor, Venice, Ferdinand and Henry VIII. of England formed a Holy League against the King of France. An English army, under the Marquis of Dorset, established itself in Ignatius' native province of Guipizcoa and a joint Anglo-Spanish invasion of France was planned. Ferdinand, seeing his opportunity, demanded free passage for his troops through the territory of Navarre. Jean d'Albret, the king-consort, refused, and sought the alliance of the French. Ferdinand's reply was to send in the Duke of Alva. The Beaumont faction rallied to the Spanish side, and without difficulty the invaders were able to take possession of the main Navarrese fortress of Pampeluna. Soon the whole little kingdom was in Spanish hands. At first Ferdinand pretended that his occupation was merely for military purposes and for the duration of the war, but after a little he judged it possible to throw off the mask and boldly proclaimed himself King of Navarre. A French expedition made one effort to reconquer the land, but it failed to take Pampeluna, and in 1513 the Navarrese Cortes swore allegiance to Ferdinand and the French abandoned their allies by concluding a truce.

Thus things remained until Ferdinand's death in 1516. The nominal Queen of Castile and Aragon was now mad Joanna. Those growlings of discontent, which always succeed a long reign, were beginning to make themselves heard. Charles, Joanna's son, was absent in Flanders. Jean d'Albret thought that the time had come for a bid for the recovery of the lost throne. He laid siege to St. Jean Pied-de-Port in French Navarre, " foot of the gate " of Roncesvalles, where is to-day the terminus of the railway and whence the motor-buses go up over the pass where Roland was trapped a millennium and more ago. During Charles' absence, however, the power in Spain was in the hands of one of the most remarkable and vigorous men of his age, the octogenarian Franciscan, Cardinal Ximenes. Ximenes easily defeated d'Albret, strengthened the fortress of Pampeluna, where he established a permanent Castilian garrison, and rased all the other fortresses of Navarre to the ground.

Some of the surrounding towns, alarmed at the hostility of the Government to their liberties, had sought to profit from the disturbance of the Navarrese revolt and had risen in rebellion. Punitive expeditions had to be sent out, and the young Ignatius was put at the head of one of them, which marched against the Biscayan town of Najera. Najera was captured by assault, and the young captain was thought to have taken the first steps in his successful military career. Honour, not riches, was his mistress, and, with a chivalric spirit worthy of a budding young Bayard, he refused to claim for himself any share in the spoils of the captured town.

In the next year, 1517, young Charles returned from Flanders. Ximenes was dismissed and the Flemish advisers installed in all the positions of power. The towns rose in revolt and for four years Spain was devastated by the horrors of the civil war of the Communeros. Perhaps the most important of the rebel leaders was Juan de Padilla, son of the Commendador, or Grand Seneschal, of Castile. Padilla's wife, seeing the desperate state of her husband's fortunes, conceived the plan of creating a diversion in his favour by appealing to the French King to revive the claims of the dynasty of Navarre. There was ample excuse for doing so, for by the Treaty of Noyon, in October, 1516, Charles in return for French friendship had promised to do justice to the claims of the d'Albrets. For five years he had made no attempt to fulfil this promise. Jean d'Albert and

Catherine were by now dead, and the Navarrese claimant was
their son, Henry. Francis I. of France therefore permitted an
army to be levied in France in Henry's name, put it under the
command of André de Foix de l'Esparre, who owed his appointment less to his military talents than to the accident that he was
the brother of the beautiful Countess of Châteaubriand, and
sent it over the frontier into Navarre. In its ranks there marched
two brothers of Francis Xavier.

Ximenes' schemes for the fortification of Pampeluna were
not yet completed, and the Spaniards not prepared to meet the
attack immediately. The population, as often happens with
the population of a small state that lies sandwiched between
two large ones, was apt to prefer whichever of its powerful
neighbours did not happen at the moment to be present. The
French had the advantage of absence, and therefore were on the
whole welcomed as deliverers from the Spaniards. They were
thus able to penetrate with very little resistance right up to the
walls of Pampeluna.

At Pampeluna all was in confusion. The Duke of Najera,
the commander, had gone off himself to see about reinforce-
ments (it seems an odd thing to have done, but there it is), and
a certain Herrera was left in charge of the fortifications. Herrera
was for surrendering at once, but Ignatius would not hear of
this. " I do not think even Æneas worthy of admiration," he
said, " when I see him escaping from the flames that consumed
his city ; for to shun the common peril is the nature of cowards ;
to perish in the universal ruin is the mischance of brave men.
I should hold him to deserve immortal glory if he had died a
holocaust of his fidelity." Ignatius demanded that the place
should be held at all costs until the return of the Duke, but at
the representation of Herrera, who argued that it was futile to
attempt to carry on battle in the midst of a hostile population,
he consented to a withdrawal from the town to the citadel.
Some half-hearted attempts at negotiation easily broke down
and the French began the siege.

There was no priest present, and Ignatius therefore took
aside one of his companions—a tried comrade-in-arms—and

made to him a confession of all his sins. Then, like a Greek general, he harangued the troops and, the speech finished, all took their places and prepared to receive the French attack. During the assault a stone, detached from the wall by a cannon shot, struck Ignatius on the left leg and, rebounding, shattered his right. The assault was successful, and on the same day on which Ignatius was wounded—Whit Tuesday, May 20th, 1521 —the French entered the citadel.

The French treated their gallant prisoner with the greatest consideration. They carried him back to his lodgings in the town and put their most skilful surgeons at his disposal for the fortnight during which he was compelled to remain there. As soon as he was able, they caused him to be conveyed back to his home in Azpeytia in neighbouring Guipizcoa. Ignatius, on parting from them, presented to them as thank-offerings his sword, his helmet and his shield.

Ignatius' father was now dead, and Loyola was in the occupation of his elder brother, Don Martin Garcia. Ignatius was well received by his brother and sister-in-law, who showed to him even more kindness than had his French enemies. Yet the journey from Pampeluna to Azpeytia can have done no good to a shattered leg, and it was from the first obvious that his cure was not going to be easy or rapid. Permanent deformity could only be prevented, the doctors told him, if he would have the bone rebroken and reset. He consented, but the pain of the operation was such that it threw him into a dangerous fever. His life was in the balance, and it was not until the eve of St. Peter and Paul that the crisis was turned. On that night, as he afterwards asserted, St. Peter appeared to him in a vision and promised that he should recover. Be that as it may, it is certain that from that moment an improvement began. Yet even after a second operation he was still deformed. A portion of the bone of the right leg projected below the knee. Ignatius was chiefly troubled, as he afterwards confessed, lest this deformity should prevent him from wearing the rich boots, or leggings, then in fashion. He asked the doctors if there was nothing that could be done. They said that there was nothing but that the wound should be reopened and the protruding bone sawed off, but they warned him that this would cause him far greater pain than any that he had experienced so far. He bade them perform the operation, and he submitted not only to the sawing but also to further and yet more painful attempts to lengthen his legs by means of an iron machine.

These sufferings Ignatius used afterwards to refer to as his "martyrdom of vanity." His mind was still fixed upon a worldly career. He had accepted his sufferings only in order to fit himself to return to that career, and indeed it is clear enough what sort of person he was during these first years. He was much as his father had been before him. Whatever the sins into which he had fallen, he had punctually repented of them. He was a good Catholic. He had recognised the obligation of the Commandments. He had written his religious poems. He had confessed his sins at Pampeluna. But, even after he had seen what he at least imagined to be a vision of St. Peter, he did not think that there was any obligation to turn away from the pleasures of this world. Obedience to the precepts of religion was merely a price that had to be paid before the pleasures of the world could be legitimately enjoyed. He was grateful to St. Peter who granted to him a recovery so that he might return to those pleasures.

CHAPTER III

THE VOCATION

As the days of convalescence dragged along, Ignatius grew weary of his own thoughts and asked for some romances of chivalry to help him pass the time. There were none in the castle, and they had to bring him instead the *Life of Our Saviour* by a certain Rudolph of Saxony and a Castilian Lives of the Saints called *Flos Sanctorum*. At first he put these substitutes from him with disgust, but at last boredom led him to read.

The story is well known. The spiritual reading had an effect on him that he had never foreseen. It was, to borrow the language of George Herbert's beautiful little poem, weariness that tossed him to God's breast. There was no immediate conversion, but gradually it dawned on him that there were spiritual adventures as well as romantic adventures. Competitiveness was strong within him. He hated to be beaten on the fields with which he was familiar. Here were new fields whose very existence he had up to now hardly comprehended. Was he to admit defeat on them? If others had been saints, why should not he be a saint, too? "If Francis did this great thing and Dominic did that, why should not I, by the grace of God, do as much?" he quaintly asked.

He hovered between the two lives, avid for the spiritual life and yet reluctant to sacrifice that of romance. Was it not possible to make the best of both worlds? Time and again he let his mind wander back over the romantic fields, but he now noticed that he always emerged from such reveries oppressed with a vague feeling of dissatisfaction. And yet he returned to them again.

It occurred to him that this after-feeling of dissatisfaction

must be a sure proof that these thoughts did not come from
God.   Romance was good, but it was not the absolute Good,
and he who had received his first glimmering visions of the true
Good could never again be content with partial good.   Like St.
Augustine, he had been " in love with love," and now, like
St. John, he had discovered that God was love.   " Love God
with all your heart and all your soul and all your will," was later
to be the often repeated peroration of his addresses.   And he
was to say that, if he were to go down to Hell, he should suffer
more from hearing the damned cursing God than he would
from the pains of fire.

Thus his meditations led him to think that he had a vocation ;
that he was called by God to separate himself from the world.
How should he do this ?   He would subdue the world in himself by the violence of his penances.   He would go barefoot on
a pilgrimage to Jerusalem and then, on return, shut himself up
in a monastery.   He must die to himself.   " First," he read in
Rudolph, " from a sense of humility a man shall deem himself
the meanest of men ;   second, he shall say so in words ;   third,
he shall bear patiently hearing it said by others ;   fourth, he
shall bear patiently being treated with contempt by others ;
fifth, he shall not only not grieve but even be glad that he is
scorned by other men."   That or Aristotle's great-spirited man,
" thinking himself worthy of the greatest things, being worthy ? "
Christ or the Renaissance ?   Which should he choose ?   There
was no room for both.

The Carthusian Order attracted him—I suppose, because it
is the strictest of Orders—and he thought that he would join
their house at Seville.   He sent a servant to Burgos to inquire
about the details of the Carthusian rule and was satisfied at the
report which he brought back.

The certain moment of his vocation was yet to come.   One
night, as he was meditating, " he saw clearly," as his dictated
autobiography records, " the image of Our Lady with the Holy
Child, at whose sight for a notable time he felt a surpassing
sweetness, which eventually left him with such a loathing for
his past sins, and especially ιor those of the flesh, that every

unclean imagination seemed blotted out from his soul, and never again was there the least consent to any carnal thought." According to his biographers—the story, I confess, does not much impress me—at that very moment a great shock was felt throughout the castle, the windows of Ignatius' room were broken and a large rent, which is still visible, appeared in the wall.

So the familiar story. What are we to make of it all?

First, let us consider the whole question of St. Ignatius' visions. I did not linger over the inquiry into what really happened at the time when he imagined himself to have received the vision of St. Peter, for it would be ridiculous to consider that incident in isolation. Had that been the only vision of St. Ignatius' life—a man at death's door, probably in delirium, saying that he had seen St. Peter—clearly one would be under no temptation to pay any very serious attention to the claim. " These ecstasies, visions and other emotional experiences," says Mr. Sedgwick, " were primarily due, unless we accept a mystical or supernatural explanation, to the weakness of his poor, ill-treated, underfed body." I quite agree. Which is it to be? To van Dyke, too, the modern psychological language alone gives the correct account ; the religious language has only a metaphorical truth. To the believer it is just the other way about. Whichever is right, the believer has at any rate this advantage over the sceptic—that the language which St. Ignatius spoke is also his language. Many years afterwards Laynez was to ask St. Ignatius whether it was true that he had an archangel for guardian. St. Ignatius, we are told, " blushed like a young girl " and said nothing. But the question did not seem to him a ridiculous question, as it must, I suppose, seem to Mr. Sedgwick. Perhaps Mr. Sedgwick agrees with Macaulay that " it is difficult to relate without a pitying smile that, in the sacrifice of the Mass, he saw transubstantiation take place, and that as he stood praying on the steps of St. Dominic, he saw the Trinity in Unity and wept aloud with joy and wonder." But even Whig historians are sometimes in need of " pitying smiles."

We must consider the problem as a whole. Let us consider it as a sober historical problem.

The problem is this. From the time of the vision of St. Peter and from that of Our Lord and Our Lady onwards for the rest of his life St. Ignatius claimed that from time to time he came face to face either with Our Lord, Our Lady or with one of the saints. His autobiography is full of the records of such visions. He made no boast of them. After his faith was firmly established, if not before, he did not even particularly wish to receive them. " I prefer," says St. Thérèse in our own day, " sacrifice to ecstasy," and similarly St. Ignatius came to bid " his sons rather to dread them than to desire or welcome visions and raptures, which often light up the soul with pride and disturb weak minds." " The devil," he said at another time, " cannot work on the soul ; but he often produces fictitious appearances on the body, betraying the foolish into illusion and pride." Yet he had no manner of doubt that God had selected him for these dangerous privileges.

We have then St. Ignatius' claim. There is no argument about the evidence. The evidence is St. Ignatius' word ; there is no other evidence, and in the nature of things there could be no other evidence. Are we to accept it or reject it ? Are such visions in some way metaphysically impossible ? If one believes in God and in the survival of the soul, I cannot begin to think of any reason why they should be. But they are, I admit, empirically extremely improbable. Thus St. Ignatius himself was extremely and, as it seemed to many of his contemporaries, unreasonably sceptical about the visions of Maddalena della Croce, a Dominican nun who laid claim to strange mystical experiences, was widely believed to be a saint, but in the end proved an impostor. If a man says that he met Our Lady, I admit, and St. Ignatius would certainly have admitted, that it is much more likely that he is either lying or mistaken than that he is telling the truth. It is true that St. Ignatius was in all the practical affairs of life a quite exceptionally shrewd, hard-headed, wide-awake man, far above the average, one would expect, in his capacity for judging evidence. Yet there is no end to the extraordinary " blind spots " of illusion which one surprisingly discovers in men otherwise most normal. I would not myself believe him simply because he was a good business man. If I accept his word and believe in the reality of his visions, it is for two reasons. First—and it is a reason which I cannot expect to weigh with any but a Catholic—because the Church has declared him a saint. Second, because his sober historical achievement was so astonishing that I cannot see any possible explanation of it other than that it was accomplished by direct supernatural aid.

Take the early history of the Church, the history of her rise within the Roman Empire. The broad historical facts are there, necessarily admitted by believer and sceptic alike. How are these facts to be explained ? The believer's explanation is that the Church triumphed through the direct, supernatural action of God. For the life of me I cannot see any other explanation which at all adequately accounts for that triumph.

This, which is true of the history of the Church at large, is equally true of the history of some of her saints. An easy example is that of St. Joan of Arc. Her achievements are matter not of hagiography but of certain and most secular history. Voltaire and Quicherat and Anatole France and even Andrew Lang and Mr. Shaw have attempted to account for those achievements and, in my opinion, have failed. To the believer she triumphed because the Holy Ghost acted through her. It is the only explanation that at all fits the facts.

St. Ignatius seems to me to fall into this class. I should not at all accept the word of any Tom, Dick or Harry who said that he had met Our Lady face to face, and one of the most troublesome of all forms of cant is that of quite ordinary people who always claim an invariable coincidence between their own desires and the Will of the Holy Ghost. St. Ignatius quite clearly was not such a man as that. Quite apart from the authority of the Church, his achievements prove that he was one of those in whom God acted—*gesta Dei per Ignatium* stand manifest in history. His life proves that he lived in the company of the things that are not of this world. And if a man of that nature tells us that he came to know in God in such a way or in such a way, even though we cannot, perhaps, fully understand what he means, yet we cannot but take his word for it.

The old Victorian rationalists would deny the possibility of such visions at all. The new fashion is rather to run to the opposite extreme and to accept with fantastic attention the most hysterical of tales. I do not wish to be accused of falling into that fashion. If I believe in the visions of Ignatius, yet I do not think that he was a saint because I believe in his visions ; I believe in his visions because I think that he was a saint.

The question of the reality of these visions is of some importance, for on it depends our whole judgment upon the nature of his experience during these months. Some biographers make much of the fact that he emerged from his illness, having shed all worldly ambitions. I see no proof of the finger of God in that. By itself it proves, if it proves anything, that he had his share of common sense. His previous ambitions had, after all, been very childish, and most people, I should imagine, in their teens and early twenties plan out for themselves great careers, in which their happiness is dependent upon the applause and consideration of other people. Then when they come to a little knowledge of the world there dawns upon them the truth that other people think about them very little one way or the other and that what they think is of very small importance, that the whole world holds no madder object for which to live than fame. St. Ignatius describes how at first, when he contemplated embracing the spiritual life, he was tormented by the thought of what his companions in arms would say of him, and that then he reflected that after all it did not very much matter what they said. The mere revolt against ambition could, I think, be paralleled in the experience of every sensible man since time began. Only intelligence is needed to show us the vanity of this world, but grace to bring us to the beauty of the next.

There comes next the question, " If true, to what do these visions amount ? " What is the lesson of St. Ignatius for us ? The difficulty about the lives of the saints to ordinary men and women is, if we honestly face the truth, that they seem to us quite fantastic. We believe in God and we wish most devilishly to save our souls. Rationally we can follow out the argument that the love of the Creator is better and more satisfying than the love of the creature. But it is a mere rattling of syllogisms to us. It means nothing.

" This kind, warm world is all I know "

and we do not in our hearts, whatever we may profess with our lips, want to be saints and to turn our backs upon it all.

In a way we are quite right. By attaching the obligation of celibacy to the priesthood the Church has very clearly shown that she does not wish all her faithful children to become priests. There are, as St. Thomas said, as many separate types of excellence as there are separate souls, and most of us are right when we feel that the only consequence of putting away the loves of this world would be to put love out of our hearts altogether. It is our vocation to love the Creator through His creatures; in such a love comes to us our opportunity of holiness.

We have all of us probably from time to time had the misfortune to meet one of those arid, loveless, methodical, pettily scrupulous religious, of whom it is impossible not to feel that he has forced himself into religion without vocation and contrary to the will of God, has put away from him the vanities of the lesser love and has yet found himself incapable of the higher. Such a man makes the whole cause of virtue seem odious, and Browning's *Soliloquy in a Spanish Cloister* is true enough of one side of the religious life (though why " Spanish " I could never imagine). It has probably been true of every age of the Church's life, as St. Augustine said that it was true of his, that there were nowhere better men than in monasteries and nowhere worse. Whatever then the lessons that we should learn from St. Ignatius, it is certainly not one of them that we should rush off without any consideration of our circumstances and strive to imitate the external details of his life. This world is for us a testing ground, and we were sent into it not only to avoid sin but also to learn to love. It is right to enjoy it, so far as it can be enjoyed, and to love whatever in it is lovable. The text is true enough for most of us that " he that loveth not his brother whom he hath seen, how shall he love God Whom he hath not seen ? " St. Ignatius' life was different to ours simply because the text did not apply to him. He had seen God—not in a vulgar, sentimental, metaphorical sense, but literally and face to face. In a fine, vivid phrase, which thirteen years later he was to use in a letter to Peter Contarini, he described himself as " I who look with both eyes upon celestial things." Naturally, therefore, a love which to us means little was to him vivid, engrossing and real.

What then, you may ask, has St. Ignatius to teach to us of the world ? The Church, though she does not demand of all of us that we give up the world, does demand that we look beyond it from time to time—even if it is only for half an hour a week while we hear our obligatory Mass. Each of us has his capacity; no one is wholly spiritually blind. But apart from that the great lesson which the saints have to teach is the lesson of deficiency. The great difference between the Christian of the world and the atheist of the world is that to the Christian there is such a thing as holiness—the most precious of virtues—even though he himself is not holy. The atheist cannot even be conscious that he lacks.

It is important that such a tribute to holiness should not be allowed to become a tribute of mere words, for it is very easy to slip into a dangerously false view of perfection. It is easy to think of the saints or of those with vocations as a kind of scholarship-class, as a class of those with especial abilities, or at the least with especial ambitions. For us, the less ambitious, Almighty God in His great mercy has, we feel, provided a very easy pass-course in the world. The standard is little more than nominal.

> " They talk of some strict testing of us—Pish !
> He's a good fellow and 'twill all be well."

It is by the saints that the experiment of the human race will be judged to have succeeded or failed. We are like those boys at the back of the class who are not taking the examination ;

nobody much minds what we do so long as we do not interrupt or make nuisances of ourselves.

Such a view has but to be stated explicitly to be seen to be dangerous and false. Perhaps

> " God's bright and intricate device
> Of days and seasons doth suffice,"

but it only suffices for those who have used it sufficiently. If I am a husband and a stockbroker and a father of three, why, then, I shall not be blamed at the Last Judgment because I have not had the visions of St. Teresa nor lived according to the rule of St. Francis; but I shall be blamed if I have been a bad husband and a bad stockbroker and a bad father. Each walk has its own difficult opportunity of holiness.

In the spring of 1522 Ignatius was sufficiently recovered to be able to leave Loyola. He went to the house of his married sister at Arancazu, twelve miles up in the Pyrenees, hoping that there he would obtain the opportunity for quiet and meditation. There was a shrine of Our Lady there and he went, as Mariani quaintly puts it, to return " the visit which his heavenly mistress had paid him." Yet he found that at his sister's house he was not as completely removed from the influences of his past life as his spirit demanded. He therefore returned to Loyola and asked his brother for leave to quit the house and make a visit of report to his late commander, the Duke of Najera. His brother, though not completely in his confidence, yet truly guessed the sort of future that Ignatius was meditating for himself. He, the head of a proud and honourable family, remonstrated with him. " I know, my brother, that you meditate some great change," he said. " I cannot believe it is because Fortune has for once betrayed you; she is fickle; it is after disaster especially that you may look for a speedy success. And why do you refuse to our house the future honours we had expected from you, when you had already given us so much ? It is worse to lose what we have hoped for than never to have hoped at all. Do not disappoint the liberal gifts of Heaven to you, your abilities, judgment, valour, the favour of princes, the applause of the people and that which seems like magic in you—the influence you exercise over all minds. I myself have no advantage over you except in being born before you ; in all other points I admit your superiority ; you may found, if you will, your fortunes on your merit alone. If you tell me you desire to become a saint, I say, there are many holy men in the army. You need not leave this house for that reason ; we are not such bad Christians that we should interfere with your good intentions ; but, if we were, you ought to convert us by your example. I oppose no obstacle to your designs ; only as an elder brother, I exhort that you will never forget that you are a Loyola." Ignatius could only answer that, whatever he did, he would never do anything unworthy of his ancestors.

He set out on mule back in the company of another brother for Arancazu. There he and his brother spent the night together in prayer in the Church of Our Lady. Then before dawn, bidding farewell to his brother, he rode on to Navarrette, where he reported himself, as he had promised to do, to the Duke of Najera. After a few days he dismissed the two servants, who had hitherto accompanied him, bade farewell to his host and set off alone with his mule in the direction of Catalonia. It was his intention to make his devotions at the shrine of Our Lady of Monserrat before departing on his pilgrimage for Jerusalem. It was on this journey that he ran across his strange adventure with the Morisco.

When the Mahommedan power had been expelled from Spain, Ferdinand had permitted Moors who had settled in Spain to remain there provided that they declared themselves Christians. Naturally a conversion, obtained in such a manner, was often less than half-hearted, and many of the Moriscos still remained Mahommedan at heart. It was such a man whom Ignatius came across as he rode out of the town of Cervera, which lies some fifty miles to the west of Barcelona. They fell into an argument in which the exact philosophical or theological position of the Morisco is not to-day clear to us and was not, I daresay, clear to him at the time, but in which he, at any rate, either denied or in some way belittled the Virginity of Our

Lady. He maintained, it seems, that She had borne other sons by natural means after the birth of Our Lord. Ignatius, of course, disputed with him. Tempers rose upon both sides until eventually the Morisco gave a shake to his reins and rode off without so much as a farewell.

When the Morisco was gone, the thought came into Ignatius' head that it might be his duty to kill the Morisco in order to avenge the insults which he had offered to Our Lady. He could not decide whether this was so or not, and determined to leave the decision to God. He soon came to a fork in the road. The Morisco, a little ahead of him, had taken the lower road. Ignatius threw the bridle on his mule's neck and let it choose the road for itself. If it took the lower road he would go after the Morisco and kill him ; if it took the higher he would let him go. How very different a method for discovering the will of God from that used later by Ignatius, the general ! The mule took the higher road and Ignatius rode off into the mountains.

Sir Walter Scott quotes the old mediæval maxim that " A Churchman should refute heresy by argument ; a Knight with his dagger," and Ignatius, even now after his vocation, still remained in some ways more knight than churchman. He had, I suppose, hardly ever before met anyone who challenged the central Christian doctrines, and this Morisco certainly seems to have challenged them in a peculiarly offensive way. If a man rejects the whole Christian revelation, then we hardly expect him to believe in the Virgin Birth. Yet, if in our presence he aggressively singles out the purity of Our Lady for especial attack, then it is natural to feel that he has behaved like a cad and deserves to be hurt. In just the same way Massinger writes that an insult to the elevated Host is a " deed deserving death with torment." He did not defend it, as we to-day are apt to argue for the necessity of religious repression under exceptional circumstances, by saying that false doctrines or impious prac- tices must be suppressed because of the danger to the public peace or to the faith of simple people. He simply said that such a deed was so horrible that it " deserved " death.

Such was also Ignatius' feeling about the Morisco. To the

modern mind, it seems, I know, a barbaric feeling, and I agree with the modern mind in so far as I am extremely glad that St. Ignatius did not kill the Morisco, but, while it is perhaps possible to be above such feelings, it is very much easier to be below them. We may hold our hands from great charity, because even the blasphemer of God is one of God's children and bears His awful image. We may equally hold our hand from indolence or cowardice or because we do not care enough whether the Mother of God was a virgin or not.

As it happens, St. Ignatius has told us just what his state of mind was at this time. He was " Our Lady's knight." He was setting out to do battle for Her against the world, by arms, if need be, against the human enemies of Christ in the world, and by a vigorous practice of asceticism and mortification against the world's vanities. As for the rights and wrongs of the debate

" Chrétiens ont droit, païens ont tort "

he would have shouted with the Song of Roland. That all asceticism and mortification were but means to an end, that the real enemies of the soul were within the soul itself, that any of the battles of the world between pagan and Christian was but a crude parody of the real battle which was fought out over each individual soul—these were things which he had not yet come to learn. Still less had he come to learn that, while there was a vocation which called the man of spiritual life from the world, there was another sort of vocation which would drive the man of spiritual life back into the world to save it.

From Cervera Ignatius rode on to the famous shrine of Our Lady of Monserrat. The hills stand up over Barcelona like the jagged teeth of a saw, whence Monserrat gets its name. Halfway up the mountain is the famous church of Our Lady of Monserrat, and by its side the great Benedictine Abbey, which contained at that date seventy monks, ninety lay brothers, and a company of thirty choir boys, known as " Our Lady's boys," and to which then, as now, pilgrims flocked from every quarter of Europe. There was no European language in which one or other of the monks was not able to hear confessions. Upon the heights above the monastery—" *elegantissimus locus est pro haeremitis*," says an old writer, somewhat as if he were advertising a desirable country residence—were thirteen cells, each inhabited by a hermit and each dedicated to a saint. Here the hermits lived a life of great austerity upon a diet of bread, herbs and flesh, " seasoned with frequent fasting," the hermit who occupied the cell of St. Benedict being the superior over the rest.

Owing to the accident of Ignatius' visit there we have a full account of the state of religion at Monserrat at this time, and the account proves how very unfair are sweeping generalisations about the evils of religious life in these pre-Reformation years. It is impossible, and undesirable, to deny, or even to minimise, the appalling corruptions of this period, and yet, if one follows through the life of St. Ignatius, one cannot but be struck with the enormous amount of holy living which even in such a period and in the midst of such corruptions such a man as St. Ignatius was able to discover both among clergy and laity.

It happened that one of the monks at this time was a certain Frenchman, Jean Chanones. He had been Vicar-General of Mirepoix at the age of thirty-two and seemed to have in him all the makings of a successful ecclesiastical careerist. But, chancing to make a pilgrimage to Monserrat, he was so edified by the life of the monks there that nothing would content him but that he should throw up the world and enter the monastery. There he lived in the greatest sanctity until his death at the age of eighty-eight.

Ignatius had somehow heard of Chanones' reputation, and on his arrival at Monserrat he sought him out and made to him a full confession of all the sins of his past life. It took him three days to exhaust the list which he had prepared. He also told Chanones, what he had not before told either to his brother or to anyone else, in confession or out of it, his whole project of devoting his life to the greater glory of God. Ignatius does not tell us what in detail Chanones said to him, but he gave, it seems, the advice and encouragement which were to be expected from a man of such spiritual experience.

In the old days of his "vanity," as he came to call them, Ignatius had been a great reader of books of romantic adventure, and of these books the most popular in Spain was the *Amadis of Gaul.* You remember how in Don Quixote, when the priest and the barber burnt Don Quixote's library, they spared only three books, the *Amadis of Gaul,* the *Palmerin of England* and *Tirante the White.* "I have heard," said the priest, "that *Amadis of Gaul* was the first book of chivalry printed in Spain and that all the rest sprung from it; I think therefore that, as head of so pernicious a sect, we ought to condemn him to the fire without mercy." "Not so, sir," said the barber, "for I have heard also that it is the best of all the books of this kind; and therefore—as being unequalled in its way—it ought to be spared." "You are right," said the priest, "and for that reason its life is granted." As for the book itself, the *Encyclopaedia Britannica* wittily summarises it. "Hacking and hewing in every page, knights always at war and seeking adventures, giants in the path, lions in the forest, damsels in durance, castles to be attacked, wizards and witches with hate in their hearts, kings everywhere plentiful as blackberries and lovely ladies abounding in tenderness."

The influence of its teaching over Ignatius was enormous, and, as has already been noted, he found it easier to abandon the world than to abandon the standards of chivalry. In the old world of the romances the newly accoladed knight would prepare himself for the responsibilities which he had undertaken by watching and praying from sunset to sunrise before the altar of Our Lady. Ignatius determined that he, too, would perform his "vigil of the armour" in order to fit him for his great knighthood. Therefore on the eve of the Annunciation, 1522, he went out after supper dressed, as he still was, like a Spanish nobleman. Many pilgrims were as usual flocking up to Monserrat for the feast, and Ignatius, selecting the most meanly clad, persuaded him to exchange clothes. Then arrayed in his new uniform, the proud uniform of Lady Poverty, he made his way back to the church and there performed his "vigil of the armour."

Bishop Stillingfleet jeeringly compared the spirit of St. Ignatius to that of Don Quixote. But there have been worse things in this world than chivalry, men too cowardly even to charge windmills or to drive sheep before them, spirits less noble than that which took Don John and Cervantes to Lepanto or Columbus and Cortes to the far corners of the monstrous world. These great men are not altogether unworthy of the greatest of their contemporaries. There is justice in the retort of the modern Spanish scholar, Menendez y Pelayo, who in his *Historia de los Heterodoxes Espanoles* writes, " If we are to choose between the maritime greatness of England under her Virgin Queen and the slow martyrdom and impoverishment of our own nation, which during two centuries was the unselfish arm of the Church, every heart that beats with enthusiasm for the noble and the beautiful will not hesitate to bestow the palm on us." I do not think that this is but sentimental rhetoric, while, if you prefer to judge by the cold canons of practical achievement—well, which of the three is it who has really achieved the most ? Cervantes or Ignatius Loyola—or Bishop Stillingfleet? The pragmatic test is not the ultimate test. It might well have been God's purpose to bring all Ignatius' efforts apparently to nothing. But it is a singularly ill-chosen test to invoke against Ignatius.

The next morning Ignatius received Communion at the first Mass at which it was possible to do so, and then slunk away from the monastery before anyone should have an opportunity of recognising him. The main road led on to Barcelona, but, fearing that if he travelled by it he might meet someone who would recognise him, he struck out instead along a little mountain path, which led, as it happened, to the small country town of Manresa, though I daresay that Ignatius neither knew nor cared whither it led.

The story of his next adventures we learn from the narrative of Juan Pascual. Pascual's widowed mother, Inez, lived normally in Barcelona, but it happened that at this time she was on a business visit to Manresa, where she owned some property. She went over that morning, in the company of three other women and two young men, to get Mass at Monserrat, and, as they were returning about noon, there rose up by the side of the road the figure of a man who, though dressed in the meanest of clothes, yet accosted them with the speech of a gentleman, and asked them if they could tell him of anywhere in the neighbourhood where he could find a lodging. Inez answered him kindly. They were on their way to Manresa, which was the nearest town. Would he not accompany them? He thanked them. They begged him to mount an ass, but he refused, lame and limping though he was. They therefore slackened their pace and he walked by their side.

They had not gone far when an official of the monastery overtook them. Was Ignatius the man, he came to ask, who had yesterday given his gentleman's clothes to a beggar-pilgrim? The beggar had been arrested on suspicion for the possession of such fine clothes. Ignatius assured the official that the beggar had told the truth and that he was no robber, but of himself or of the motives of his action he would give no further explanation either to Inez or to the official than was contained in the words, " Ah, sinner that thou art, thou couldst not even do thy neighbour a service without causing him an injury." Inez rode on, wondering who this strange companion might be ; Ignatius hobbled at her side.

When they reached Manresa Inez took Ignatius to the hostel of a friend of his, called the Hospital of St. Lucy, where she arranged that he should be given a bed and a room and promised herself to furnish him with food from her own table.

Ignatius does not seem at first to have had any suspicion that extraordinary experiences awaited him at Manresa. His intention was to stay there for a few days to recruit his health and then to continue on his way, nor are we anywhere told the reason which caused him to change his purpose. We come to the period of his life most difficult for the normal reader to comprehend. It is best first to record the facts without comment and then afterwards to discuss the possible explanation of them.

Installed at the Hospital of St. Lucy, Ignatius proceeded to give himself up to a life of the greatest devotion and asceticism.

Every day he heard Mass and attended vespers and compline. Apart from the time spent in assistance at these services, he knelt by himself for seven hours every day in private devotion. He slept always on the floor, using a stone or a log of wood as his pillow. Inez Pascual had promised to furnish him with food, and every day she sent him a pullet and a bowl of broth, but he gave these away to the sick or poor, eating himself nothing but some hard black bread once a day and drinking only water. This diet was only varied on Sundays, when he took a glass of wine and some herbs ; yet, lest the indulgence should prove too great, mixed earth and ashes with the herbs. He wore neither hat nor shoes. Beneath his sackcloth dress he had a hair shirt, and round his waist a heavy iron chain, for which he would sometimes substitute a girdle that he had woven for himself of sharp and prickly leaves. He associated only with the foulest and lowest of the people. He let his hair, his beard and the nails of his hands and feet grow until even the beggars insulted him for the lowness of his condition, and the children in the streets shouted out after him " Look there at Father Sack."

He used to visit the sick in the hospitals. Once, he records, the Devil sent into his soul a sudden wave of disgust against the filthiness of the sores and diseases of those to whom he ministered. To overcome this feeling he rushed into the midst of the sick and embraced them all.

Just across the River Cardenero was a cave about twenty feet long by six wide, eight feet high at the mouth but rapidly narrowing. The entrance was almost obscured by briars and bushes. Hither, after a time, Ignatius made his way, feeling the need of even greater solitude, and, living here, he carried his mortifications to an almost incredible pitch. It was here that he was called upon to undergo those strange and terrible conflicts with the Devil for the possession of his soul, the record of which seems so incredible, so nonsensical, and perhaps so naive to normal men and women, but without the experience of which it seems almost impossible to achieve any high degree of sanctity, those experiences which St. John of the Cross has described under the vivid phrase of " the dark night of the soul." One day, as Ignatius was entering a church to hear Mass, a voice said to him, " How will you be able to support this for forty years or more ? " He answered the Devil, " Can you promise, O wicked one, another single hour of life ? And what are forty years of suffering compared with the ages of eternity ? " It was Pascal's wager accepted by a fierce Spanish soldier. The Devil, baffled for the moment, returned to the attack by afflicting him with moods of despair and desolation ; Ignatius replied with the attempt to drive him out by increased mortifications. So severe were they that they seriously endangered his health. Then the Devil tempted him with presumption. Such had been his mortifications, he suggested, that Ignatius might safely pray God that he might die, in the certainty that his soul would now be received. In order to strengthen himself against this temptation Ignatius begged some pious women who were attending upon him that, if they should perceive him to be in danger, they should repeat into his ear, " Remember, O sinner, all the evil thou hast committed in the sight of God."

After presumption scruples again assailed him. He began to have doubts whether the general confession which he had made at Monserrat was a good confession. He sought counsel of a priest, who advised him to write down all the sins which he could remember to have committed, confess them and forget about them. Let him, said the confessor, only accuse himself of those things which he knew to be sinful. It was not possible to commit a mortal sin without knowing that one was doing so.

But this advice did not at all relieve Ignatius' mind, for, in spite of it, concerning every smallest action of his life he was now tormented with the thought that it might perhaps be a mortal sin. When he received Communion he was terrified lest perhaps he was eating to his own damnation. One day, as he was waiting in the Dominican Convent at Manresa, he cried out to God in the greatest agony, asking that He should reveal His will. There came no answer, and the thought entered Ignatius' mind that in his despair he should cast himself down a large opening that there happened to be in the ground near the place where he was kneeling, and thus end all. But he had strength to put the temptation from him with horror, crying out, " No, never, never will I so offend Thee, Lord."

He determined to drive out the Devil by neither eating nor drinking until he was compelled to by the necessities of health. He kept up his fast for a week until his confessor said that he would refuse him absolution unless he took the sustenance that his health required. Ignatius humbly obeyed, and by this submission to proper authority, and therefore to the will of God, the power of the Devil against him was broken. Scruples vanished; peace invaded his soul. Only once more—three days later—did the Devil return for a last desperate struggle. After that he left him untroubled.

So far the story, which I have told in a précis of St. Ignatius' words. What are we of the 20th century to make of it? The normal reader will, I daresay, be repelled by at least two things— by what will seem to him the morbid and unnecessary excess of the saint's asceticism and by the language in which he speaks of the Devil, which will sound childish and unreal.

First, as to asceticism. The case for a mild asceticism under certain circumstances is a case of common sense. Everybody admits that health is desirable, and that, if a certain dish is harmful to a particular person's health, it is then wise in him to give it up. Lovers of boxing agree that it is wise for the boxer to go into training before his fight, and those who jeer at the athlete's training only jeer because they think that the rewards of athletic success are not sufficient to deserve such sacrifices. All must agree that human nature is such that it is sometimes only possible to attain the highly desirable by sacrificing the less highly desirable, which is, nevertheless, in itself good. Asceticism is the sacrifice of some pleasure or other of the world for the love of God. The attack on it comes from those who do not believe in the possibility of attaining to the love of God, or from those who do not understand that the sacrifice of the lesser good is made for the greater good and who therefore think of the ascetic as an unreasonable person who denies his own end of happiness.

Now there is no doubt—and all the sadness of life comes from it—that we do all become attached to the things of this world. And, as Rupert Brooke says,

> " These shall pass
> Whatever passes not, in the great hour,
> Nor all my passion, all my prayers have power
> To hold them with me through the gate of Death.
> They'll play deserter, turn with traitor breath,
> Break the high bond we made and sell Love's trust
> And sacramental covenant to the dust."

As I have already argued, there is no help for it with the most of us. God has not given us the gift of loving Him save through the love of His creatures, and we must take the sadness with the gladness and make the best of it that we can. For that reason the Church only demands of us, as it were, the mildest little hints of asceticism—tells us to abstain from meat on Friday, recommends a little further private asceticism in Lent, and, where she imposes a discipline in affairs of sex, offers us at the same time the joys of matrimony. We are rather encouraged than otherwise to indulge in such pleasures of the world as are not either sinful or occasions of sin, and God is glorified in our enjoyment.

St. Ignatius himself was no Puritan, either at the great moment of Manresa or at any other time in his life. If he had been a Puritan, he would have said that the enjoyment of broth was evil, and would presumably have thrown the broth away. But such enjoyment was not evil ; it was in itself good, even though bad for him at that moment. Therefore he did not throw it away, but he gave it to the poor, who might legitimately enjoy it. He did not burn his fine clothes ; he gave them to the beggar.

St. Ignatius in his later days was no friend to extravagant asceticism—certainly no friend to it in others—and seems to have come to think that it was only his ignorance of the spiritual life which led him to some of the excesses into which he then fell. "Though it be charity which impels you to undertake things beyond your strength," he was to write to his nephew, Araoz, "yet even this, conjoined with obedience, obliges you to moderate these (works) so that you may preserve your health longer in God's service," and it was to be laid as a serious complaint against the Jesuits by Melchior Cano that they under-flagellated. However that may be, Ignatius, if he had admitted to error, would have admitted no error save in degree. The general truth remains that each special grace demands a special condition of the soul. Just as things that are permitted to a layman are forbidden to a priest, things permitted to a secular forbidden to a regular, so, too, with Ignatius who had received a quite special vocation from God. He could not come in, "not having on a wedding garment." We are by no means called upon to imitate every external act of his. Much that was demanded of him by his nature would in us be affectation. He had seen God face to face. He was soon to see Him again. It is easy to understand how such a man must have felt a strong desire to purge himself of every affection of the world, lest it come between him and his great love—a desire that is quite beyond our imagination.

So, too, with the Devil. I have brought the Devil into my narrative because St. Ignatius brought him in. St. Ignatius did not think that during these days he merely wrestled with temptation ; he thought that he wrestled with the Devil. God is the author of everything ; therefore in a sense every act is an act of God. Yet theology has drawn a distinction between the supernatural and the natural, between acts of His special inter-vention and acts of His general responsibility. In the same way the Devil is the father of all evil, and all temptation is from the Devil. Yet it is possible to believe that the Devil does make a special, personal attack on certain souls which are subjected to trials quite different in their nature from those ordinary temptations to which normal men and women are subject. St. Ignatius certainly believed that he was the victim of such attacks, and that it was not until he had defeated the Devil that God gave to him the revelation of the fullness of His vocation.

I can understand the instinct of the modern mind to dismiss the whole of such language as unreal. I have such an instinct myself. Yet, when we examine it, we surely see that the argument for its unreality is circular. An agnostic friend of mine often tells me that he cannot help feeling that the Apostles were the sort of people with whom it would have been very easy to " put over a story." It is, I always think, a fair answer that he knows nothing about the Apostles except that they believed the Christian story. For that reason alone he thinks them gullible, and his feeling is therefore not so much an argument against the evidence for the Christian story as a refusal to accept any evidence in favour of the Christian story. To him anyone who bears witness in its favour becomes, by the mere doing so, untrustworthy. So with St. Ignatius. There is no kind of reason for doubting his veracity or his sanity except for his extraordinary claims to spiritual experience. By every other test he was the sanest of men, and, if we think of him as morbid and neurotic, we only do so because we are previously determined to think of anyone who lays claim to such experiences as morbid and neurotic. That we ourselves or our friends or a gentleman in Bermondsey or a Mayfair hostess have never had such experiences is little to the point. God has not chosen to make us of such a nature as to receive them : perhaps it would be more honest to say we have never tried to receive them. It is as if one were to express astonishment that people who have always remained in England have never been to Australia. When we have tried to love God in any sort of sense at all similar to that in which St. Ignatius tried to love Him, then we shall have earned the right to criticise the spiritual experiences that accompanied that love.

Meanwhile, perhaps the best way to treat of these experiences is not to linger too much over this and that detail of what of its nature can hardly be comprehensible to us, but to say that St. Ignatius sought after and obtained the awful and personal love of God in some sense wholly beyond our understanding, that he was only admitted to that love after he had suffered a purgation more terrible than any that we are called upon to undergo.

The result of his experiences was to leave him throughout life, in his dealings with ordinary men, admirably aware of the great dangers of over-scrupulousness. It was the Devil's trick, he thought, to play on the consciences of those who were too scrupulous, always suggesting to them that this, that and the other little things that they did were sinful, until at last, hopeless of grace, they abandoned themselves to despair and were lost. He afterwards wrote :—

" The enemy carefully studies the nature of the conscience he attacks, examining whether it is strict and delicate or easy and obtuse. The first he endeavours to contract and intimidate still more, until he shall have reduced it to a state of such intolerable anxiety that it ends by abandoning itself to despair and is lost. Thus, when he observes that, far from consenting to the slightest fault, it flies even from the shadow of one, he will make it believe that sin exists when really there is no sin ; as, for example, in certain expressions or in sudden and unguarded thoughts. . . . He who wishes to advance in the spiritual life should follow the path which is exactly the contrary to that towards which the enemy endeavours to attract him. . . . If it (his conscience) be too contracted, he should labour to expand it."

In 1536 he wrote to the same effect to Teresa Rejadella of the convent of St. Clare at Barcelona :—

" To illustrate this in some way I will mention another of the enemy's devices. If he finds a person with an elastic conscience who passes over sin without consideration, he does all in his power to make venial sin seem nothing and mortal sin, even very serious mortal sin, of no account ; so that he turns to his purpose the defect he finds in us, that of a too elastic conscience. If in another he discovers a conscience over-tender—a tender conscience, be it noticed, is no fault—and if he sees that such a one will have nothing to do with mortal sin, nor even with venial sin so far as it is possible—for it is not in our power to avoid all—and that he even tries to cast off every slight semblance of sin in the shape of imperfection or defect, then the enemy makes an effort to confuse so good a conscience, suggesting sin where there is none and defect where there is even perfection, anything to be able to disturb and afflict us; and in many instances, where he cannot induce a soul to sin and has no hope of ever bringing it about, at least he endeavours to torment."

CHAPTER IV

THE REPULSE FROM CALVARY

ONE day soon after his last overthrow of the Devil St.
Ignatius was sitting on the banks of the River Llobregat.
"Suddenly there fell upon his soul an illumination of supernatural light," and at once, as he said, he understood a number
of things, both about the supernatural life and also even about
"*litterarum peritiam*," whatever exactly that may mean, of
which he had previously been quite ignorant. It was in this
vision, as he told Nadal, that God revealed to him the future
constitution of the Society of Jesus, and afterwards, when any
questioned him on any detail in the constitution, he would
answer, "I saw it thus at Manresa."

He ran at once, as he told Gonzales, and threw himself at the
foot of a crucifix near by. He saw above the Cross a vision
which he had often seen before—a vision of a luminous spiral
trail like a serpent, spotted with eyes of fire and sensually
beautiful. Seeing it above the Cross, he then understood, what
he had not understood when it appeared to him before, that
this vision was from the Devil, and he was easily able to reject
it. The history of the next few days one can but record, not
pretending to understand. He claimed that a pure spiritual
radiance conveyed to him the sublimest of the mysteries of
faith. Divine signs and interior lights visited him. In particular, as he waited for a procession one day on the steps of the
Dominican church at Manresa, in a sudden vision he saw clearly
the whole mystery and beauty of the Trinity, "figured by
three keys of a musical instrument." Thenceforward for the
rest of his life he lived in close and intimate communion with the
Three Divine Persons.

Later, while hearing Mass, he saw the Body of God in the

elevation of the Host and understood the mystery of Transubstantiation. From twenty to forty times, he told Gonzales, during these days he enjoyed the vision of Our Lord " always by an interior perception and without sensible distinction of the corporeal members." He also enjoyed the vision of Our Lady.

Then for a week he fell into a trance, lying as one dead and only recognisable from the dead by the faintest palpitations of the heart. On emerging from the trance all that he said was " Oh, Jesus, Jesus," nor would he ever reveal to any man what he had seen during that week. Like him of whom St. Paul speaks, he had seen " things unspeakable," and with Dante

> " il mio veder fu maggio
> Che il parlar nostro ch'a tal vista cede."

With St. Teresa he had tasted " intimate joys, known only to the souls that taste that ineffable sweetness." We of the world are not worthy and cannot hope to understand.

The extraordinary experiences of these days, combined with the vigorous asceticism of his life, brought about a breakdown in his health, and he was taken first to the house of a certain Andres Amigante and afterwards to that of a man called Ferreira. Warned by experience, he moderated his ascetical practices, though still refusing to eat any meat, in spite of the fact that for some odd reason he had an almost uncontrollable desire to do so.

Meanwhile, although they did not know the full story of the experiences which he had suffered, yet St. Ignatius' life there had been quite sufficiently striking to arouse the violent feelings, on the one side or the other, of the citizens of Manresa. Some—especially some ladies of wealth—moved by his example, enrolled themselves as his followers, and, attracting attention by the frequency of their presence at the Sacraments, earned for themselves the nickname of " las Initas." Others, those of the world, mocked and reviled. This, like every other movement of religious reformation in history, had its scoffers. To suffer from the misunderstanding, even of good people, seems to be a part of the necessary price to be paid in the apprenticeship of sanctity. Attacks were made on the family of the Amigantes, who had sheltered him, and on Inez Pascual. At the same time St. Ignatius found once more even among his friends none fitted to share in the work which it was now his task to take up. He therefore determined to leave Manresa. As soon as he received the news that an epidemic of the plague, which was raging at Barcelona, had abated and the port was again declared free, he went thither with the intention as soon as possible of sailing for the East in order to make the pilgrimage to the holy places which he had promised.

The years of St. Ignatius' youth were, as has been said, the years of the final defeat of Mahommedan power in Spain. A very different tale had to be told in the East of Europe. The gigantic military power of the Turkish Sultans had made itself master of the Balkan Peninsula, of all the Asiatic Mediterranean seaboard and of African Egypt. The efforts of Christendom to unite against the great menace had all ended in disappointing failure, and it looked by no means improbable that our European life, victorious in the West, would go down in complete destruction before the invasion from the East.

In the Eastern Mediterranean there remained but one Christian power, the Knights of St. John, who ruled over the little island of Rhodes. In 1480 Mohammad II. had sent against this island an armament whose artillery was the wonder of the world, but the attack had been driven off by the Grand Master of the Order, the gallant Peter d'Aubusson. Mohammad was preparing a second attack when in the next year he died, and thus Rhodes was spared for forty years.

The projects of Mohammad were taken up again by his grandson, Selim. Selim, however, died in 1520. Yet the accident was of little advantage to Rhodes, for to Selim there succeeded his son, Soliman, "the Sultan of Sultans, the Sovereign of Sovereigns, the distributor of crowns to the monarchs of the surface of the globe, the shadow of God on the earth, the Sultan and Padishah of the White Sea, the Black Sea, Roumelia, Anatolia, Caramania, Rum, Sulkadr, Diarbekr,

Jerusalem, all Arabia, Yemen and other countries which my
noble ancestors (may God brighten their tombs) conquered,
and which my august majesty has likewise conquered with my
flaming sword, Sultan Salayman Khan, son of Sultan Selim,
son of Sultan Bayazid," as he modestly described himself.
Rhodes lay across the line of his communications between
Constantinople and Egypt ; its continued independence was
intolerable, nor could the Knights look for any help from
Christian allies. The great national powers were rendered
impotent by their own divisions and jealousies, and Venice,
once the mistress and defender of those waters, had now for
commercial advantage adopted the policy of friendship with the
Turk, foolishly hoping that she would thus be able to preserve
her empire over her two remaining islands, Cyprus and Crete.

In the summer of 1522, while St. Ignatius was wrestling with
the Devil at Manresa, Soliman, with an army of twenty thousand
and a fleet of three hundred ships, set sail for Rhodes.   The
Grand Master of the Knights was now Villiers de l'Isle Adam,
of the same family as that Jacques Villiers de l'Isle Adam,
Provost of Paris and, as Mr. D. B. Wyndham Lewis well says,
" man of wrath," who in 1463 did his best to hang the immortal
François Villon as an incorrigible poet and public nuisance.
De l'Isle Adam had locked the harbour with an iron chain, and
outside it floated a boom of timber.   All the houses outside the
harbour had been demolished, and the forces of the Knights,
concentrated within, awaited the attack.   The first great assault
in September was repelled with enormous loss, but Soliman
then settled down to the siege of slow starvation.   Abandoned
and hopeless of relief, de l'Isle Adam surrendered in December.
Soliman promised free departure to the garrison, but in violation of the promise parties of Turks broke into the town on
Christmas Day and massacred the inhabitants, shouting as they
did so, " Italy, Italy, on to Rome ! "   The Venetians congratulated Soliman on his new conquest.

Naturally enough this catastrophe greatly increased the
difficulty of St. Ignatius' pilgrimage.   Nevertheless in February,
1523, he left Manresa for Barcelona.   Arriving at Barcelona, he

found that he would have to wait some days before he could embark. He had by now greatly moderated both the asceticism and the strangeness of his life. The two lessons which he claimed to have learnt were, first, that just as a moderate regimen is good for health but excessive rigours can be even more damaging than excessive indulgence, so too with asceticism and the spiritual life ; the purpose of asceticism is to expel all desire save that for the love of God, but an asceticism so rigorous as to impair health and the full powers of perception weakens, along with other capacities, the capacity for love. Secondly, he had learnt that the purpose of a sober and inexpensive dress was to prevent people's attention being distracted to a contemplation of the merely externally magnificent. A dress extravagantly poor was as likely to distract attention as a dress extravagantly magnificent. Therefore St. Ignatius now cut his hair. He wore shoes, a coarse grey cloak and a sombrero of the same colour. Dressed thus, he differed little from many a poor scholar—a common figure in the streets of that day—and could go about Barcelona without attracting any especial attention.

The days of his enforced waiting he spent partly in visiting the sick, partly in visiting any monks or hermits in the neighbourhood, from whom he hoped that he might receive any further light upon the spiritual life. He made the acquaintance of many people—among others, of one who was to play a considerable part in his future life, Isabel Roser.

Isabel Roser was the wife of a rich but blind nobleman, and lived in retirement from the world entirely for his service and for that of God. She went one day in Lent to the cathedral at Barcelona to hear a sermon, and, as she sat listening, her eye was caught by a man sitting on the steps of the altar. His head seemed to be surrounded by a circle of light, and she felt a strong impulse to go up to him. However, she resisted this impulse, but, going home, told her husband of her odd experience. He advised her to find the man out, which Isabel therefore the next day did. The man was, of course, St. Ignatius. Isabel, having found him, told him nothing of her strange experience, but begged him as an ordinary act of hospitality and charity to come home with her. St. Ignatius seems to have made it a rule always to accept such invitations. He therefore consented, and they went back to dinner, where he spoke to them, as was his custom, of the mysteries of divine things.

Isabel learnt that her guest was about to leave for Italy on a small brigantine. She tried to persuade him at first not to go at all; afterwards, when he was obstinate in this, at least to wait and travel in a larger vessel in which her husband's kinsman, the Bishop of Barcelona, was soon to set sail. This St. Ignatius consented to do, and fortunately so, as the brigantine went down with all hands on board a few hours after leaving port.

The captain of the ship agreed to give St. Ignatius a free passage on his ship for the love of God, provided that he brought his own food. Refusing to accept provisions from Isabel Roser, he begged in the streets sufficient for his needs on the voyage, and then when the time came, went down to the ship. So determined was he to set out upon his pilgrimage penniless that he left four or five little coins, which he still possessed, on a stone bench in the harbour, so that the first comer might take them, and then went on board.

The vessel made a rapid passage of five days to Gaeta in the kingdom of Naples. In that ancient harbour, famous since the time of Cicero as *portus celeberrimus et plenissimus navium*, in the town to which 350 years later Pius IX. was to fly for refuge from the Masonic Republic of Rome, St. Ignatius disembarked in order to journey up the Appian Way to Rome herself. He set out in company with three other pilgrims—a young man and a mother and a daughter. After some adventures and some difficulties owing to the plague which was then raging, and with which St. Ignatius was suspected of being contaminated owing to the worn looks with which his austerities had marked his features, he reached Rome on Palm Sunday.

His business there was to get from the Pope a pilgrim's licence. The Pope of the time was Adrian VI., the last *pontefice barbaro*, as Guicciardini calls him, or non-Latin Pope, old school-fellow of Erasmus at Deventer, the Flemish tutor of Charles V., whom the vigorous Ximenes had prevented from his share in the Regency of Spain after the death of Ferdinand of Aragon. His was to be a brief and unhappy reign of eighteen months, and he died in September of this same 1523, of shame, as it was said, that Christendom had been unable to prevent the fall of Rhodes, and leaving behind him the wish that on his tomb should be inscribed the quaint but Catholic inscription,

HERE LIES ADRIAN VI.
WHO ACCOUNTED IT THE GREATEST MISFÒRTUNE OF HIS LIFE
THAT HE WAS FORCED TO GOVERN

the product of a spirit very different from that in which his predecessor, Leo X., childishly exclaimed, " *Questo mi da piacere, che la mia tiara.*" The epitaph that actually was composed for Adrian's tomb in Santa Maria dell' Anima by his servant Cardinal Eckenvoert was, " *Proh dolor ! Quantum refert in quae tempora vel optimi cuiusque virtus incidat.*"

St. Ignatius received the licence and the Papal blessing, and then, having visited the several churches of the Stations, set out on the ninth day for Venice. His friends had induced him to take with him seven or eight gold crowns in case of accidents, but soon he came bitterly to reproach himself for the smallness of faith in God's providence which such a precaution implied, and therefore distributed the money among the first poor people· whom he met, and went on empty-handed, a form of recklessness which he was later sternly to condemn in his followers. The difficulties of his journey were enormously increased by the prevalence of the plague, which naturally made people everywhere reluctant to receive a casual stranger into their houses, or even into their cities. When he and his companions reached Venetian territory at Chioggia, they were told that they would not be allowed to enter Venice unless they could produce a certificate of freedom from infection. They had to go to Padua for examination and to obtain such a certificate. Owing to the feebleness of his health, St. Ignatius was unable to keep up with the rest, or to reach Padua before nightfall. They pushed on, leaving him alone. However, during the night, as he records, Our Lord appeared to him in a vision and told him not to worry, for no hindrance should come to him in his journey. Therefore when he rejoined his companions the next day, instead of waiting behind in Padua, he travelled on with them, much to their astonishment—an astonishment which was greatly increased when, on reaching Venice, the papers of all the rest of the party were examined, but St. Ignatius was allowed in without any questions being asked.[1]

St. Ignatius at this time knew no Italian. He was therefore at a great disadvantage in begging or in inquiring for lodgings. Yet as it was the middle of the summer, he perhaps thought it no great hardship if he should spend the night under the arcade of the Procuratori in the Piazza of St. Mark. A certain senator, Marc-Antonio Trevisani, a man of pious life, twenty years afterwards to become Doge of Venice, was lying in bed on this night when a voice came to him which said, " What ? Dost thou sleep comfortably in thy bed when my poor servant lies so near stretched on the bare stone ? " Trevisani therefore rose and went out with his servants. He found St. Ignatius, as it had been told him, lying on the pavement, and insisted on bringing him back to his house.

St. Ignatius spent that night in Trevisani's house, but would remain no longer, thinking that it would be contrary to his profession of poverty to do so. He took to the streets once more. The question now was how to obtain a passage for the East. The problem was solved for him by a chance meeting with a merchant who came from some place in his own part of Spain. This merchant took St. Ignatius back to his house and fed him. He then pressed upon him food and clothes. These St. Ignatius refused, asking only that the merchant procure for him an interview with the Doge, Andrea Gritti. This the merchant did, and St. Ignatius begged of Gritti that he should procure for him a free passage on the Admiral's ship which was soon to sail in order to take the Lieutenant-Governor out to Cyprus. Gritti readily granted this request.

---

[1] So one story. According to another version the quarantine regulations were suspended on the very day of St. Ignatius' arrival.

Of Venice at the time of her glory Wordsworth says in his
great sonnet

. " Once did she hold the gorgeous East in fee."

Hers was the great commercial Empire of the Middle Ages, and
the commerce of the Orient passed from the Venetian settlements
of the Eastern Mediterranean up the Adriatic to Venice herself,
and thence over the Alpine passes down to the cities of the
Rhine and of the Netherlands.   By St. Ignatius' time, Venice,
though by no means in evident decline, had yet passed her day
of supreme greatness.   The discovery of a route to India round
the Cape of Good Hope in 1498, when St. Ignatius was seven
years old, altered the whole centre of gravity of the world's
commerce, greatly to Venice's disadvantage.   But a more
immediately noted cause of alarm was, as has been said, the
advance of the Turk.   In 1479 the Turks had taken from
Venice the greater part of her Ægæan Islands as well as Eubœa
and the Morea.   They had even advanced right up to Friuli on
the Venetian mainland.   In panic the Venetians abandoned
their traditional rôle of " guardians of the West," left Rhodes
to her fate, as we have seen, sought the friendship of the Turk
for commercial advantage, and devóted their political attention
to an attempt to profit from a support of the French schemes
of aggression in Italy.

Yet even in the Eastern Mediterranean these years had
brought them one consolation.   In 1489 Caterina Comaro,
widow of James III., the last of the Lusignan Kings of Cyprus
and Jerusalem, ceded the island of Cyprus to Venice.   In the
long run the acquisition did the Venetians little good, for the
inhabitants were of the Greek Church, and the Venetians found
that their acquisition brought them little save the heritage of a
struggle between Catholic and Orthodox, so bitter that when
the Turks were to conquer the island in 1571, they were
generally welcomed as deliverers by the Greek population.

What with conflict in Cyprus, the Turk triumphant everywhere else, the menace of the plague, the temptations to any
Christian to take a trip to the East were not large.   The

disadvantages were urged upon St. Ignatius, but he only answered, " God is my sole support ; I would not hesitate to set sail upon a plank." When the time came to sail he was, as it happened, very ill, and his doctor prophesied that the voyage would be fatal to him. Nevertheless, Ignatius insisted on going on board, and they set sail on July 14th, 1523.

His fever soon left him, but the saint got himself involved in troubles of a different kind. They were a lewd lot on board, it seems, and Ignatius did not spare to rebuke them for their evil ways and the looseness of their conversation. They got so tired of him that they formed a plan to drop him on an un-inhabited island and leave him there. Some Spaniards came to warn him of his danger, but St. Ignatius was indifferent, willing to accept whatever fate God might send, and, as it happened, a wind arose and blew them past the island and on to Cyprus.

There is no subject upon which Christian traditions have been, and are, more utterly divided than that of Rabelaisian talk, and this is natural enough, for person varies from person in physical make-up, and a joke which to one will be merely amusing will fill another with awkwardness. To a third the indulgence in it will be truly dangerous. Yet the wiser, and on the whole the more persistent, tradition has been within limits rather to encourage such talk than otherwise. " No man can live without pleasure," St. Thomas teaches us. " Therefore a man, deprived of the pleasures of the spirit, goes over to the pleasures of the flesh." And—he might have added—a man deprived of the legitimate pleasures of the flesh goes over to the illegitimate. Rabelaisian talk is not, it is true, for saints, but most men are not saints. It is hard enough to get them to keep the Commandments, and they are on the whole more likely to keep them if they allow themselves to break out a little in easy Rabelaisian jests than if they keep their thoughts bottled up uncomfortably and morbidly in their own souls. Whatever may be false in the teachings of the modern psychologists, they are certainly right when they tell us that if you repress the innocent expressions of an instinct, then that instinct is sure to break out in a more harmful fashion.

Of such truths St. Ignatius was well aware three hundred and fifty years before modern psychology, even as St. Thomas Aquinas had, as has been shown, been aware of them three hundred years before him. Indeed it was afterwards to be a complaint made by those of less understanding, and is still a complaint, that the Fathers of his Society were too tolerant towards the weakness of the flesh. Jests about physical love could not be expected to appeal much to him—not because they were necessarily wrong in themselves, but because they were wrong for him with his very special devotion—for him who had wrenched his mind away from all consideration of physical love, light or serious, to the undivided contemplation of the Divine Love. Yet he never fell into the error of imagining that his standards ought to be the standards of normal men. It may be that, had he met them later, St. Ignatius would have dealt less harshly with the Rabelaisian sailors. Or it may be that their sins were by no means the unmeant jest or even the casual sins of too strong passion, but that they had abandoned the whole vision of right living and not only followed but also approved the worse.

Arriving at Cyprus, he found that the pilgrim-ship had not yet sailed. It was at Salamis, ten leagues away across the island. Thither he made his way, caught the boat, and without further adventure reached Jaffa on August 31st. At Jaffa, the city in which St. Peter raised Tabitha from the dead, and in which he had the vision of the unclean animals, St. Ignatius was for the first time in his life in the presence of the world of the New Testament. Jaffa had itself been in Mohammedan hands since it had been captured from the Christians in 1268. Yet the Sultan Omar at the Arab conquest of Jerusalem in 636 had promised the Patriarch Sophronius to grant toleration to Christians, and Saladin, on his conquest of the Holy City from the Crusaders in 1187, had held himself to be still bound by Omar's promise. Pilgrims were then admitted to the Holy Land under certain conditions even in such troubled times as those in which St. Ignatius landed. He and his companions were therefore able to make their way without trouble from

Jaffa up to Jerusalem. As they approached the Holy City, they were met by a Spanish gentleman, Diego Nunez, who admonished them that they should set their consciences in order and enter the city in silence. Their casual conversation was therefore hushed, just as Chaucer's pilgrims, after they had passed " Bob-up-and-down " and drunk in from the Maunciple the world-old Tale of the Crow, hushed their voices to listen to the Person's sermon on Penance as they came near to the shrine of St. Thomas, and turned their minds away from " the enditings of worldly vanities." So the pilgrims to Jerusalem marched on, and when a body of Franciscans met them, carrying a cross, they dismounted and finished their journey on foot. It was September 4th when St. Ignatius entered Jerusalem.

We have Ignatius' own account of the effect produced upon him by the holy places of Jerusalem in a long letter which he sent to Inez Pascual. It is hard to paraphrase without giving a falsely sentimental picture. When, for instance, he tells us how he was so overcome by emotion at the place of Our Lord's agony in the Garden that he kissed the blessed ground again and again, we are apt to have a feeling of the unreality of such an emotion. It is, I am sure, wrong to have such a feeling. Such demonstrativeness in us would, I daresay, be false sentimentality, but the defect is in us, not in St. Ignatius. It is not thought false sentimentality if a man kisses his dead wife, nor can we understand a word of St. Ignatius' life if we do not understand that the Son of God was constantly present to him, as real as person is present to person, and as beloved friend to beloved friend.

Yet it was not only in order to gain an inspiration to holiness from a visit to the holy places that St. Ignatius had come to Jerusalem. It had been revealed to him by God at Manresa that he was to found a Society, but God had not told him the place of that Society. His hope was that it might be God's will that it should be founded at Jerusalem. And as commentary on those uncomprehending views which think of the Jesuits as a company of competent election-agents for capturing votes for their political party, the Catholic Church, or as recruiting sergeants for an army, it is interesting to notice that the very reason why St. Ignatius wished to found his Society at Jerusalem, was to expiate the error of Christendom which had imagined that the battle of Christ was fought only with material weapons between Christian and non-Christian, and had forgotten the real battle—the battle for mastery within each soul.

There was a difficulty about his plan which proved insuperable. During the period of the Latin kingdom, the supreme Catholic authority in Jerusalem had been the Latin Patriarch. After the capture of Jerusalem in 1187, the Latin Patriarch left the city and lived at whatever place was the capital of the Latin king. After the final overthrow of the kingdom by the capture of Akka in 1291, the Latin patriarchs retired to Rome, where they continued as merely titular dignitaries, using the basilica of St. Lawrence Without the Walls as their church, until Pius IX. sent them back to Jerusalem in 1847. The patriarchs of the Latin kingdom were for the most part not very edifying people, and the Church was well rid of them. During the large interregnum between 1291 and 1847, the Catholic cause in the Holy Land was upheld entirely by the Franciscans. The Franciscan provincial bore the title of *Custos Terrae Sanctae*, and the Turkish Government recognised him as head of the " Latin nation " in Palestine.

The position was no sinecure. For the Turks, faithful to the promise of Omar, allowed rights of pilgrimage to the unbelievers, but they allowed them only on very definite conditions. Any pilgrim who at all violated these conditions —went out of the prescribed bounds or visited any place at other than a permitted hour—was at once seized, perhaps killed, perhaps sold into slavery, perhaps ransomed by the impecunious Franciscans. Life was never easy under such circumstances.

St. Ignatius, strangely enough, seems to have arrived at Jerusalem ignorant of the ecclesiastical constitution there. He found that he could establish nothing without the consent of the Franciscan provincial. The provincial happened to be away at Bethlehem, and St. Ignatius was given leave to remain in the convent until his return, when his request could be considered.

The provincial returned, and on the day on which the other pilgrims were to depart, St. Ignatius was sent for by the provincial and told, with the greatest kindness, that after full consideration of his request it had been decided that he must go along with the rest. The Catholics in the Holy Land lived under strictly conditioned toleration, and the provincial thought that obedience to those conditions would impose upon a person of St. Ignatius' zeal an intolerable strain, while disobedience might involve the whole Christian community in disaster. St. Ignatius was at first a little inclined to truculence. He said that he was determined to abide by his resolution if to do so would not be to offend God. "But you would indeed offend God," answered the provincial, "if you persisted in remaining contrary to my will, who have authority from the Holy See to determine who shall be allowed to remain and who not, and even to excommunicate those who refuse to comply." He offered to show St. Ignatius the Papal Bull in proof of his claim, but Ignatius refused to look at it, and meekly obeyed.

The story is interesting, for on his visit to Jerusalem, St. Ignatius was for the only time in his life brought into personal contact with a non-Christian culture. Many people think of the Jesuits as a society especially formed for fighting the battles of the Church against her external enemies. Such a notion is false and unhistorical, and it is interesting that on the only occasion in his life in which he was brought face to face with such a non-Catholic culture, he was judged exceptionally unsuited to deal with the problems of such a situation. The Christian at Jerusalem at that date had to learn to tolerate something which only people of a particular temperament are capable of tolerating. He had to learn to be content with less than his rights. If the Christian religion was true, then certainly Christendom had a right to the ownership of the Holy Land. It had a duty to vindicate that right, if necessary in arms, yet the divisions of Christendom made such a vindication impracticable. The Christian in Jerusalem had to be content with compromise, and compromise in such a matter St. Ignatius' temperament was not well suited to accept.

Before he left Jerusalem he was guilty of an act so rash that the provincial, when he heard of it, must have been devoutly thankful for the decision which he had taken. On the Mount of Olives were to be seen what tradition averred to be the last footmarks of Our Lord before He ascended into heaven. St. Ignatius felt a great longing to venerate these footmarks alone, even though it was very dangerous to venture beyond the city walls without a Turkish escort. He therefore bribed the guards with a penknife, and was allowed to go to the Holy Place alone. After he had finished his adoration and was coming away, it entered his mind that he had not sufficiently observed in which direction Our Lord's feet were pointing when they last touched the earth. He felt an inexpressible longing to go back and see, and giving to the guard a second bribe of a pair of scissors, he made his way back. As he was returning from his second visit, he was met by one of the Armenian servants of the Franciscans, who angrily caught hold of him and led him back to the monastery. By his devotion and his violation of the rules, he had thrown into danger the whole Christian community in Jerusalem, and the Armenian cannot be blamed for his anger. Yet, as St. Ignatius was being led back, he saw Our Lord moving before him in the air, presumably to reassure him lest his rash love should lie hardly on his conscience.

St. Ignatius returned from Jerusalem to Jaffa and thence to Cyprus. From Cyprus three vessels were sailing for Europe, one Turkish, two Venetian, the one large and well equipped, the other old and small. Winter was coming on, and most of the pilgrims took their passages on the large Venetian boat. St. Ignatius could not afford to do so, but the others told the captain that he was a saint, and begged that he might be given a free passage for the love of God. The captain replied with more humour than charity that if he were a saint, then he could walk on the water as other saints had before him, and St. Ignatius had to sail on the smaller vessel.

At sunset on the first day a storm took them all. The Turk went down with all hands on board. The large Venetian vessel

was wrecked on the coast of Cyprus, and those on board
escaped only with their lives. St. Ignatius' vessel made the
Apulian coast and thence continued on her way to Venice,
which she reached in January, 1524.

They were two and a half months on the voyage, and there
was thus plenty of opportunity for reflection. The saint was
now in a bewildered state. He had dedicated himself to the
service of God, and he had persuaded himself that it was God's
will that he should serve Him at Jerusalem. Now it seemed
that this was not so. What next then? Whither should he
turn? His one desire was to imitate Christ. How learn to
do that better than by learning the life of Christ? So he
turned to the Bible. He read and came one day to the 18th
chapter of St. Luke—that amazingly dramatic, pathetic chapter
in which we get a more vivid insight into the everyday life of
Our Lord than we do perhaps anywhere else in the Gospels.
It begins with the sad, half-humorous, half-satirical parable of
the unjust judge who would do nothing for the widow for
justice's sake, but remedied her grievances because she made
such a nuisance of herself. After that the parable of the
Pharisee and the publican, and then the rich young man comes
up to Our Lord and asks how he can be saved. One can see in
one's mind's eye across two thousand years the little buzz of
satisfaction of the Apostles as they nudged one another in
approval at the doctrine of the camel and the needle's eye.
They were not rich; they had renounced the world, its pomps,
its follies and its vanities. "With God all things are possible."
Why, yes, that was only fair; a rich man would squeeze in
here and there by the mercy of God, but his chances were very
much smaller than those of one who had on earth already given
up everything to follow his Master.

Yet what harm could it do to make assurance doubly sure?
They push forward St. Peter; perhaps he steps forward of
himself. Master, it is all right, isn't it? Then Peter said,
" Lo, we have left all and followed Thee." Nobody could
ask more of us, could they?

Jesus answers, " Verily I say unto you. There is no man

that hath left house or parents or brethren or wife or children for the kingdom of God's sake, who shall not receive manifold more in the present time and in the world to come life everlasting."

What a relief ! We can imagine the sigh that went round the Apostles. Why, this was better than they had dared to hope. Theirs was the best of both worlds with a vengeance.

Then immediately Our Lord takes the Twelve apart and pours out to them that terrible prophecy of the Passion that awaited Him. What on earth was this ? They could not make head or tail of it. It seemed to be in complete contradiction with what had gone before. " And they understood none of these things." " *Et ipsi nihil horum intellexerunt.*" *Nihil*—not a single word of them.

As St. Ignatius read this great story—read it with all the passion and more than all the passion with which he used to read the *Amadis de Gaul*—it suddenly flashed upon him that he was as the Apostles. Strongly emotional by nature, he had yearned for love, but even the emotion of love was not satisfying, because it was unsupported by reason.

The word " love " is loosely used in common talk. When we say " I love such and such a picture," we merely mean that we get pleasure out of looking at it. But love of a person implies more than pleasure in the lover. The pleasure and the emotion indeed are there, but they can be there where no love is. What differentiates love from what is not love is that in love there is an identification of wills. The happiness of the lover is made dependent on the well-being of the loved. The perfect expression of love is in the words, " Not My Will, but Thine, be done." " What's to come is still unsure," writes Shakespeare in answer to the question, " What is love ? " True enough of the love of the creature, only untrue of the love of the Creator, for God alone is unchangeable.

Now love in this full and proper sense, which demands the identification of the wills, clearly demands both the training and the exercise of the intelligence in order to discover what God's will is. In the most satisfying love, the *amor intellectualis*, the soul loves that which reason tells it that it ought to love; reason, in the Aristotelian phrase, "gives an account" of the emotion. All these truths St. Ignatius had not at all grasped. Up to this time he had studied little and casually. He was an uneducated man in the sense in which most so-called educated men in England to-day are uneducated. That is to say, he was not an illiterate, but, on the other hand, the things of the intellect played no part in his life. Now if he was to love God fully, he must learn to understand. And in order to learn, he must be willing to start from the beginning.

CHAPTER V

LEARNING IN SPAIN

In order to carry out his project, it was necessary for St. Ignatius to return to Spain; in order to return to Spain, to cross Italy from Venice to the west coast. The task was no easy one, for the uncertain peace of Noyon was now at an end. Hapsburg and Valois were again troubling Europe with their interminable wars, and Northern Italy was one of the many theatres of those wars. The Battle of the Bicocca on April 27th, 1523, had enabled Francesco Sforza to establish himself as ruler of Milan, and had reduced the French force there to a few garrisons. In order to restore the French position, Admiral Bonnivet was sent in at the head of a motley army of twenty-five thousand Swiss, Germans, French and Italians. The Imperial troops, who were to oppose him in support of Sforza, were under Colonna, and both Venice and Pope Adrian VI. declared themselves on the Imperial side. In the very month of September, however, in which Bonnivet entered Italy, the situation was thrown into confusion by the death of Adrian. Colonna abandoned the Northern Milanese and retired on the city of Milan. Bonnivet's attempt to capture Milan was a failure, as was Bayard's to capture Cremona. The Imperialists rallied their forces. At the end of the year Charles de Lannoy succeeded to the leadership in place of Colonna, who had died, and the first months of 1524 saw the two armies in conflict round the waters of the Ticino and the Imperialists driving the French back from Albiate-Grasso to Vigevano and then from Vigevano to Novara. It was just these months which St. Ignatius chose to make his journey from Venice through the Milanese to Genoa.

St. Ignatius set out from Venice probably some time in

February, 1524, taking with him some fifteen or sixteen giulii which a friend had forced on him, probably the Biscayan merchant who had befriended him during his previous stay in Venice. In order to avoid the country of operations as much as possible, he struck south across the Po to Ferrara, at that time ruled by Alfonso d'Este under the suzerainty of the Pope, a suzerainty which it had been the ambition of Julius II. and Leo X. to convert into real ownership. Under Adrian VI. the Papacy had for the moment forgotten its Italian political ambitions, but it was confidently expected that they would be revived by the new Medici Pope, Clement VII., the controller of the policy of Leo X., that he would throw his forces on to the Imperial side, and that Alfonso would by consequence join the French. For the moment all was unsettled.

St. Ignatius, arriving at Ferrara, went into the cathedral to pray. A beggar came up and asked alms of him, which he gave. Others tried their luck, and the saint gave to each of them until very soon all his little wealth was exhausted. The beggars were much impressed at such generosity in one who seemed poorer even than themselves, and when St. Ignatius told them pathetically that he had now nothing left either for them or for himself, they raised loud cries of " A Saint ! a Saint," but made no motion to restore the money, allowing him to go on his way enjoying the advantages of holy poverty.

In spite of his southerly route, he fell in with both Spanish and French troops before he reached Genoa. By the Spaniards he was suspected of being a spy, but after examination was contemptuously dismissed by the officer who said to those who had arrested him, " Cannot you tell a fool from a spy ? Take him and set him free ! " Among the French he fell in with an officer who came from his own part of the world, from some place just to the French side of the Pyrennean frontier, and was most kindly treated.

It was only in the previous year and not far away, on the banks of the River Sesia up in Piedmont, that the great Chevalier himself had died, and some have amused themselves with the thought that perhaps Bayard's gallant spirit had been allowed to

LEARNING IN SPAIN

infect the whole French army. It is more pleasant than probable. Yet one cannot but regret that coincidence did not stretch her long arm just a little longer, and bring face to face these two great knights without fear and without reproach, the knight of the lilies of France, and the knight of the lilies of the Mother of God, the one splendid and the cynosure of all eyes, the other mean, draggled, unkempt and yet more splendid and of a prouder uniform.

At Genoa, St. Ignatius met a certain Don Rodrigo Portuondo of Biscay with whom he had been acquainted in his courtier days. Portuondo was in charge of the Spanish galleys, and obtained for St. Ignatius a passage on one for Barcelona. Even then his troubles were not at an end. Genoa was in Imperial hands, but Andrea Doria, the famous Genoese seaman-adventurer, afterwards to become the liberator of his native town, was at that date still in the service of Francis I., with whom he was not to quarrel till 1528. Doria was on the watch in the Gulf of Genoa, and gave chase to the Spanish flotilla, but it managed to escape him and arrived safely in Barcelona towards the end of February or the beginning of March.

As soon as he reached Barcelona, St. Ignatius at once sought out Isabel Roser and told of his failure and of his new plan. She approved and offered to get a certain Geronimo Ardebalo as tutor for him. But St. Ignatius wished to be taught by an old Cistercian whom he had got to know during his stay at Manresa. He went up to Manresa for the purpose of arranging this, but, arriving there, found that the Cistercian was dead. He therefore returned to Barcelona and took up his residence with his other great friend among the ladies of that town, Inez Pascual. Antonio Pujol, Inez' priest-brother, furnished him with books, and St. Ignatius, thirty-three years old, entered himself at a local school as one of the ordinary pupils, taking his place in the class along with the boys.

One is inclined to say that this was a very stupid bit of affectation, and so I have no doubt, from the narrowly educational point of view, it was. A man of thirty-three learns in one way, a boy of fourteen in another. To tie the former down to the methods of the latter is but wantonly to handicap him. Doubtless, St. Ignatius either understood this from the first or else came very soon to understand it. For he never recommended such a practice to any other grown student. He did what he did—or at least, he persisted in what he did—in order that he might teach by a striking example. I will not say that the lesson which he was anxious to teach was that of the supreme importance of education, for to say that would be to give a false impression. The lesson was rather that reason must be the ruler of the emotional life. In society those with understanding must rule those without; in each individual, according to his capacity, the emotions must be the servants of the reason. For thirty-three years St. Ignatius had not understood this. It was important therefore that he should show by vivid example that he was now beginning to work out his whole system of life afresh.

The progress of his studies was not at all satisfactory. He was well down the class. Partly, no doubt, this was simply because the exercises were suited to growing boyhood where the memory is strong and the reasoning power weak, and we should none of us make much of a showing at examinations and lessons in " by heart." There was a further reason, and a peculiar one. St. Ignatius found himself unable to concentrate on his lessons because he was continually distracted by the thoughts of God which he could not banish from his mind. As his biographers say, " He was for ever practising the *Amo*, *Amas* which he was incapable of conjugating." The little story is, I think, important as illustrating how exactly true it is to say that St. Ignatius loved God as the rest of us love a person. The surest sign of a schoolboy's first love is that he is unable to learn his lessons because of the domination of his mind by the thought of the loved one.

All affections, in the Ignatian view, can be inordinate, save only the love of God. We cannot love God too much. But even in such a love there is a trick that the Devil can play on us. Though we should do everything for the greater glory of God, yet it does not necessarily conduce to God's greater glory that we should always be thinking of it. There are the tasks of Martha to be done as well as those of Mary. So St. Ignatius saw in this preoccupation of his mind a device of the Devil. " Satan is transformed into an angel of light," he said. Therefore, one day he took his tutor, Ardebalo, to that Church of Santa Maria de la Mar, and there told him of his faults and begged him, if he ever found him inattentive in the future, to beat him as he would beat any of his other pupils.

Whether Ardebalo ever did beat him is not, I think, recorded. But certainly from the time of Manresa onwards he frequently beat himself, and during the time of his schooling he was particularly severe upon himself. It is impossible, if one would give a full picture of St. Ignatius or indeed of any other saint, to omit the story of such self-disciplining ; at the same time it is hard to comment on it. To our sturdy ancestors, with no nonsense about them, the birch played its honourable part in the education of an English gentleman, but the self-flagellation of a grown person was " mad "—and there was an end of it. We of a later Freudian day do not let things slip by so easily as that. In every virtue the eagle eye can detect a secret, lurking and twisted vice. In every feat of mortification, at which previous generations have stood amazed, the sophisticated modern can discover a new form of sexual perversion, and where we used to read such words as " saint " or " ascetic," we now read " coprophilist " or " masochist."

Now it is very easy to make jokes about modern psychologists —and not bad fun either. But if we face the question honestly, we must admit that there is some truth in what they say. Whether we are the better for thinking so much about the oddities of sexual perversion is, I think, doubtful, but that in point of fact the influence of sex is present in many actions in which Victorian novelists did not see fit to recognise it at all cannot be denied, and I should not think it at all a healthy sign in most of my acquaintances if I heard that they had taken to flogging themselves. For to those who have in their nature the appropriate twist, there is a physical satisfaction to be got out of all these acts of mortification.

No attitude towards life is more horrible than that of the psychologist, who combines intense Puritanism with intense prurience, who can detect the influence of sex in every action, and who thinks that for some reason or other he has stripped an action of all its virtue, if he can only show that the sexual was one among its motives. Yet at the same time it is a risky thing for those to indulge in such practices who are not quite sure of themselves—who are not quite sure that they have first purged their nature of physical affections, and that the intensity of their spiritual life is such that their emotions find a purely spiritual and not a physical satisfaction. Intensely wise was the reply of Strada, who disapproved of the extravagant acts of mortification in which Rodriguez permitted his students at Coimbra to indulge. Rodriguez argued that there was precedent for all that they did in the life of St. Francis. Strada replied, " St. Francis acted under a special inspiration from God, and these practices will do when another St. Francis comes, or God grants a fresh inspiration."

Thus St. Ignatius did not, it seems, begin to flog himself until he had first had the vision of his vocation, one result of which was, as he himself tells us, to free him entirely and for the rest of his life from all carnal desires. It is probably true that no high sanctity has ever been achieved without the practice of some or other of these extraordinary acts of mortification ; it is as true that these acts can only be safely practised by spirits which have already purged themselves by more normal asceticism. The fallacy of the modern psychologists, we are often told, is that they generalise from abnormal cases. It may be true, though I am inclined to suspect that most of us are the victims of our whirling complexes of one sort or another, and my complaint against the psychologists is rather that they generalise only from a certain class of abnormal cases. It may be true of most of us that if we rolled about naked in the brambles we should be doing so for some obscure and not creditable sexual reason, but that does not alter the fact that when St. Francis rolled, he rolled solely for the love of God. Nor, if the only motives that could bring us to flog ourselves would be mixed and morbid motives, does it prove that those are the only motives that brought St. Ignatius to flog himself.

In the course of his studies, St. Ignatius was advised to read Erasmus' *Enchiridion Militis Christiani* both for the sake of its Latin and for the sake of its content. He did so on his confessor's advice, but disliked the book extremely, nor, though Nadal was to be able to introduce Erasmus' treatise on grammar as a text-book into the Jesuit College at Messina, would St. Ignatius as a general rule allow any but the most senior of the Fathers of the Society to read Erasmus. His own favourite author during these years was Thomas à Kempis. It is important that we should try to understand St. Ignatius' enormous lack of sympathy for Erasmus. The lack of sympathy was partly to his credit, partly to his discredit.

It is a superficial view which thinks that St. Ignatius disliked Erasmus because Erasmus scoffed at corrupt religious. No one was more keenly alive to the corruptions of ecclesiastical life than was St. Ignatius, and, even though he might have objected that in Erasmus' attacks there was not sufficient of that almost intolerable sadness which the truly devout believer would feel at the thought how unworthy were the instruments of the divine dispensation, yet he never argued that the person of an unworthy priest should be exempt from criticism. Nor did he object to Erasmus' demand that religion should win for herself the support of sound learning. St. Ignatius, no lover of learning himself, was to win for the Church just that support of learning for which Erasmus was always clamouring. He saw very clearly that the weapon of learning in the hand of the unorthodox could in the long run only be met by the weapon of greater learning in the hand of the orthodox.

The point is more subtle. Erasmus was no heretic. If we are of those who are amused by listing our authors into columns of Catholic and non-Catholic, then Erasmus must come in the Catholic column. And certainly by the time that St. Ignatius came to read him, he had quite definitely broken with Luther by his *Diatribe De Libero Arbitrio*, written in 1524. Yet there was in Erasmus a spirit subtly dangerous to the Church. We all of us in England to-day know of Catholics—very likely in a sense, exemplary Catholics—who punctually perform every obligation which the Church lays upon them, who piously accept all the teachings of the Church that they are absolutely compelled to accept but who, the moment that they get outside what one may call the area of the *ex cathedra*, betray the fact that unconsciously they draw their opinions from an anti-Catholic culture. So with Erasmus. He was a scholar, and by that I mean not merely that he was a learned man, but that in his standard of values, learning came first—above holiness. St. Ignatius was concerned that the Church should be supported by sound learning, but Erasmus was rather concerned that sound learning should be supported by the Church.

Erasmus was a Catholic, but he was what one might call a negative Catholic. He formed his own views on life and then allowed to the teachings of the Church, as it were, a veto upon them, shedding with reluctance such opinions as he was quite compelled to shed. Nor can one be quite certain that he was not in the last resort a political Catholic. Now it is an important truth that ultimately the Church is the one safe bulwark against chaos, anarchy and revolution. But she is only a safe bulwark because she is so much more than a bulwark. No spirit is more alien to that of the Church than that of the man who supports her merely because he is, say, a Conservative.

It is significant that St. Ignatius turned from Erasmus' work to that of Thomas à Kempis. For the imitation of Christ is a feat that it would never have occurred to Erasmus to attempt. St. Ignatius' objection to Erasmus was that there was nothing Christlike about him. To him to be in a state of grace was the end of religious duty ; to St. Ignatius it was but the beginning, the necessary condition before it became possible to receive the grace of God, to co-operate with it and thus to fashion the soul more nearly in imitation of the Beloved Master.

" Give ear, thou knight-errant of Christ," Durer wrote to Erasmus. " Ride on for the Lord Christ's sake ; defend the truth ; reach forth to the martyr's crown." But Erasmus had other plans. He had no ambition to be a martyr, whether for the Protestant or for the Catholic faith. His true religion was the religion of scholarship. The revival of learning, in which he played so honourable a part, was, in so far as it was a revival of learning and not a mere substitution of learning for thinking, a movement for the benefit of mankind. Yet it brought into Europe a new dogma—a dogma which has played a more important part in the development of Protestant countries than any Protestantism ever taught by Luther or by Calvin—a dogma which I can only describe in all reverence as that of the Immaculate Conception of the expert. The men of the Middle Ages, with all their faults, did not have that fault. St. Thomas Aquinas thought that his task was to teach the doctrine of the Church, not, since he was a man with a first-class mind, to tell the Church what her doctrine ought to be, and at the end of it all he was quite ready to genuflect and say " Credo," if his superiors showed him that he was wrong. Thomas à Kempis did not say, " I am Thomas à Kempis who have a right to self-expression." Villon was a sad scoundrel, yet to do him justice, he never pleaded that the fact that he was a great poet excused him for being a great scoundrel. With the Renaissance —and more than anybody else, with Erasmus—came in the notion that the great question who was the final authority should be settled not by the choosing of the Holy Ghost, but by purely human qualifications. While there is nothing in this world better than the love of learning, there is nothing worse than the worship of it. Even though Erasmus did not wholly know what he was doing, it was through his mouth that the kingdom that was of this world issued its challenge to the kingdom that was not of this world.

In this, as in all ethical problems, the Catholic way is the middle way. The Church, opposed to the divine right of experts, is equally opposed to some mad equalitarianism which pays equal attention to everybody's opinion, quite irrespective of his qualifications for forming it. The expert—the scholar or any other sort of expert—has an all-important function to perform in society, but he must perform it within the framework of society. The very nature of God's revelation is that He has revealed to us what we could not know of ourselves, and before revelation an Aquinas or an Erasmus, an Acton or a Döllinger must bow and accept like any Breton peasant-woman or Goanese illiterate.

So, too, with corruptions in the Church. Ecclesiastical corruption is gross ; it is unpardonable ; reform is necessary. Yet " it must needs be that offences come." They are in the very nature of the Church militant here on earth, and to say that Man is corrupt is but to say that he has fallen. Our Lord did not choose for His Apostles " twelve good men and true." He chose eleven good men and a traitor. Nor did He select for the leadership of his Church some Platonic saint-philosopher-king. He chose one whom He Himself accused of savouring of those things that be of Man in protest against which He erected His Church—one who even on the worldly code of honour was to fail miserably before a trial which the average English gentleman would rightly think himself quite strong enough to surmount. So, too, of the scandals of Erasmus' time. They did not unchurch the Church. Indeed in a way I cannot imagine a more vigorous tribute to the strength of the Christian tradition in Europe than the fact that people were willing to pay deference to Alexander Borgia because he was the Vicar of Christ, and that for generations the revenues of abbeys, bishoprics, prebends were handed over to swindlers, infants, debauchees, pluralists for no better reason—in the long run—than that they demanded them in the name of Christ. The less admirable is the Church in her temporal nature, the less is the danger that we shall forget her mystical nature. The less we think of Christians, the more we are compelled to think of Christ, and the less is the danger that we shall imagine that the ultimate authority is with Man.

So far then St. Ignatius was right in his suspicion of Erasmus. Yet at the same time it is but right to admit, as I have already admitted, that he seems to have been quite inhumanly insensitive to intellectual pleasures. The temptations of the flesh he knew and had conquered. But all those high delights in discovery, achievement and creation, which were so strong a

life to such a man as Blessed Thomas More—the love of the
colour and form, the warmth and laughter of the passing world
which filled the grand souls of Cervantes, of Chaucer and of the
gorgeous Rabelais—these were nothing to Ignatius, even as
they had been nothing to Savonarola before him. What is
there sadder or more striking than this total lack of sympathy
between the grand spirits of their age, Ignatius and François
Rabelais? "The bad odour of the Spaniards overcockcow-
leedooed by Brother Inigo," Rabelais includes among the
library of St. Victor.

The true, inward spirit of the Renaissance St. Ignatius did
not welcome as a friend, nor fight as the temptation of the Devil.
He simply never heard about it. In Paris, among the haunts of
which Villon and Rabelais had written, in Rome with Michelangelo and Bramante, on the hills above Bologna which Dante
had made famous, in Venice with Titian and Cellini, he betrays
not one flicker of interest in all the great dream that was coming
to birth around him, and in which his own disciples were to
play so notable a part. For all the Jesuits were not as Ignatius.
Turn to Francis Xavier and you have turned to a different
world. Le Jay could hold his own at the court of Ferrara,
where Clément Marot had delighted the Este blue-stockings,
and perhaps the most convincing of all arguments that was ever
penned for the futility of a policy of mere intellectual repression
by Edict and Index was to come from the pen of the great
Canisius. But St. Ignatius, if he ever heard of Dante, must,
one feels, have wondered why on earth he imagined that Virgil
was going to receive any special favours in the next world. If
there was one side of Erasmus' character which he understood
only too well, there was another side which he did not understand at all.

After his strange interview with Ardebalo in the Church of
Santa Maria della Mar St. Ignatius' studies took a turn for the
better. At the same time he was attempting to continue the
life of devotion. He lived in a room in Inez Pascual's house,
and Juan Pascual has recorded how one night he looked into
St. Ignatius' room through a chink in the door. As Juan

afterwards deposed on oath, a dazzling light which radiated from the saint himself seemed to fill the air. Ignatius was lifted up two feet from the ground, and Juan heard him cry out, " O Lord, if men did but know Thee," and " Ah, my God, how infinitely good Thou art to bear with a miserable sinner such as I am."

It is a first feeling that of all miracles those of levitation are among the most pointless. And just as people often ask why God should wish the blood of St. Januarius to liquefy, so we are inclined to ask who was the better off for St. Ignatius' floating about in the air. But in truth nothing could be more impudent nor less scientific than this wish to dictate to God how He should interfere with the workings of His own laws. Our task is to discover what did happen and to record it—not to deduce what ought to have happened. I cannot myself, I must confess, see much sense in levitation. Who is the better for floating ? Yet I mention it but as a confession. If I cannot see, so much the worse for me.

At Barcelona, as previously at Manresa, St. Ignatius on the one hand attracted to himself many followers, and on the other aroused the enmity of those who had no wish for reformation. He made it his study to behave towards his enemies according to the precepts of the Gospel. Once when they stopped him in the street, reviled him and threatened him with physical violence, he made no answer except to thank them. And in the same way, when Inez Pascual discovered some of her servants abusing him and would have dismissed them, St. Ignatius pleaded for them, saying that when they called him a great sinner, they had but spoken the truth.

His chief conflict during this time was that over the Convent of the Angels. The Convent of the Angels was a Dominican nunnery just outside the gates of Barcelona. Like so many religious houses in all parts of Europe at that time, it had fallen into corrupt ways. Young men of bad reputation frequented it at all hours of night and day. St. Ignatius determined to reform it. So, instead of writing a witty little book about the nuns as Erasmus might have done, he went every day to their church and knelt there before the Blessed Sacrament, praying for their conversion. After a time the nuns began to notice him, made inquiries who he was, and at last questioned him. He then took his opportunity to speak to them on their life. Christ died for all, he said, and sin in any one was horrible, but they had accepted a special vocation, and God offered to them a special grace that they might live worthily of that vocation. If they neglected to co-operate with that grace their condition would be far worse than that of the man or woman to whom it had not been offered.

After a time St. Ignatius' exhortations had their effect on the nuns, and they decided once more conscientiously to enforce their rule and to refuse admission to the convent to the dissolute men. This naturally infuriated the men, and twice they attacked St. Ignatius on his way to or from the convent. In the end they determined on a more desperate remedy. They hired two Moorish slaves, and, as St. Ignatius and Antonio Pujol were returning from the convent one day, these two Moors fell on them just outside the city gate of San Daniel and so beat them that Pujol died of his injuries and St. Ignatius was for a long time thought likely to die.

St. Ignatius was brought back to Inez Pascual's house by a kindly miller who happened to pass by, and there he lay for thirty days at death's door. On the thirtieth day, there being no longer any hope of recovery, he received the Last Sacraments. Immediately he began to recover. Three weeks later he was declared out of danger and soon after was able to leave his bed.

Throughout he had refused to give the name of his assailants, praying only that they might be pardoned and might come to repentance. And, as soon as he could walk, he insisted that in spite of the danger he would go again to the convent. Inez Pascual besought him not to do so, but he insisted, and the result was a great triumph of grace. As he left the convent, a certain merchant named Ribeira met him, knelt down before him and confessed that he was the author of the attack. He asked for St. Ignatius' forgiveness—which the saint readily gave—and promised amendment of his life for the future—a promise which he is said to have kept. He added that he was moved not so much by the horror of his crime as by St. Ignatius' forbearance.

Ever since God had revealed to St. Ignatius that he was to found a religious order, he had been on the look-out for those who might be associated with him in his work. So far he had found none. Now in Barcelona he came across three who he thought might be suitable—Calisto, Arteaga and Diego de Cazares their names. None of them, as it happened, persevered. At the same time he rejected two who wished to join him. The first was Miguel Rodis, to whom he answered, "You will not follow me, but one day a son of yours will enter the religious order which by God's grace I shall found." This prophecy was fulfilled. In years to come, Miguel's youngest son came to him and told him of his desire to be a Jesuit. Then for the first time Miguel told him of St. Ignatius' prophecy. Curiously enough the boy then changed his mind and tried to become a Carthusian, but twice an accident prevented his reception into a Carthusian monastery, whereupon he reverted to his original intention and became a Jesuit.

The second whom St. Ignatius rejected was that Juan Pascual whom I have quoted. Neither St. Ignatius nor any other wise spiritual director has ever believed that souls should be collected higgledy-piggledy into religion, irrespective of their vocations, and he told Juan Pascual that it was God's will that he should remain in the world. He prophesied for him neither joy nor success in it, as the world counts joy and success, but prophesied that through sorrow and failure he should come closer to God. "You will marry a woman of great virtue and will have many sons and daughters ; and on their account you will have many sorrows and misfortunes, which will be sent you by God out of love for you and for remission of your sins." This prophecy, too, was fulfilled. Juan's eldest son was born deaf and dumb ; his second went mad ; his third led a dissolute life and one day fell dead at his father's feet. His daughters drained his resources to provide them with marriage-portions, and, as a result, at the end of his life he was reduced to beggary—to a beggary for

which, as St. Ignatius had prophesied, he thanked God Who
had spared him the temptations of wealth and success.

After two years of study Ardebalo told St. Ignatius that he
was now fit for higher studies. St. Ignatius, having passed an
examination before competent theologians, therefore decided to
go to the University of Alcala. The University of Alcala
traced its history back to Sancho IV. of Castile in the 13th
century. But the establishment of the College of San Ildefonso,
or the Renaissance University of Alcala, in 1499 was the work
of the great Cardinal Ximenes, at that time Archbishop of
Toledo, and afterwards, as has already been said, to become
Regent of Spain. Ximenes brought to Alcala a scholastic
colony from the great University of Salamanca and imported
professors from Paris and Bologna. He established a hostel in
honour of the Mother of God for the students, and on his death
in 1517 left to the College of San Ildefonso 14,000 ducats.
As Francis I. said a year or two before St. Ignatius' arrival at
Alcala, when he was taken there during his captivity in Spain
after his capture at Pavia, " Only a line of kings could have
done in France what has been accomplished here by a single
Spanish monk." In consequence of Ximenes' munificence the
University was able to make especially liberal provisions for
poor scholars, and for that reason, probably, St. Ignatius elected
to go there rather than elsewhere.

St. Ignatius arrived in Alcala in August, 1526, and found that
the University term did not commence until October 18th. He
therefore determined to fill in the intervening two months in
devotion and works of charity. Ignatius refused to go to a
college like other students, but instead lodged in the old hospital
of the city. There he was able to minister to a certain young
Frenchman of the name of Jean, page to Don Martin of Cordova,
Viceroy of Navarre. The result of his ministrations was that
Jean threw up his position at the Viceroy's and begged St.
Ignatius to accept him as the fourth member of the Society.
Ignatius consented. St. Ignatius and his companions went
about dressed in a loose tunic of coarse grey serge which won
for them the nickname of " *los Ensacados*," or the people in

sacks.   He also soon after made the acquaintance of two others
—Diego d'Eguia, cousin of Francis Xavier, and Emmanuel
Miona—who were afterwards to be of the Society, though they
did not join at this time.

At Alcala, as at Manresa and at Barcelona, St. Ignatius soon
found himself called upon to face hostility.   A priest this time
was at the head of the opposition to him, but he was befriended
by the warden of the hospital of Antecana, in whose house he
was given refuge.

When the University term opened St. Ignatius attempted to
combine the life of study with that of charity and devotion.
Indeed not only that, but he attempted in addition, in order to
get his degree as soon as possible, to take courses in logic,
physics and theology at one and the same time.   The spiritual
prospered more than the academic life.   From his first arrival
in Alcala he began to exercise an influence upon those around
him greater than he had ever attempted to gain at Barcelona or
elsewhere.   It is a difficulty for the biographer of St. Ignatius
that of all his natural gifts by far the most striking, by unanimous
testimony of his contemporaries, was one which it is quite
impossible to account for—the power to influence others.   We
can often tell why a certain person is unable to exercise any
influence over others, to point out the crudity in his character
which causes him to set about his task of persuasion in just the
wrong way or at just the wrong moment.   But it is easier to
account for the lack of this gift than for the possession of it.
Yet it is certain that this gift St. Ignatius pre-eminently possessed.
There was, for instance, a certain young man at Alcala who, in
the grossly scandalous fashion of those times, had obtained by
influence one of the prebendal stalls at the cathedral, though he
was not in orders and of course performed no duties.   On the
contrary, his life was a scandal to the town.   St. Ignatius went
to him one day and, desiring to speak to him alone, rebuked
him for the wickedness of his life and told him what people
were saying of him.   The young man at first burst out into a
temper of fury at such impudence, and threatened to throw him
out of the window.   St. Ignatius spoke again.   How exactly

the conversation developed we do not know, but the end of it was that the young man admitted himself to be wrong and St. Ignatius right, and that, when the servants were called back into the room, they found him speaking to the saint in tones of the deepest respect. He bade the servants lay an extra place for supper, as his guest was going to do him the honour of eating with him. St. Ignatius remained to supper. The young man from that day wholly reformed his life and lived to become a powerful and generous protector of the Society of Jesus.

There is one tale, and it would be easy to tell other similar tales of St. Ignatius. To some it may not perhaps make him seem very attractive. It is common and just to dislike self-righteous busybodies, but any who imagine that St. Ignatius should be put in that class should observe the difference between him and the offensive type of social reformer. We shall speak later of one quite exceptional campaign of his—the campaign against gambling in Guipizcoa. With that exception he never interfered without clear reason with people doing something that amused them. At the Convent of the Angels, here and elsewhere throughout his life, he was concerned only with a definite thing—the purity of the Church of Christ. He interfered to prevent people in ecclesiastical position from giving scandal by conduct unworthy of that position, nor do I think that he ever interfered except where the grossest immoralities were notoriously being committed. He had more serious work to do than to try and prevent such things as mixed bathing or poor people having an occasional drink. His task was to vindicate the law of God where it was being violated. He did not claim, as is so often the modern habit, the right to make up sins as he went along, and so to name any habits which he happened to dislike.

More interesting is the problem why, right or wrong, the young man did not throw him out of the window. The weaker such men's arguments, the more ready they are, as a rule, to resort to violence. And to this problem the only answer is that, as the phrase goes, St. Ignatius " had a way with him." He had the strange gift of getting on with people and influencing them. We may, if we will, ascribe his success to the grace of God, and doubtless the grace of God went with him if ever it went with any man. Yet we have the evidence of his brother that he possessed this gift as a natural gift before he turned in any especial sense to God. " That which seems like magic in you," it will be remembered, his brother called it. There is a phrase, much abused and yet possessed of very real meaning, in which we are told that such a one has " a genius for friendship." We have all of us met one or two of these happy persons. We go with them into a certain environment. We find them the centre of the society there. They do not push or press people for confidences, yet it is to them that everybody naturally turns with his tales of joy or sorrow. We go to another environment, to a society of quite different interests, and again it is to these men or women with their " genius for friendship " that all instinctively flock. There seems no boundary to their power of sympathy, no limit to the number who gain strength from feeding on that power. Such a man, possessed of such a power, was St. Ignatius. If you want further proof of it, read the letters of St. Francis Xavier, and see the terms in which he speaks of his great and most beloved master. Possessed of this power, Ignatius could have led men to great evil, had he chosen to do so. He chose instead to lead them to the love of God.

Perhaps the most important development in the history of the Europe of our day is the exhortation by the ecclesiastical authorities to the faithful to more frequent participation in the Sacraments. Similar exhortations by St. Ignatius in his own day had in these early years no such official support. Not until the great reign of Paul III. was St. Ignatius' campaign to enjoy the advantages of official patronage. Yet even now he always used to urge his followers to communicate every Sunday and holiday. It was the theory, even among conscientious Churchmen, that a too frequent participation in the Sacraments would lead to an irreverent familiarity with them. A certain Doctor Alonso Sanchez, of the Church of San Just, therefore publicly refused communion to one of St. Ignatius' followers who wished to receive it on the octave of a feast as well as on the feast itself.

However, shortly afterwards, as he was dispersing the Bread, some interior feeling of devotion took hold of him, and, convinced that he had been wrong in his previous action, he went up to St. Ignatius after the Mass and invited him home with him. So moved was he by the saint's discourse on spiritual matters that he confessed himself in fault, and ever afterwards entertained the greatest reverence for him.

Yet St. Ignatius was not thus easily freed from difficulties. The position of the ecclesiastical authorities was honourable and intelligible. St. Ignatius was a man of no official position, and yet he was advising those whom he could influence to indulge in a religious practice which was not at all recommended by the regular ecclesiastical authorities. That he was probably a pious man and in good faith might be admitted, but had little to do with the question. Most heresies had been started by pious men in good faith, and dangerous heresies came not from rank falsehood but from an over-emphasis on one aspect of truth at the expense of the balance of the whole. Protestantism was far away and touched either Spain or Ignatius but little, but even Spain, as the great work of Menendez y Pelayo adequately shows, had her own heresies and the troubles which they brought to pious souls. Only three years before, down in the south of the country, there had been " *los Alumbrados*," or the Enlightened, who had taught that interior prayer was the one fulfilment of the law of God. To the man who had attained to that state of prayer, neither good works nor the Sacraments were necessary, and the foulest immoralities might be indulged in without sin. The teachings of St. Ignatius certainly did not seem to be the same as those of *los Alumbrados*, but it was only common sense to investigate and find out exactly what they were. The treatment of St. Ignatius was not unique. Every Spanish spiritual adventurer of the time—Blessed John of Avila, St. Teresa, St. John of the Cross, Luis de Granada—was quite properly compelled to submit his or her experiences to the judgment of the Inquisition.

Whether in matters ecclesiastical, political or artistic, it is absurd to complain of an official machinery for being cautious and conservative. It is the duty of an official machinery to be cautious and conservative, and thus to guard society from the innovating cheap-jack out for notoriety. It is the duty of the true reformer to be prepared to prove his worth by enduring some preliminary discouragement and disappointment.

Therefore the Inquisition at Toledo, the archidiaconal see of the province in which Alcala was, very properly thought that it was right to inquire into the activities of St. Ignatius. A commission was sent down under Don Alonso de Mexia. Mexia was very easily convinced that there was nothing seriously amiss, and handed over the task of completing the informations to Juan Rodriguez de Figueroa, Grand Vicar of the Archbishop of Toledo, he himself returning to Toledo. Figueroa, too, reached the same conclusion as de Mexia, and, summoning St. Ignatius, told him that no evidence had been brought of anything reprehensible in the lives of St. Ignatius and his followers or erroneous in their teachings. They were at full liberty to continue their pious practices as before. He only suggested that, since they were not a recognised religious order, they should not give the impression of a uniform by dressing all alike but should wear different coloured hoods.

St. Ignatius was a little annoyed at the bother of this second examination. " What have you gained by all these question-ings ? What wrongdoing have you discovered in me ? " he asked Figueroa. " Nothing. If we had you would have been punished. You might even have been sent to the stake," said Figueroa. " You, too, would go to the stake if you were a heretic," answered Ignatius.

Yet they all readily agreed to the verdict, as they did also to a subsequent suggestion that they should wear shoes.

A further accusation of a busybody that a certain lady of rank was in the habit of going to St. Ignatius in a mantilla and then removing the mantilla while she conversed with him, Figueroa dismissed as baseless, not even bothering to tell St. Ignatius that the accusation had been made. So far, as he was the first to admit, St. Ignatius had no grievance of any depth against the Inquisition. Thinking that the acquittal was final, he went off to Segovia to visit Calisto, who lay there dangerously ill. On his return to Alcala he was met by an officer of justice who, giving no reason, told him that he must come with him to the clerics' prison. Astonished and understanding nothing, St. Ignatius nevertheless obeyed without question.

As he was being led through the streets to prison, there occurred an incident to narrate which it is necessary to interrupt the story of the saint's dealings with the Inquisition. Making their way down a narrow street, St. Ignatius and his guards had to step to the side for a minute while there swept past them a brilliant cavalcade in the midst of which was the young seventeen-year-old son of the Duke of Gandia, Francis Borgia, on the way from the palace of his uncle, the Archbishop of Saragossa, to the court of the Emperor Charles V. at Valladolid.

It is the business of the Christian faith to challenge the values of the world. And in all the great dramatic scenes of Christian history—of which this was surely one—there has always been present this immortal paradox of Christian values. Since first the astonished shepherds found lying in a manger the little Child Who was Very God of Very God, the lesson of the Christian tableau has been always the same. He who appears strong is always the servant; he who appears weak is always the master. So now the two passed each other and each went his way, Borgia to the Emperor, Ignatius to prison.

What an amazing thing is the mystical nature of the Church! What vileness do we continually find in places where it is least to be pardoned! What sanctity in places where it is least to be expected! If an anti-Catholic pamphleteer wished to expose the filthiness of Catholic life he could hardly do it better than by publishing the genealogical table of Francis Borgia; only he does not do so because of the flower that flourished from that filth. On his father's side his great grandfather was Alexander VI.; on his mother's side, Ferdinand of Aragon. His maternal grandfather was Ferdinand's illegitimate son whom the King made Archbishop of Saragossa when he was nine years old. This eminent ecclesiastic had himself at least four children, two sons and daughters. The two sons were both Archbishops of

Saragossa in their turn, though one of them at any rate never was even ordained priest.   Of the daughters, one married the Duke of Gandia and was the mother of Francis Borgia, one of the greatest saints in the calendar of the Church.   Yet at the age of seventeen Francis still saw before him only a brilliant courtier's career.   He went on, as I have said, to the Emperor's court, Ignatius to prison.   We shall return to him again.

St. Ignatius was taken to the prison of the Inquisition.   In such detention there was no hardship save that of the loss of liberty.   His friends could come and go as they pleased; he could live as he liked ; his free use of his time was not interfered with.   He was merely detained lest he should leave the country before the investigation was concluded.   He soon learnt what was the new charge against him.   Among his disciples were two pious women, mother and daughter, named Maria del Vado and Luisa Velasquez.   These women had conceived the project of devoting their lives to a perpetual pilgrimage from hospital to hospital, ministering to the sick.   But when they asked St. Ignatius' advice he advised strongly against the plan, and imagined that he had caused them to abandon it.   However, towards the end of Lent, without his knowledge or that of their guardian, the two women set out alone on a pilgrimage to beg their way down through Toledo to the shrine of Our Lady of Guadalupe and thence into Andalusia to Jaen, which they hoped to reach in time to see the Santo Rostro, or handkerchief of St. Veronica, exhibited in the cathedral on Good Friday, as was the custom.

The guardian of these women, Don Pedro Guerillos, the professor of theology at the University, was naturally enough very angry when he heard of the madcap scheme which his wards had undertaken, and since he knew that they were in the habit of going to St. Ignatius for spiritual advice, not unreasonably imagined that they were acting on the saint's suggestion. He denounced them to Figueroa.   Many people of influence offered St. Ignatius their services in order that he might regain his freedom, but he was in no special anxiety to do so, and quite content to let things take their course.   Eventually,

Figueroa came to examine him. He asked him "whether he and his companions kept the Sabbath." For St. Ignatius made it a custom to keep Saturdays in special honour of Our Lady, which aroused some suspicion, as among professing Catholics in Spain were many secret Jews who—as the Jesuits were afterwards to discover—tried to pervert Christian teaching from within the Church. St. Ignatius now answered, "I keep the Sabbath in honour of the Blessed Virgin, but I know nothing of Jewish customs, for we have no Jews in my country." (The Jews were mostly in the parts of Spain that had been recently under Mahommedan rule; they did not penetrate much up into the Basque country.)

Figueroa next asked St. Ignatius if he knew the two ladies in question; he said that he did. Was he aware of their project before they set out? "By the oath by which I bound myself when you began your interrogation I was not," he answered. Figueroa replied kindly, "That is the sole cause of your detention here; yet I should have been better pleased had you been more careful to avoid all novelty in your discourses." St. Ignatius had some reason to be amazed at this stupid answer, for, if the question of the two ladies was the sole cause of his detention, then the novelty of his discourses had nothing to do with the case. Besides Figueroa had told him at the previous inquiry that no fault could be found with his discourses and he was encouraged to continue them. He therefore replied with a tartness worthy of his disliked Erasmus, "My lord, I should not have thought that it was any novelty to speak of Christ to Christians." Figueroa answered, as out-debated superiors always do answer, with a sad and silent smile.

St. Ignatius still had to remain in the Inquisition prison for another five weeks until the ladies returned to Alcala and verified his story. He made no objection to the detention. What he did object to was the sentence of the Inquisition which he then received. He was told that his life and doctrine were found to be above reproach and he was free to leave the prison. At the same time he and his associates were at the end of ten days to lay aside the long gown and adopt the ordinary dress of students, and they were also forbidden from holding any public or private conferences until they had finished their theological courses.

The first command was in itself not unreasonable, had not Figueroa in his previous decision already given to them the command to change the colour of their gowns. They had the right to think that that first decision had settled the question once and for all. St. Ignatius answered, " When you bade us dye our clothes, we did as we were told ; but what you now order we cannot do, because we have not the money wherewith."

The second command was a much more serious affair. St. Ignatius and his companions, it must be remembered, had at this time taken no vows of obedience. They were ordinary laymen. Now the stand which Figueroa took is confused by modern talk about every man's right to his own opinion. The machinery of the Church certainly has the right to restrain the professing Catholic from teaching heresy under the guise of Catholic truth. There may even be extreme occasions when because of some grave scandal it is right to prevent even the telling of the truth. But the weapons for the suppression of falsehood should only be used in cases of the most desperate necessity. How much more sparingly still should those weapons be used for the suppression of truth !

We are told by honest men that there is a grave risk of scandal if such and such an evil thing in the life of the Church is freely talked about, if such a thing, in which there is admittedly nothing in itself wrong, is permitted. What these honest men are apt to ignore is the enormous mountain of scandal which is built up by this continual preoccupation with policy. " Great is Truth," they seem to argue, " and it will prevail—in the days of our great grandchildren. For the moment there are most urgent reasons against allowing it to get out." And those who are most anxious to be of the faithful come to feel that it is hopeless to attempt to penetrate to the truth past the shield after shield against it, erected by policy for the prevention of scandal.

Surely this preoccupation with policy is itself bad policy. How small, argues the enemy, must be the trust in God of men who will not even leave it to Him to see that good shall come out of the practising of virtue? In spite of popular chatter about the Jesuits nothing could be more contrary to the Ignatian spirit than such a preoccupation. " Whoever would do a great work for the glory of God must not be overwise " St. Ignatius was afterwards to say. It was Figueroa's fault that he tried to be " overwise." I repeat that the Inquisition was right to be cautious and conservative and to insist on the fullest investigation before acquittal. St. Ignatius could not object to that. The complaint is only of its illogical conduct after full acquittal.

There is something horribly reminiscent of Pontius Pilate in a verdict of " Not guilty but do not do it again." It was not only the infamies of Borgia Popes and worldly monks which brought on the troubles of the 16th century. They were brought on just as much by rows of honest Figueroas dismissing Ignatiuses without a stain on their characters but bidding them keep quiet for the sake of peace, until at last the satire of an Erasmus rises uncontrollably or the ill-balanced mind of a Luther explodes in despair that justice can ever come out of a regular machinery.

While Ignatius was in prison, " the infant of Spain " was born —the prince who was afterwards to be King Philip II. The celebrations of the birth in Alcala coincided with his release. A friend of Ignatius went round the town begging for alms and clothes for the saint. He asked, among others, a certain Lopaz de Mendoza, but Mendoza answered that Ignatius was a rogue, and prayed that he might himself be consumed by fire if Ignatius did not deserve the stake. That very evening, in preparing fireworks for the illumination of the city, Mendoza accidentally set light to some powder and perished in the explosion.

This horrible coincidence confirmed St. Ignatius in the purpose which he had already formed to leave Alcala. He did not argue with Figueroa about his decision. Instead he went off to the Archbishop of Toledo, Don Alonso Fonseca, who happened then to be at Valladolid. Fonseca, an Erasmian reformer and no friend of the ecclesiastical big-stick, received him most kindly and promised to get the sentence revoked. But he could not move unless St. Ignatius lodged a formal appeal. This the saint refused to do. There was therefore no remedy. Fonseca asked him what then he proposed to do. He said that he would transfer to the University of Salamanca. Of this the Archbishop approved ; Salamanca was his own university and he gave him letters to people there. St. Ignatius thus left Alcala, a town famous in the history of his Society, for from it came Laynez, Salmeron and Bobadilla ; soon one of the most notable of Jesuit colleges was to rise up there. St. Francis Borgia was to preach to its townspeople, and in the lecture-halls of its university the imperishable greatness of Suarez was to lay down anew those principles which shall yet astonish and rebuild our Europe. Nor was its great history exclusively connected with the Society of Jesus. For twenty years almost to the day after St. Ignatius shook its dust from his feet was born there Miguel de Cervantes, who, like Ignatius, thought in youth to face life under the easy discipline of a false chivalry and, like him, was brought through suffering to a sterner and a truer love. Alcala is nothing now ; the university has gone to Madrid.

In the late summer of 1527, that same summer in which the Emperor Charles V. let loose his hordes for the sack of Rome, St. Ignatius went on from Valladolid to Salamanca. Salamanca, the first University of Spain and one of the first of Europe, the university which Dr. Johnson two hundred and fifty years later told Boswell that he loved, possessed a greater name than its more modern rival, Alcala. At Salamanca, as at Alcala, there was provision for poor students. In 1401 the then Bishop, Diego de Anaya Maldonado, had founded for them the College of San Bartolomé, afterwards known as the Old College. Two generations after St. Ignatius, Miguel de Cervantes wrote for us a description of the life of the Salamanca undergraduate. " Lack of shirts and no superabundance of shoes," he says. " Their dinner a penny piece of beef amongst four of them ; a pottage made of the broth of the same, with salt and oatmeal and nothing else." They had no fires and " were fain to walk or run up and down half an hour to get a heat into their feet " before going to bed.

St. Ignatius was probably guilty of a blunder in not formally appealing against the verdict of the Inquisition. As it was, that verdict stood uncorrected. He was now in the province of Valladolid and outside the jurisdiction of the Inquisition of Toledo, but it was natural enough that, with such a verdict pronounced upon him, authorities at Salamanca should begin to ask questions the moment that he started to teach. Before he had been in the town a fortnight his confessor, a Dominican of the monastery of St. Stephen, told him that his brethren wished to speak with him. St. Ignatius and Calisto therefore went to dine at the monastery on the next Sunday. After dinner the sub-prior, who was superior as the prior was away, the confessor and one other member of the community took St. Ignatius and Calisto down into the chapel and there began to question them.

Why was Calisto so oddly dressed ?

St. Ignatius explained that Figueroa had forbidden them to wear the gown, that Calisto had given away his student's clothes to a poor priest, and that therefore he had to clothe himself as best he could.

" Oh," said the sub-prior, " Charity begins at home."

Then, turning to Ignatius, he spoke to him of the great pleasure with which he had heard of his manner of life and of his holiness. Ignatius must pardon him if he put to him a few questions on matters of detail. What course of studies had he followed ?

St. Ignatius told him of what he had done at Barcelona and Alcala, of what he intended to do at Salamanca, freely confessing his lack of education.

" How, then, is it that you preach ? " asked the sub-prior.

" We do not preach," said St. Ignatius ; " we only converse with people in a familiar manner about divine things, as, for instance, after dinner with those who ask us to their houses."

" And about what divine things ? For this is what we want to hear."

"We speak of this or that virtue in such a way as to make people love and practise it, and of this or that vice in such a way as to make them hate and avoid it."

"You own you are not learned and, nevertheless, you hold public discourses about virtues and vices. These are subjects about which no one is able to speak unless he has been taught in the schools or by the Holy Spirit. You have not been taught in the schools; it therefore follows that you have been taught by the Holy Spirit. Now this it is that we seek to know."

An Erasmus might easily tell this tale as if it were that of a vile plot to entrap a good man. I do not think that such an interpretation would be fair to the sub-prior. Inquisitiveness was perhaps really the motive which led him to cross-examine St. Ignatius, but there is no reason to think that he had not deceived himself into imagining that it was his duty as a priest to probe into the secrets of St. Ignatius' soul. St. Ignatius' attitude was, on the other hand, perfectly correct. At this, as at all times, he was ready to submit his every word or deed to the judgment of the Church through her regular officials. But this fellow was not the Church. He was not St. Ignatius' confessor nor his bishop nor an inquisitor nor anything else. He was just a busybody who had asked him to lunch. Therefore Ignatius replied:

"It were better to speak no more of these matters."

"What," asked the sub-prior, angry at being baulked of his secrets of the soul, "in these times, when the errors of Erasmus and so many others are being spread abroad and deluding the people, do you refuse to declare what it is you teach them?"

"Father," said St. Ignatius, "I will say no more than what I have said already, except before my superiors who have a right to interrogate me."

"Remain here then," said the sub-prior, "we will soon make you tell everything," and they locked St. Ignatius and Calisto into the monastery and kept them there for the three days while they were arranging for an investigation by the authorities. They treated them as guests and many of the monks declared themselves openly on their side. But kindness was neither here nor there. The sub-prior had every right to demand an investigation; he had no right at all to detain them pending the investigation.

After three days Frias, the Grand Vicar, sent for them to the prison of the Inquisition. They were not indeed put in the common dungeon, but in a room just above it, where their feet were fastened by a chain some eight or nine feet long to a pillar in the middle of the room, " and," as Polanco records, " so they remained for the whole of that night in company with small, most disgusting animals, which would not let them sleep." St. Ignatius was not merely detained, as he had been as Alcala; he was punished. For what offence he was punished it was impossible to say, but the truth was that his treatment was an example of the application of that appalling principle which panders to the insolence of man, by which those in authority must be supported by their superiors, even when they have exceeded their authority. The sub-prior was in a position of authority, therefore he must not be humiliated.

Obedience is a virtue, and it is often a noble thing for the subordinate to obey and not to kick even against the foolish commands of those above him, but it is no virtue for those in higher authority to shield their subordinates who have been guilty of such foolish commands.

Cazares and Arteaga were also arrested and put in the dungeon. The four were then called up one by one and interrogated. They questioned St. Ignatius on theological points. He began by saying that he was unlearned and submitted himself in all things to the judgment of the Church. But he then proceeded to answer their questions with unimpeachable orthodoxy. As satisfactory were his replies on canon law.

The only objection that the Inquisitors could bring against his teaching was that in the discourse on the General Examination of Conscience in the *Spiritual Exercises* he had drawn a distinction between venial and mortal sin, saying that it was but a venial sin when there was " some negligence in rejecting an evil thought," and that a mortal sin was committed only when a man gives his consent with the intention of acting afterwards according to that consent, or with the desire of doing so if he could. Such a distinction, they said, a man without theological qualifications had no business to draw. St. Ignatius pertinently replied that it was not his qualifications but the truth that was in question. Was the distinction true or false? He did not question their right to judge; he only asked that they should do so. "Whether what I have said is true or not, it is for you to judge; if therefore it be not true, condemn the definition."

Since his day St. Ignatius' distinction has received philosophical defence from the great authority of Suarez. But, even apart from such defence, it could not be pretended that his teaching was at all heretical. Unable to meet his challenge, the Inquisitors passed on to their next test. They bade him give them an example of his methods of instruction by delivering a discourse on the First Commandment. St. Ignatius therefore spoke to them of the love of God with such power and sweetness that his judges were, it seemed, for the moment shamed out of whatever designs they may have had against him. Instead of sentence they spoke to him some words of encouragement and respect and left the court.

Yet, strange as it may seem, in spite of such a conclusion Ignatius was not set free. He was led back to prison and the chains were put on him again. There was indignation throughout Salamanca at the way in which he was being treated, an indignation that was, it seemed, felt by everybody except St. Ignatius himself, who bore all gladly for the love of God. Frias himself came to see him accompanied by Francesco Mendoza, afterwards to be Cardinal and Archbishop of Burgos. When Mendoza asked the saint if he did not find it difficult to bear cheerfully such undeserved sufferings, he replied, " I will say to you what I said just now to a noble lady who pitied me because she saw me bound with this chain—' It is a sign that you have but little love for Jesus Christ in your heart, or you would not deem it so grievous a thing to be in bonds for His sake '—and I declare to you that all Salamanca does not contain as many fetters, manacles and chains as I long to wear for the love of God."

After twenty-two days St. Ignatius and his disciples received their sentence. It was the same old sentence as that of Alcala, " Not guilty, but do not do it again." This time they were told that they might teach but that they must not draw distinctions between mortal and venial sins. St. Ignatius saw that such a prohibition would stultify all his teaching. He replied that he would be obedient as long as he remained within the jurisdiction of Frias' court, but that he could not grant to it interior assent, unless Frias was able to declare his teaching false and heretical. He made it clear that he was not willing to remain in Salamanca under the conditions imposed. Frias begged him to remain, and told him that he need not construe the prohibition too rigidly.

One searches in vain for any principle upon which Frias' muddled and disastrous ruling can be defended. It was his duty to prevent the teaching of false doctrine—but he knew that St. Ignatius did not teach false doctrine. Either St. Ignatius ought to be stopped from drawing his distinctions between different kinds of sins, or he ought not. Officially to forbid him to draw such distinctions and privately to tell him not to pay too much attention was to leave him in an intolerably false position. The judgment would stand, ready for any enemy to use against him in the future.

Why did Frias behave in this extraordinary manner ? There was, no doubt, stupid authority's feeling that its own dignity should not admit that nothing at all was wrong. There was, too, its feeling that, however exceptional the case of St. Ignatius might be, it yet did not want to create any precedent of encouragement to unqualified people to go about teaching religion. There was, in fact, as there always is in the whole catalogue of such judgments, volumes of policy and no spark of confidence in the greatness of truth. But there was also, I think, another thing of which Frias was afraid and of which curious accident has preserved a record.

St. Ignatius' trouble with the Inquisition of Salamanca took place during the month of October, 1527. The sub-prior of St. Stephen's, it will be remembered, in his argument mentioned the name of Erasmus. Now it so happens that letter 338 in the

second series of Erasmus' Letters is a letter written from Burgos
—not so very many miles distant from Salamanca—on September 1st of this same year, 1527, by one Juan Maldonado—
not of course the famous Jesuit of that name, who was not born
till 1533.   Maldonado writes: "They (the theologians) tell
them (noble ladies) that they cannot have their sins pardoned
unless they go on their knees to some sophisticated friar—only
friars, they say, can distinguish the qualities of sins.   Not a man
from the meanest pot-boy to the Emperor will they count a
Christian unless he takes a monk for a director."   In fact in the
eyes of such men—perhaps the sub-prior of St. Stephen's was
one of them; perhaps they were powerful, and Frias feared
them—the fault of St. Ignatius, as a layman, was not that his
opinions were heretical, but that he had any opinions at all.
Laymen thinking were a nuisance and to be discouraged.

I do not know if the Inquisitors at Salamanca had the record
of the inquiry at Alcala before them.   But, if so, they would
have found that St. Ignatius did not shrink from interference
between penitent and confessor when he thought it necessary.
The record of May 2nd, 1527, recounts the cross-examination
of Maria de la Flor.   Maria de la Flor gave evidence that " she
had related to Inigo a thought that she had had and that she had
confessed to her confessor and the confessor had told her that
it was a mortal sin, and she had confessed and had received the
Holy Sacrament the same day.   And Inigo had said to her,
' Would to God you had not got up that morning,' because
the fault she said she had confessed was not a mortal sin nor even
a venial one ; on the contrary, it was a right thought."   There is
no record of the point upon which St. Ignatius quarrelled with
the confessor's theology.

His experience at Salamanca, coming on top of that at Alcala,
convinced St. Ignatius that there was nothing for it but to leave
Spain altogether.   He determined to go to Paris.   He therefore
returned first to Barcelona, where he was gladly welcomed by
Isabel Roser and his other friends, and then, in spite of their
efforts to dissuade him, set off again somewhere about the turn
of the year for Paris.

CHAPTER VI

PARIS AND THE FIRST DISCIPLES

THE journey over the Pyrenees was full of peril. Francis I. had been freed from his captivity in Spain by the Treaty of Madrid in January, 1526, but, returning to France, had at once broken his word. War recommenced, and brigands, taking advantage of the confusion, established themselves all along the Pyrenæan frontier and made life horrible by their atrocities, while the regular French troops, giving an unpleasantly literal twist to the old saw about the frying-pan and the fire, were reported to be clapping into an oven all Spaniards on whom they laid their hands. Now, at any rate, Bayard had been dead some time. However, St. Ignatius was lucky enough to escape adventures and reached Paris in safety.

There can be no doubt that the petty persecution which led St. Ignatius to leave Spain was providential. The Pyrenees were then, as they are to-day, the strongest frontier in Europe. The Spanish, in some ways the most charming, in many ways the wisest of the nations of Europe, is not, and never has been, truly European. To-day, in the growing cosmopolitanism of our modern world, it is Spain alone who keeps herself as a distinctive nation. She rejected the gospel of the French Revolution and refused the enlightenment of the *roi philosophe*. It was the same in the 16th century. The Renaissance touched her but little, the Reformation not at all. Happiness is the end of Man, and it may well be that the Spaniards were lucky to be free of these disturbances of the mind. Yet the result is that it is hardly possible for any Spanish town to be the headquarters of a great intellectual movement which shall shake Europe. The capital of such a movement must be in one of the great central cities, of which the two chief are Paris and Rome. And, if it be true that

Ignatius of Loyola saved Europe, then meddlesome Figueroa and timid Frias deserved well of mankind when they drove Ignatius, exasperated, across the Pyrenees, to Paris first and then to Rome.

The University of Paris, in the 13th century the first centre of learning of the world, still survived at St. Ignatius' day in all outward magnificence. It was a town within the great town of Paris, comprising fifty schools or colleges, in which resided masters, professors and scholars, and a total student roll of from 12,000 to 16,000. All Paris south of the Seine was university; no authority was recognised there save university and ecclesiastical authority. The students were divided into four " nations," the French, the Picard, the Norman and the German, each under its own procurator. The French included all those from South France and from Italy and Spain (Ignatius was of it), the Picards those from Flanders and Brabant, the Normans those of Northern France, and the German, which up to the Hundred Years' War had been called the English, those from the Northern European countries. The work of the university was divided between Four Faculties, each of which had its dean—the Faculties of theology, law, philosophy and medicine. There were also courses in metaphysics, natural history, the Semitic languages and the classics, but the Collège Royal for the study of the learned languages was not to be founded by Francis I. until three years after St. Ignatius' arrival in Paris.

The golden age of the university had passed. Learning and discipline were little regarded either by professors or students. The rattle-tattle of the dry bones of the great scholastic philosophy echoed round empty lecture-rooms. The undergraduates behaved like François Villon and the dons like St. Francis Xavier's tutor, who died, the saint tells us, of " the shameful complaints " which he had contracted when debauching in the company of his pupils.

St. Ignatius recognised the mistake which he had made at Alcala in trying to combine too many subjects at once and to combine the life of a student with that of a mendicant. He, therefore, consented to live upon the charity of his friends—to begin with, his friends at Barcelona—and, determined to begin all over again, attended classes at the Collège Montaigu.

He was not the first of the college's interesting students. Erasmus had been there a generation before and grumbled at the bad eggs, and Rabelais makes Ponocrates complain to Grangousier of the " lousy college " and of " *l'énorme cruauté et villennie que j'y ai connu.*" [1] He had another and an even stranger old school-fellow, for, just about the time that Ignatius went up to the college, John Calvin came down from it. The name reminds us that at Paris St. Ignatius found himself, for the first and the last time in his life, in the presence of those forces of the new religion, the conflict with which played so large a part in the life of his followers, if only a small part in his own. Paris was the capital of the kingdom of ideas, of the foolish as well as the wise. Francis I. in a somewhat undiscriminating zeal had invited in professors from Germany of all and every opinion ; 1529 was to be the year of Calvin's sudden conversion. He was to be back in Paris, it seems, about 1531 and again about 1535. In the latter year he was to issue his famous *Open Letter to Francis I.*, which is the Prologue to the *Institutes*. " *Le crime d'hérésie pullule et croît en la bonne ville de Paris,*" the King was to complain, and later he was to turn from patron to savage persecutor. In the university, too, there was a fashion of confused thought even at this earlier date, but we know little or nothing of St. Ignatius' opinion of, or policy towards, the new speculations. Ignorant of any language but Spanish, it is probable that he came across them but little.

His own personal policy towards heretics was one which is, I daresay, the most effective of all policies, but is certainly not the policy of those who place their main hope in the weapons of the intellect. It was to convert them not by controversy but simply by showing them the Christian life. In 1541 in Rome a certain young Lutheran was to fall into the hands of the Inquisition. St. Ignatius begged that the Jesuits should be allowed to entertain him as their guest. He went to live with them,

[1] Rabelais, according to Mr. Mangan, the biographer of Erasmus, was not there as a student.

soon afterwards was re-converted to orthodoxy and bore witness that his re-conversion was due not to argument but to " the
holy and charitable life he had seen around him." He could not
believe that its foundations lay in anything but truth.

Ignatius infected his disciples with a similar spirit. The
Jesuits received a young Jewish convert in their house in
Venice in 1542, and an angry brother came to claim him back
for the family. The Fathers received the brother as their guest
and insisted on humbly washing his feet. He was so impressed
by such courtesy under such circumstances that he himself
became converted and devoted his life to missionary labours in
the East. It was in St. Ignatius' spirit that Faber was to write
many years later, " On the day of St. Elizabeth, Queen of Hungary, I worshipped long and held in my thoughts eight [1] persons, without regard to their errors, while I prayed for them—
the Pope, the Emperor, the King of France, the King of England,
the Grand Turk, Bucer and Philip Melanchthon. The reason
was that I knew they were condemned by many, and so a holy
compassion sent by the Holy Ghost sprang up within me."

At Paris St. Ignatius was soon in difficulties. He had brought
with him a Barcelona bill for twenty-five ducats. This he
entrusted to a fellow-lodger who spent it and was unable to
repay it. He wrote to his followers who had remained behind
in Spain, telling them of his misfortunes and bidding them complete their studies where they were. But, separated from St.
Ignatius, all four of them deserted the Ignatian life, the French
page, Jean, it is true, to die piously in a convent and Arteaga to
become a bishop in America, but Calisto and Cazares for lives
in the world of no great edification or repute. Meanwhile in
Paris St. Ignatius was compelled, willy-nilly, to take once more
to begging. He had tried to attach himself to the personal service of some professor but was unable to obtain a master. Yet
he knew no French, and begging was therefore not only an
unsatisfactory but also a difficult means of livelihood to him.
When, therefore, the summer vacation came he determined to

---

[1] *Sic.* It will be noticed that he only mentions seven.

go to Flanders, the nearest Spanish territory to Paris, and there collect from his fellow-countrymen sufficient to keep him through the next year. This he did with success for two years, and the third year he came to England.

Meanwhile troubles of another kind had fallen upon him. Three of his fellow-countrymen had insisted on sharing with him his way of life. They were Juan de Castro, of Toledo, a bachelor of the university; Peralta, a student; and a Biscayan, called Amadores, who lived at the College of Sta. Barbara. These three had sold all their possessions, even to their books, distributed the money to the poor and embraced poverty. St. Ignatius was a great deal older than any of his disciples, and, not altogether unnaturally, his influence was held responsible for the very rash step which the young men had taken. Pedro Ortiz, the tutor of de Castro and Peralta, and Govea, the Rector of Sta. Barbara, took up the case and demanded that Ignatius be restrained as a public danger.

It was no doubt true in a sense that it was St. Ignatius' influence which had caused these young men to embrace poverty, but he had never advised them to do so. All that he had done had been to cause them to make the Spiritual Exercises—in which it is most carefully forbidden to the director in any way to force the thought of a vocation upon the recipient of the exercises. The vocation, if it comes at all, must come from God alone. "He who gives the Exercises," writes St. Ignatius, "must not move him who receives them more to poverty or to any other promise than to their contraries, nor to one state or manner of life than another; for, although outside the Exercises we may lawfully and meritoriously urge all who are probably fitted for it to choose continency, virginity, the religious state or any other kind of evangelical perfection, nevertheless in these spiritual exercises it is more fitting and much better, in seeking the Divine Will, that the Creator and the Lord Himself should communicate Himself to the devout soul, embracing and drawing it to His love and praise and disposing it for that way of life in which it will best serve Him for the future; so that he who gives the Exercises should not turn or incline himself to one side or the other, but, keeping in the middle like a balance, should allow the Creator to work immediately with the creature, and the creature with its Creator and Lord."

Nevertheless, the university authorities were perfectly right in demanding an investigation into St. Ignatius' activities. Only it happened that, when the clamour was raised, St. Ignatius was himself absent from Paris. He had gone to Rouen on a characteristic mission—to relieve the necessities of, and to pay a visit of charity to, the young man who had robbed him of his twenty-five ducats and reduced him to beggary and who was now himself lying ill and penniless at Rouen. A messenger found the saint at Rouen with a letter telling him that he had been delated to the Inquisition. There was no regular Inquisition in France, but visiting Inquisitors from time to time held commissions. Their conduct was, as a rule, more intelligent than that of the regular courts in Spain, and St. Ignatius saw in the charge not so much a cause for fear as an opportunity of establishing himself once and for all as above suspicion. The only inconvenience was that the Parisian authorities had been informed that he had already been in the hands of the Spanish Inquisition and therefore, if they did not hear the full story, might entertain a prejudice against him.

St. Ignatius saw that it would be important to be able to prove that he had not attempted to escape from legitimate ecclesiastical authority. He therefore went first to a notary in Rouen and obtained from him a certificate, countersigned by two witnesses, stating that he had started for Paris at the first possible moment. He then made his way back and, as soon as he reached the city, went straight to the Inquisitor, Matteo Ori, a Dominican, whose strange fate it was to be to sit in judgment on St. Ignatius, on Servetus, whom Calvin denounced to him, hoping that Ori would do his burning for him, and on the famous Duchess Renée of Ferrara. Ignatius now told him that he understood that charges had been made against him and asked that they might be investigated at once in order that he might enter upon his next term's course of philosophy, free from distractions. Ori was very easily satisfied and told him at once that he was free, that there was no charge against him that would bear investigation, and that he could take himself untroubled to his philosophy.

Meanwhile, however, their friends had forcibly compelled St. Ignatius' disciples to resume normal life. In the end they agreed to do so and to take a fresh decision at the end of their university career. What became of Amadores is not known, but de Castro eventually became a Carthusian and Peralta a secular priest, ending his life as a most exemplary canon of Toledo. None of them returned to St. Ignatius.

When the summer came, St. Ignatius went, as has been said, to the Netherlands. By the marriage of the daughter of Charles the Bold to the Archduke Maximilian in 1477 the Netherlands had passed under Hapsburg rule, and St. Ignatius lodged with Spanish merchants during his visits. Bruges was his headquarters, but either during this or a subsequent trip he certainly visited Antwerp, for there it was that a curious incident occurred that was afterwards attested during the process of his canonisation. He met at dinner a certain Pedro Quadrato, whom he led aside from the rest and told that he was under infinite obligations to God for having chosen Pedro to be a founder of one of the colleges of the future Society of Jesus. Pedro did afterwards found a Jesuit college at Medina del Campo. Opinions will differ whether St. Ignatius' prophecy was mere coincidence, whether Pedro acted as he did because St. Ignatius put the notion into his mind, or whether the saint truly foresaw the future. But, whatever be the true explanation of this particular incident, he certainly believed himself to be (and there seems little doubt that he was) one of those strange persons who have the gift of breaking through the barriers of time and seeing the future with the eyes of the present.

In October, 1529, on his return from the Netherlands, St. Ignatius began his course of philosophy at the College of Sta. Barbara, where George Buchanan, the Scotch Latin poet, was at this time teaching Latin under difficulties. "While the professor is puffing over his teaching," writes Buchanan, " these

lazy boys go to sleep, or into daydreams of play and amuse-
ment. One boy stays away and has bribed his neighbour to
answer for him; another has lost his stockings; a third is
gazing at his foot that peeps out from a hole in his boot; a
fourth pretends to be ill; a fifth is writing home. No help but
in the rod, then sobbings and tear-stained cheeks for the rest of
the day. . . . Now a troop of loafers from across the river
tramps in, the clatter of hobnail boots announces their approach.
They come in and pay as much intelligent attention as Marsyas
did, listening to Apollo. They are ill-humoured because they
did not notice the announcement of the course, although it be
placarded at the street corners, and they are offended because
the professor does not read out of an enormous tome scribbled
all over with marginal comments. So they all get up and with
an infernal hubbub walk across the way to Montagu where an
odour of soup prevails."

St. Ignatius' difficulties were of a different sort from those of
the more normal student. The study of philosophy brought
back to him those trials from which he had suffered in his first
school days at Barcelona; his mind was continually distracted
from his task by the delights of spiritual contemplation. However, he was now more practised at dealing with his own
problems than he had been then. Had the trials of his own
temperament been the only trials with which he was afflicted,
he would have lived out a peaceful life.

In order to devote himself to his studies, he had decided to
abandon for the time any attempt to make converts, and to
confine his discourses on spiritual things to those who were
already his friends. The result was that his doings ceased to be
of interest to the world at large. Yet St. Ignatius was under no
illusion. When a friend, a Dr. Frago, congratulated him that
he was now left at peace and none tried to interfere with him,
he answered, " They leave me in peace because I do so little for
my neighbour's salvation; but wait till I set to work again, and
then see what will happen."

Dr. Frago had not long to wait. While they were still talking
a monk came up and asked the doctor to help him in finding a

new lodging, as several people had died in his present lodgings and it was suspected that the cause was the plague. A nurse who was sent to investigate reported that the monk's suspicion was correct. As soon as he heard this St. Ignatius went straight off to the house and began to dress the sores of a sick man whom he found there. He soon felt a violent pain in one of his hands and feared that he had himself been infected. At first he was terrified, but, to cure himself of his fear, he put his hand into his mouth, saying, "If you have the plague in your hand, you shall have it in your mouth also." The pain at once vanished. Yet it was not surprising that, when he returned to Sta. Barbara, everyone fled at his approach, and they compelled him to go and live elsewhere.

In spite of his determination to refrain from any attempt to make converts, St. Ignatius, merely by mixing with the other students, could not help himself but have a profound influence upon them. Every feast-day the students had to hold public disputations before their masters, as tests of the progress that they had made in their studies. Now after the coming of St. Ignatius many of them, instead of attending these disputations as they were supposed to do, used to go to the Sacraments and spend the day in prayer. Pena, St. Ignatius' tutor, several times told him that his influence was reducing the whole life of the college to chaos, and bade him mind his own business and let the other undergraduates mind theirs. At length, when nothing else seemed of use, Pena reported him to Govea, the Rector.

Amadores, the Biscayan, had, it will be remembered, been a student of Sta. Barbara, and Govea had therefore been one of those who had delated St. Ignatius to the Inquisition the year before. Whether Govea had born any lasting grudge against St. Ignatius for his seduction of Amadores, or whether he was as completely satisfied as Matteo Ori, we do not know. At any rate, it is but fair to Govea to admit that St. Ignatius had given most ample cause for complaint since his entrance into Sta. Barbara. It was an outrageous thing to have returned to the college from the plague-infected house. If one student, from however high a motive, was to be free to prevent others from performing

one of the regular duties of student-life, all would be thrown
into chaos. Govea, it must be remembered, was concerned with
St. Ignatius not as a Catholic but as an undergraduate. His
problem was not one of heresy but of university discipline.
Therefore he decided, not at all unreasonably in my opinion,
that, since St. Ignatius had been repeatedly warned by his tutor
and had paid no attention to the warning, there was nothing for
it but that he should be publicly birched. It is true that to
modern notions birching seems an inappropriate punishment
for a man of thirty-five, whatever his offence, but we must be
careful not to ascribe to 16th-century characters such 20th-cen-
tury feelings.

St. Ignatius flogged himself such a lot that, from the point of
view of physical pain, it could not make much odds if he was
flogged by somebody else for a change. Yet the public birching
was a great disgrace, and the tale is that St. Ignatius, when first
he heard that he was to receive it, flared up in anger. But almost
immediately, recognising the folly and injustice of such anger, he
mastered himself, saying, ". Ass that thou art, it is vain for thee
to kick against the pricks. Forward and get thee on, or I will
drag thee to the spot." Yet, though he was willing to receive
his birching, as he was willing to receive any other suffering for
the love of God, he nevertheless saw that the effect of it would
be to throw ridicule upon the pious practices which he had
introduced. Therefore, when all the students were assembled
to witness the sight and waiting for the Rector and culprit, he went
up to Govea's room and said to him, " As far as I am myself concerned, I should desire nothing better than to bear stripes and
shame for the sake of Jesus Christ, as indeed I have borne
imprisonment and chains, and have never uttered a word in self-
exculpation, nor would I allow any advocate to plead on my
behalf.   But now it is not my interest or honour only that is at
stake, but the eternal salvation of numerous souls. And I ask you
whether it be an act of Christian justice to permit a man to be
publicly disgraced whose only crime is to have laboured to make
the name of Jesus better known and loved ?   Is it right, as you
would answer before God, to put this open shame upon me

solely with a view to detaching from me those whom I have drawn to myself only that I might bring them to God ? "

As this tale is told, St. Ignatius was not putting the question at all fairly. The charge against him was that, from whatever motive, he had caused students to absent themselves from compulsory disputations. Yet, as the tale goes, Govea, a wise man, recognised that under the circumstances more harm than good would be done by a strict interpretation of rules. He was moved to tears by St. Ignatius' sincerity, and, leading him by the hand into the hall, there threw himself on his knees before him in the face of all the students and asked pardon for his misjudgment. The evidence for the tale is scanty and its truth improbable. Only two things seem fairly certain—one, that Ignatius was not birched; the other, that Govea was ever afterwards a great supporter of the Jesuits, and that it was by his advice that John III. of Portugal asked for members of the Society for the mission-work in Goa.

Pena, too, was won over to the support of St. Ignatius, as were other professors—among them the professor of theology, who was so struck by the depth of St. Ignatius' theological learning that he urged him to take his degree as doctor of theology before completing his course in philosophy. This St. Ignatius very wisely refused to do. He foresaw that the work which he was proposing to himself would quite certainly bring upon him much opposition, and that it was of the first importance that his opponents should not be able to discover any irregularity in his qualifications.

In the long vacation of 1530 St. Ignatius paid his visit to London. The state of war between Henry VIII. and Charles V. had been brought to an end by the Treaty of Cambrai in the previous year. English politics were dominated by the question of the annulment of Henry's marriage with Catherine of Aragon, which had already brought about the fall of Wolsey, who died a few months after St. Ignatius' visit, and which was in the next year to bring about the secession of England from the Roman obedience. It would be fascinating to know what a mind so acute as that of St. Ignatius made of these tangled and tragic politics, but unfortunately we know nothing of his English visit except that he was entertained by the Spanish merchants, whose colony was near the river in Old Broad Street, round the Spanish Embassy at Winchester House, and that he found them more generous than the merchants of Bruges or Antwerp. He knew no English, and probably hardly mixed at all with the natives. After this year his Flemish friends saw to it that he was provided with the necessities of life without putting him to the trouble of making long journeys each year in search of them.

St. Ignatius remained on at Paris for the full course. On March 13th, 1533, he passed the examination known as the *petra* or *rigorosum*, and was able to take the degree of licentiate. On March 14th, 1534, having passed with credit the further examination, he became a Master of Arts. During these years he, according to his plan, refused any systematic work of preaching or conversion. Yet he could not help influencing greatly those with whom he came in contact. Stewart Rose tells three picturesque tales of St. Ignatius' life during these years.

The first is that of the libertine who used to go and spend the night with a married woman on the further side of the Lake of Gentilly. One night in cold winter, as he came to the bridge, he saw below him a man standing up to his neck in icy water. It was St. Ignatius. " Go," said the saint, " and enjoy your odious pleasures at the peril of your life and your immortal soul. I meanwhile will do penance for your sin. Here you will find me when you return; and here every evening until God, Whom I shall never cease imploring, shall bring your crimes, or my life, to an end." The sinner was so struck and astonished that he abandoned his mistress and all his former way of life.

The second story is that of the scandalous priest. St. Ignatius went to him, fell on his knees before him and confessed the sins of his own life. The priest was filled with shame at the thought that the sins of this man, a layman, were so much less than those of himself, a priest, and that such little sins could arouse such true and terrible penitence, while he himself was so indifferent to his great sins. Therefore, when St. Ignatius had done, he threw himself on his knees, confessed himself a great sinner, and begged the saint to teach him how to amend his life. This St. Ignatius did by conducting him through the Spiritual Exercises.

The third—the quaintest of the stories—tells how he called one day on a doctor of theology and found him playing billiards. The doctor asked St. Ignatius to join him in a game. Ignatius agreed, but on a very peculiar condition. " I will consent," he said, " but a poor man like me has nothing he can stake, and yet a stake there must be. Now I have nothing I can call my own except my own person. If then I lose I will be your servant for a month to obey your orders. If I win you shall do just one thing for me, and it shall be something to your advantage." The doctor agreed, and they played. How strangely true was found the Ignatian theory that the qualities which make for success in the world are the same as those which make for success in the spiritual life ! St. Ignatius, though but little practised, won the match. As payment of his stake he demanded that his opponent should go through the Spiritual Exercises for a month. The doctor, though doubtless feeling that he had got more than he bargained for, loyally agreed and obeyed, and the result was a very notable reformation in a life hitherto lax. One of the most certain marks of a modern Jesuit college is the number of billiard tables which are provided for the pupils to play upon—an intentional imitation, I hope, of holiness even in its more secular successes.

So far the influence which St. Ignatius had exercised upon those around him had been immense, but his attempts to attract companions who would share with him the especial work which God had called him to do had not been successful. The three whom he had attracted in Spain had left him ; the three whom he had attracted in Paris had been forcibly taken from him. It was during these years that he found the first of those who were to persist as his companions.

Peter Faber was the son of a peasant of Villaret in Savoy.

From infancy he was of extreme piety. At twelve he took a vow that he would dedicate himself to the service of God, and he would, when still a boy, mount upon a stone and preach publicly to the people of the neighbourhood. At first he used to keep his father's sheep, but his father, finding him afflicted with what his biographer calls " an inordinate desire of learning and knowledge," at last agreed to his earnest request that he should be educated, and he was put under the tuition of a certain Peter Vellardo, who seems, it must be confessed, to have confounded piety with squeamishness to a somewhat unnecessary extent, and who taught Peter Faber the classics in such a way that his innocence could not possibly be corrupted by anything that he read. " The pages seemed purified as they passed through his lips," said Faber.

Let us be honest enough to admit that the whole story is not enormously engaging. Holiness is the highest of virtues, but, for all that, pious little boys preaching are not attractive. His father would have stopped it, if he had had more sense; as for the much-praised Peter Vellardo—I have always a feeling that there is something left-handedly salacious in all this exaggerated trouble lest the ears of the young should be contaminated by the mildest of indecent tales. At least I am certain that, if the object be to keep the young from sexual sin, then such tactics as those of Peter Vellardo are the worst possible. You do not drive out sex by making it taboo as a subject of conversation; you merely bottle it up, and a boy can hardly be expected to escape unscathed from his early trials if he is forced to fight them out as a horrible and lonely battle. It is far wiser to encourage— or at least to allow—him to use the safety-valve of easy-going conversation, which pays to sex the important insult of treating it, when jokes are on, as a joke—much the best way of treating it for those who are safely able to do so.

Anyway, what happened to Peter Faber was very much what one would expect to happen. At nineteen he went from Vellardo to the University of Paris, to the College of Sta. Barbara, where he soon found many people saying many things that were by no means " purified " as they passed through their lips. The world seen from Paris was very different from the world seen from Villaret, and Peter Faber sometimes found it very difficult to resist with vows of chastity taken at the age of twelve the immediate temptations of twenty or twenty-one. Not only the temptations of sex but also those of good living and of the world in general attracted him.

Yet he did not by any means go completely to the bad. He shared lodgings by a curious chance with Francis Xavier, his contemporary—they were born within a week of one another in April, 1506—and Xavier never abandoned himself to the practices of vice, even if, as he afterwards confessed to the chaplain of St. Tomé, it was only the fear of disease which prevented him from doing so. Nor even under temptation did Faber abandon his desire for goodness nor his belief in his vocation. He seems rather to have lived in a condition of continual conflict between the higher nature which called him to his vocation and the lower which called him to sensual joys.

It is a dangerous condition—this condition of internal conflict—in which evil seems intensely more attractive than good, and the soul only refrains from it through fear of hell. Sooner or later there is sure to come into the struggler's life some glib talker or clever book which will offer to show him that this fear is an illusion, and the struggler, thinking thus to resolve the intolerable conflict, will abandon both faith and morals on grounds that pretend to be intellectual but in reality are far from being so. Only too late does he discover that he has freed himself from conflict only in order to submit himself to a dominating tyranny.

Faber might perhaps have gone this way had things been different. But all through this same time he was making good progress in his studies. He was Pena's favourite pupil, and Pena, by now friendly to St. Ignatius and very likely knowing nothing of Faber's private troubles, suggested that Ignatius' philosophy would greatly benefit if the two were to get together after the classes and discuss the lecture that had been delivered. This was in the year 1530, when Faber was twenty-four and St. Ignatius thirty-nine. In order to bring them the more easily together, they were put to share the same room. At first Faber was far from keen on the plan—presumably because he knew both St. Ignatius' reputation and his own false conscience, and feared that his self-justification would be stripped from him. However, he was induced to consent.

Never did St. Ignatius more strikingly show his masterly understanding of human nature than in his handling of Peter Faber. Most of us would have been content to explain to him that his childish vows were of no validity, that his troubles were the outcome of a morbid conflict induced by an obstinate attempt to preserve a vocation which he had never really possessed, and have advised him as soon as possible to try matrimony as a solution—and we should have prided ourselves on our worldly wisdom in giving such advice. But St. Ignatius somehow or other discerned that, in spite of the nonsense of cocoon-piety, Faber really had a vocation. He led him on through two years of conflict, guided him through the Spiritual Exercises up to the priesthood, and took him for the first of his companions. The calendar of the Church to-day bears witness to the penetration of St. Ignatius' discernment.

It is characteristic of Faber's temperament that he should have tried to usher in his converted life with feats of exaggerated mortification. In a bitterly cold winter he would kneel in a little courtyard throughout the night and refused to go near a fire. He fasted for six days on end. It is as characteristic of St. Ignatius that two of the first orders which he gave to his new disciple were to eat regularly and to have a fire.

After Peter Faber, the next follower whom St. Ignatius gained was Francis Xavier. Francis Xavier was born, as has been said, at Sanguesa in Navarre, and was thus a neighbour of St. Ignatius. His family, though gentle, had been impoverished by its obstinate support of the kings of Navarre against the Spanish policy of absorption. Xavier's brothers, it will be remembered, had served in the army that marched against Pampeluna when St. Ignatius was wounded there in 1521. As a scholar Francis was as brilliant as his room-mate Faber. Less troubled than Faber by the temptations of the flesh, he suffered instead in these early years from the less pardonable temptations of intellectual ambition. He was destined for the Church, and both his father, a gentleman of lineage but little wealth, and he himself hoped and expected for him a brilliant career.

At about the time when in 1530 St. Ignatius and Faber were working out together their problems of philosophy, Xavier, having taken his degree, began to give lectures on Aristotle. The academic world, such as it was and is, was at his feet, and but for the grace of God, Who destined him to be the greatest of Christian missionaries since St. Paul, he might have gone on giving lectures on Aristotle for the rest of his life. When he came across St. Ignatius through Faber, he despised him as an eccentric ascetic endowed with only very ordinary academic qualifications. With some astuteness, St. Ignatius in spite of this, persisted in behaving with friendliness towards him, treating his academic pride as a passing fault, induced all but inevitably by his unfortunate knack for passing examinations. Xavier was gradually won over by goodness, and when one day in conversation St. Ignatius quoted to him the text, " What shall it profit a man if he should gain the whole world. and suffer the loss of his own soul ? " the question sunk into Xavier's heart and turned his whole life.

His father asked him to come back to Spain to enjoy the career that they had planned together. But he refused, and his sister Maddalena supported him in his refusal, prophesying that " God had elected him to be His messenger to the Indies, and a strong pillar of His Church." His friends at Paris, too, were angry at his changed life, and imputed the blame to St. Ignatius. One of them, Michel Navarro, even went so far as to attempt to murder the saint.

Further additions to the company were not long delayed. St. Ignatius' reputation had spread to his old university of Alcala. Two of the students, Laynez and Salmeron—both in later years to play their dominating parts as Papal theologians at the Council of Trent—determined to come to Paris and see this Ignatius for themselves. Laynez was by blood a Jew from Castile, though his family had been Christian for many generations; Salmeron a native of Toledo. They came, saw and were conquered, went through the Exercises shortly after Faber, and joined the Society. Next came Nicholas Alfonso, commonly known as Bobadilla, after a little village near Valencia in Spain where he was born, " *semper strenuus, semper et ubique sibi similis Bobadilla.*" He had already lectured on philosophy at Valladolid, and had come to Paris to study theology. He too joined St. Ignatius. After him, Simon Rodriguez, a Portuguese, drawn to St. Ignatius partly by his friendship for Bobadilla, partly by the desire which he shared with the saint to devote his life to God in the Holy Land, and to his admiration for what he called St. Ignatius' " *immensum hominum salutis desiderium.*"

To these six St. Ignatius greatly desired to add a certain Nadal, a native of Majorca, of whom he had the highest opinion. So strong was his desire that he allowed himself to break his rule of waiting for God to suggest a vocation to a soul rather than pressing it on him himself. He took Nadal with him one day to a deserted church and there begged him to be of their company. Nadal answered, pointing to a New Testament, " I hold fast to this book; it is sufficient for me; I will not follow you unless you have something better than this to offer." Nadal did follow, but it was not until ten years later that he did so. St. Ignatius learnt the lesson that it was a mistake to try and compel anyone to a vocation.

In the days of generalship, St. Ignatius was sometimes to be accused of being too ready to refuse admittance to, or to expel, novices. He would expel people at a moment's notice, even pulling them out of their beds in the middle of the night. Certainly he was not guilty of the opposite fault. When at length his vocation did come to Nadal, fortune, as so often happens in these matters, succeeded where calculation had failed. A copy of one of the letters of St. Francis Xavier, in which he spoke of his life among the heathen of India, chanced to fall into Nadal's hands. " This is indeed a great work," he said. And, setting off to Rome, he there went through the Spiritual Exercises in order to discover in what way God called him to His service.

After making the *Meditation on Two Standards*, he felt within himself a vocation to the Society of Jesus.

St. Ignatius spoke privately to each of his six companions, bidding them prepare themselves by prayer and fasting for the great decision of the form which their future was to take.   Then on the Feast of the Assumption, 1534, they all met together at the little deserted Church of Our Lady of the Mount of the Martyrs, or Montmartre, where some thirteen hundred years before St. Denis had shed his martyr's blood for the cause of Christ, and where four hundred years afterwards English tourists and American tourists were to foregather for more secular purposes, but whence to-day shines out across Paris, like the gate of heaven, the great votive basilica of the Sacred Heart, which the faithful of France have offered in expiation for the sins that brought the disaster of 1870.   With them was another who wished to be of the company, Jean Codure.

We have accounts of that great meeting from the pens both of Faber and of Rodriguez.   When all were assembled, St. Ignatius said on behalf of all a short prayer.   He then told them that it was his design to go to the Holy Land and there to live, bound by solemn vows of poverty and chastity, in the service o God.   The others gladly agreed to go with him.   It was decided that if after a time it should be found, as St. Ignatius' previous experience showed to be most probable, that there were difficulties about their residence in Palestine, then they should take a vote of the seven, the whole company to abide by the verdict of the majority, and according to the vote either remain in the Holy Land and face the difficulties or else return to Rome and put themselves at the disposal of the Pope.   They were all to meet at Venice on January 25th, 1537, there to embark for the East.   But if the disturbed state of things made it impossible for them even to reach the Holy Land within a year, then they were to go straight to Rome and offer themselves to the Pope.   St. Ignatius insisted on postponing the departure until 1537 in order that all might first complete their university courses.   In the meantime, in order that all might persevere in their purpose, they were to meet again in this same place on the

Feast of the Assumption, 1535, and again in 1536 and renew their vows.

All agreed to what St. Ignatius proposed. Among them, Faber alone was a priest—he had been ordained a few months previously. They descended to the crypt beneath the church where Faber said Mass. All communicated and, as Faber held the Body of Our Lord before him, each repeated aloud vows of poverty, of chastity and of obedience to the Pope, a vow to go to Palestine, and a vow never to take money for the dispensing of the Sacraments or any pious work. They then left the Church and went together to a small fountain on the side of the hill, where they ate a frugal breakfast and talked for a time on spiritual matters. They then dispersed to their usual tasks.

A mind as alien to such a life as that of Balzac has paid its tribute to this great moment when our world was saved. "Who is there," he writes, "that would not admire the extraordinary spectacle of this union of seven men animated by a noble purpose, who turn towards Heaven, and under the roof of a chapel lay down their worldly wishes and hopes, and consecrate themselves to the happiness of their fellow-men?" (They did nothing of the kind. They consecrated themselves to the service of God.) "They offer themselves as a sacrifice to the work of charity, that shall give them no property, nor power, nor pleasure; they renounce the present for the future, looking forward only to a hereafter in heaven, and content with no happiness on earth beyond what a pure conscience can bestow."

In humility before the weight of new responsibilities which God was thrusting upon him, St. Ignatius immediately after the taking of the vows submitted himself once more to the practice of an extreme asceticism. He passed days in the Carmelite church on Montmartre, and loved to hide himself in the gypsum quarries there, which reminded him of his own cave at Manresa. The result was a complete breakdown in health, and the doctors told him that only a return to his native air could possibly save his life. Laynez, Salmeron and Xavier all had private affairs to settle up before they could enter into the practice of their vows of poverty. It was therefore decided that St. Ignatius should go to Spain and settle these affairs.

Before he could set out he had to face another of his constantly recurring troubles with the Inquisition. Where it had before been the publicity of his life which had aroused suspicion, it was now its secrecy. He was denounced to Laurent, the Inquisitor, for wishing to found a new sect. Laurent, a very sensible, level-headed, unexcitable man, as were most of the French Inquisitors, refused to take the charge seriously, but St. Ignatius determined to seize the opportunity in order to get a clear and official certificate of orthodoxy. This Laurent was willing enough to give, and wrote for him on January 23rd, 1535 : " We, Brother Thomas Laurent, professor of theology, priest of the Order of Preaching Brothers, Inquisitor-General in France, delegated by the Holy See, certify by these presents that after an inquiry made by our precursor, Valentine Leivin, and by us, his council, into the life, morals and doctrine of Ignatius of Loyola, we have found nothing that is not Catholic and Christian ; we also know the said Loyola, and M. Peter Faber and some of his friends, and we have always seen them live in a Catholic and virtuous manner, and observed nothing in them but what becomes a Christian and virtuous man. The Exercises also which the said Loyola teaches seem to us, so far as we have looked into them, to be Catholic."

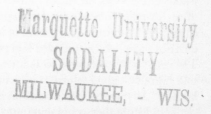

CHAPTER VII

VENICE

St. Ignatius set out from Paris round about the end of March, 1535. When he had reached Bayonne, he was recognised by some people who took the news of his coming to Don Martin Garcia at Loyola. St. Ignatius went on to an inn six miles from Azpeytia, where he was again recognised, this time by a certain Juan Esquibar. His brothers and nephews prepared to ride to welcome him with a great cavalcade, but, thinking that if they came thus he would refuse from humility to ride with them, they sent instead a worthy priest called Balthazar d'Arabeya to meet him. They also sent two armed servants round by a mountain-path, infested by brigands, in case St. Ignatius should in humility prefer to come by that way.

When he reached Azpeytia, he refused to sleep at Loyola, as all had half-suspected that he would, saying that he had taken a vow of poverty and his life must henceforth be lived with the poor. He went therefore to the Hospital of Sta. Maddalena, where he lodged, refusing to make use of the rich bed or the provisions which his family sent him. Only once, or possibly twice, during his visit did he sleep at Loyola.

To some the violence and completeness with which he broke with his family may seem harsh and unnecessary. He went so far as to fasten a piece of paper over a picture of Our Lady, which reminded him of his sister-in-law, Donna Maddalena, and though he did not demand of his followers imitation of his conduct in every detail, yet he did demand that they too utterly abandon parents and relations for the love of Christ. Yet we must remember that he did what he did not because he despised the ties of family, but because he honoured them. For those who have not the special vocation to the priesthood the family is the refuge from the folly of the world. He was a great lover himself; his company was to be a company of lovers; " the company of love" was the very phrase by which St. Francis Xavier was afterwards to describe it. The souls whom he wished to attract to supernatural love were then the very souls which would naturally feel the ties of family most intensely. The servants of Christ must for Christ's sake deny themselves not only what was empty and foolish in this world, but also what was beautiful and noble. To renounce the world meant for St. Ignatius not merely to renounce worldly ambition, to recognise the unbalanced insanity of the competitive life, whose primary object is money, or, worse still, fame—which means what other people say about you—or success. It meant also to renounce all the jolly life of "laughter and the love of friends," to renounce the beauty and sanity of this world every bit as much as its madness and its horror.

St. Ignatius suggested that he should preach to the people. Don Martin advised against the plan, saying that nobody would come to listen. The story brings a pleasant little breath of everyday into this record of wonders and the works of God. There is something delicious about Don Martin's Melbournian attitude towards enthusiastic activities—the attitude which looks on such activities not so much either as good or as bad, but rather as merely a waste of time. It is perhaps the wisest attitude with which to face nine-tenths of the activities of life, but it is useless for facing an Ignatius. For in such a spirit there are things that are not dreamed of in the Melbournian philosophy. St. Ignatius did preach, and the people did come.

He told them that one of the reasons why he had returned to Azpeytia was to appease a conscience which had never ceased to trouble him because of the evil example which his worldly youth had given to the neighbourhood, and in particular to ask pardon of a certain man who was imprisoned for damage to an orchard which was really done by St. Ignatius and his companions. To this man he gave in restitution two farms which had been left to him.

He attacked the immorality of the priests—in especial, the

scandalous custom by which many of them kept in their houses mistresses who wore veils on their heads as if they were married women.   He procured from the governor an order forbidding any but properly married women to dress as such.

Less obviously justifiable was his attack on the gaming habits of the people, as a result of which no cards nor dice were seen in Azpeytia for three years.   It cannot fairly be denied that betting and gambling, though like all good things capable of abuse, yet contribute enormously to the happiness of mankind, and on the whole bring with them more pleasure than pain.   When one considers in how many worse ways people might occupy their leisure than in gambling, it might be thought that St. Ignatius would have done better to have left the people to their pleasures. It is sometimes argued that if one eschews such pleasures one is at least " on the safe side."   I do not think that this is so. The teaching of the Church is that betting and gambling are not in themselves sinful, and I once heard a wise old priest, eighty years of age, say from his experience of life that there was no graver sin than for a confessor to be stricter than the mind of the Church.   If we link virtue up with a lot of irrational and petty prohibitions, we incur the grave responsibility of making her whole cause ridiculous.

It was also during this time that St. Ignatius founded at Azpeytia the Confraternity of the Holy Sacrament, for the relief of the " bashful poor," or " *poveri vergognosi*," as the Italians call them—the poor who will not beg or call attention to their poverty.   The duty of the members of the Confraternity was to search out such people and to give them relief in secret.

There are many other stories of St. Ignatius' doings during this time at Azpeytia.   A catalogue of such wonderful tales serves little purpose, and, whatever may be true or false, it is sufficient to say of them that St. Ignatius himself quite expressly denied that he ever worked a miracle or had power to work one. He remained three months at Azpeytia.   Then in late summer he went on his journey, first to Xavier in Navarre, the home of Francis, thence to Almazano in Castile, the family home of Laynez, and to Toledo, that of Salmeron.   At each of these

places he settled the financial business for which he had come.
His sanctity had already won him fame in his native country.
Somewhere or other during these journeys—it is not certain
where—he happened to run across the nine-year-old boy who
was afterwards to be Philip II. His nurse bade Philip note
him and ask his prayers. "That," she said, "is a saint."

From Toledo he travelled down into Valencia. He made it
his first business to visit his old friend and companion, Juan de
Castro, now a monk at the Carthusian monastery of Valdecristo
at Segovia, some seventy miles north of the town of Valencia.
St. Ignatius told Juan of all that he had done, and asked him if
his work was in accordance with the will of God. Juan said
that he would tell him the next morning, and after a night spent
in prayer, in the morning told him that it had God's blessing,
and begged to be allowed a second time to become one of
St. Ignatius' companions—for he had not yet taken his last
Carthusian vows. This request St. Ignatius refused. It was
probably during this visit that St. Ignatius discovered that two
of the monks were plotting to break their vows and abscond.
He denounced them before the whole community, and the
offenders, smitten with remorse, confessed their fault and
handed over their disguises.

From Segovia he went down to the town of Valencia. At
Valencia, it will be remembered, was the palace which King
Ferdinand had given to the Queen of Naples and her daughter,
Princess Joanna, the object, if conjecture be true, of St. Ignatius'
devotion in his courtier days. She was still there at this time
and it would be a pleasure to those who are lovers of the
romance of history to record a last meeting under these strange
circumstances. But there is no such record. Princess Joanna
had gone the way of all the world from St. Ignatius' affections.

The seas of the Western Mediterranean were at that time
dominated by the pirate Kahir-ed-din, Hayradin Barbarossa.
This strange adventurer, the younger son of a Roumelian *sipahi*,
had in company with his brother embraced Islam and established
himself in the island of Mytilene, after its capture by Mahomed II.
Thenceforward the pair pursued a wild, adventurous and highly

successful career, the result of which was to bring the elder brother to an untimely death at a moment of victory, but to establish Hayradin as Begler-beg or ruler of Algiers. To Algiers he soon added Algeciras, and the war between the Sultan and Charles V. in 1533 had given him the opportunity to extend his power to Tunis as well, whence he was able to descend in devastating raids upon the Spanish and Italian coasts. At Valencia St. Ignatius could see visible evidence of the terror which he inspired by turning his eyes towards the citadel which was built to defend the town against his incursions.

So great a nuisance was he that in May, 1535, Charles sailed from Barcelona at the head of a great fleet. He was joined by Andrea Doria from Genoa, who, it will be remembered, had in 1524 chased St. Ignatius from Genoa to Barcelona on his return from the Holy Land. Doria had then been in French service, but in 1528 had deserted Francis, and now served Charles. The fleet was also aided by contingents from Portugal, from Venice, from the Knights of St. John, now established at Malta, and, in especial, from Paul, the new Farnese Pope, that tremendous ruler of imperishable strength, whose piercing and commanding eyes, whose face of grand intelligence we can still see on the canvas of Titian and in the stone of Michelangelo, and beneath whose rule the majesty of Rome was to return to Europe. The Armada defeated Hayradin, and drove him out of Tunis, but he still held Algiers, and from it as a base swept out in pirate raids upon all the shipping of the Western Mediterranean.

St. Ignatius was lucky enough to escape his attentions. Instead they fell into a violent storm. The sailors gave themselves up for lost, but St. Ignatius himself, as he afterwards told Gonzalez, felt no fear but only a profound grief that he had co-operated imperfectly with the graces which God had offered to him. In spite of the storm they at last reached Genoa. Thence he made his way across the Apennines to Bologna. It was now late winter, and in crossing the mountains, he lost his road and suddenly found himself on the brink of a precipice whence it was almost impossible to go either forwards or back. He had to clamber up a steep rock on hands and knees with a

sheer precipice for some hundreds of feet below him. Only
with the greatest difficulty did he escape, nor, even when he
reached Bologna, were his troubles at an end. Entering the
town, he slipped on a bridge and fell into the moat. Ill,
emaciated, unkempt, dripping wet, he made his way to the
Spanish college, where he was kindly received. He remained
there a week to recruit, and then, rejecting the notion which he
had at one time entertained of continuing there his interrupted
theological studies, went on to Venice, which he reached on the
last day of 1535.

For a time he lodged with a " learned and worthy man "—
probably, it seems, Diego d'Eguia, afterwards of the Society
and St. Ignatius' confessor—but as soon as he was sufficiently
recovered from the hardships of the journey, he transferred
himself, according to his usual custom, to a religious hospital—
in this case to one which was under the directorship of St.
Cajetan de Thienne, founder of the Theatine Order. St.
Cajetan, or Gaetano, was a native of Vicenza, where he was born
some eleven years before the birth of St. Ignatius. After taking
his degree at Padua, he lived in the circles of Papal diplomacy
up till the death of Julius II. in 1513. He then withdrew from
the diplomatic world, and occupied himself with the institution
of an Oratory of Divine Love to embrace priests and prelates,
who by the piety, austerity and charity of their lives would
recall the corrupt among the clergy to more edifying ways;
for, as he truly said, " e cosi maltrato il culto divino." Eleven
years later, in 1524, he, in company with three others, of whom
one was Giovanni Caraffa, afterwards that Pope Paul IV. who
ruled the Church so furiously during the time when Mary Tudor
was on the English throne, obtained from Clement VII. a Bull
for the erection of the new Order of the Theatines. Three
years later the house of the new Order was destroyed in the
great sack of Rome and its members had to flee to Venice,
where he assisted St. Hieronymus Aemiliani in the establishment
of his Congregation of Clerks Regular, the Somaschi.

From Venice he was to go to Naples, where in 1547 he died.
He lived in his last years a seraphic existence, culminating in a

kind of mystical crucifixion for the sins of the world, the exact nature of which it is not possible for us to comprehend, but the story of which is well known. His great desire was to receive the grace of martyrdom, and as he lay on his death-bed there entered the room the wounded Form of Christ. " Behold Me, Cajetan," He said. " I come to bestow on thee the grace thou dost desire." And those around saw the saint receive an embrace and kiss the Blessed Wounds. Cajetan reopened his eyes and Christ was now before him, hanging on the Cross. " Dost thou weep, Cajetan ? " He asked. " Thou dost ask me, Lord ? " he answered. " I weep because I see Thee dying yet again. Blot out this scene. I cannot see Thee in the midst of such torture and still live." " Cajetan," said Our Lord, " I have given thee My Cross ; it behoves that someone should be fastened thereupon." " Lord, Lord, wilt Thou die again ? " cried Cajetan. " Know that my sole ambition is martyrdom. But I would that it were by some other death more cruel than the Cross, for of that which is Thine I am not worthy. Lord, I bend me to Thy will." And Christ leant down and raised him up to the Cross, granting him to feel every one of the pains of Calvary—the nails, the thirst, the anguish, the last agony, and even the awful and mystic desolation of the *Lama Sabachthani*. So Cajetan died.

Yet here our business is with the Theatines whom St. Ignatius found established at Venice. The purposes of the Theatine and the Jesuit Orders were very similar to one another, and the suggestion was made more than once that they should amalgamate. There was even a story that St. Ignatius at this time sought admission to the Theatines—though it does not seem to be true, and in view of his vow it would hardly be possible for him to have acted thus without consulting his companions. In 1545 the Theatines suggested to Laynez that they should all join the Jesuits, and Laynez carried the request to St. Ignatius, but St. Ignatius answered that it was more for God's service that each Order should remain as He had been pleased to consecrate it. As it happened, while it was in the providence of God that St. Ignatius' Society should so greatly increase, the Theatine Order always remained small, and is to-day almost extinct.

St. Ignatius found in Venice three further companions—Hosez, a Malagan, who died soon afterwards, and the two d'Eguia brothers, one of whom at least St. Ignatius, it will be remembered, had known at Alcala, and whom he now met returning from a pilgrimage to the Holy Land. The elder, Diego, afterwards became, as I have said, St. Ignatius' confessor.

St. Ignatius, when he left Paris, had entrusted the authority over the rest of the company to Faber, as the only priest among them. Faber during these months had added to the rest two more companions—Le Jay and Brouet. Their zeal, piety and ability had won for them a considerable position in the world of Paris, and when the time for their departure drew near, many urged upon Faber that to desert a field in which their labour had shown itself so fruitful would be a clear defiance of the will of God. Faber answered that their vows left them no alternative but to go to Venice to their master, Ignatius. And, as it happened, circumstances took the decision out of their hands.

It will be remembered that when we spoke of St. Ignatius' crossing of the Pyrenees on his way to Paris from Barcelona in 1528, we mentioned how war had again broken out between Charles V. and Francis I. On August 3rd, 1529, the two monarchs had signed a peace at Cambrai, but Europe was not large enough to contain their silly ambitions. In 1536 Francis began to prepare for a fresh attack upon Savoy, and Charles replied by defensive works in Navarre and Rousillon. On July 25th of that year the Imperial army crossed the frontier into Provence. Montmorency, the French commander, shut himself up in two fortified camps at Avignon and Valence, and Charles, though he devastated the country round about, was unable either to attack him or to capture Marseilles. The Imperial army advanced as far as Fréjus, and in the fighting there the greatest of Spanish poets, de la Vega, was mortally wounded and died in the arms of a gallant fellow-officer, the Marquis of Lambay, the Duke of Gandia, Francis Borgia, whom we last heard of as he drove through the streets of Alcala, and whom we shall hear of again. In the north the Count of Nassau, marching from the Netherlands, had invaded Picardy, captured Guise and laid siege to Peronne.

Of the ten companions at Paris under Faber's leadership six were subjects of the Emperor. They were warned by their friends that it would be best to leave the country that autumn, as next year the development of more extended operations might block the roads against them. They therefore started on November 15th. It was agreed that all should assemble at Meaux, a little town on the Marne, twenty-eight miles east of Paris, which had already gained for itself a certain reputation as the headquarters of a movement for reform within the Church, soon to become a centre of Huguenotism, and a century and a half later to be first the episcopal see, afterwards the last resting-place, of one of the greatest of the Jesuits' pupils, Bossuet. The journey was not begun without difficulties. Rodriguez was one of the first to arrive. On the night before the others were to come, he was seized with an intense fever. He lay on the floor, which was his bed, rolling in agony, but after he and the rest had prayed he at last fell into a quiet sleep, and by the morning was completely recovered and able to set out with the rest. Before he could start, however, he was overtaken by his brother and a college friend, who tried to dissuade him from so foolish a life, urging that he had an obligation to his mother and relatives and to the King of Portugal, who had provided the money for his education, and that he should satisfy it by a less abnormal life. But Rodriguez who, like St. Ignatius, had renounced the ties of family, refused to be persuaded.

They set out, and on their way met with various strange adventures. St. Francis Xavier accused himself in his conscience for the many sins of pride in his past life. Not only had he been guilty of intellectual pride, but he had also, so he thought, taken too great pleasure in his success in the university athletic sports. As penance he therefore tied his legs together with a rough cord and proposed to walk, thus hobbled, to Venice. It was a pity that St. Ignatius was not at hand to check such an extravagance, for the effect of it was so to reduce the pace of the whole company that it would have taken them most of the rest of their lives to have got to Venice. After a time he sank exhausted by the wayside, and it was found that the cords had so bitten into his ankles that the flesh had closed over them. The doctor refused to remove them, but after a night's rest the cords were found to be removed and the flesh healed.

The party travelled east towards the Franco-German frontier, and soon fell in with some French soldiers. There might have been difficulties had not a passing peasant shouted to the soldiers the delightfully contemptuous question, " *Ne voyez-vous pas que ces messieurs sont réformateurs? qu'ils vont réformer quelque pays?*" The soldiers, learning that they were only "reformers," let them go.

They crossed the frontier somewhere near Verdun, and travelled down through Lorraine and Alsace, then of course Imperial territory. They came down eventually to Basle. The famous Carlstadt had three years before settled there as Zwinglian pastor and professor of theology, and he visited the Jesuits at their inn and invited them to a public controversy. It was their usual custom to accept such invitations, but whether this disputation ever took place it does not seem possible to say. If it did, it is not likely that it bore much fruit, for Carlstadt, though in some ways not an unattractive man, was yet one whose religious opinions varied throughout his life with the growing resources of his vocabulary of invective, until eventually he had the considerable honour of breaking off his friendship with Martin Luther on the ground that Luther's controversial language was not sufficiently violent.

From Basle they went on towards Constance, walking, as was their custom, two and two, now praying, now singing, now conversing of spiritual things. The Swiss Confederate States, still nominally a part of the Empire, had in effect established their independence of Imperial authority by the Suabian War of the previous century, though that independence was not to be expressly recognised until the Treaty of Westphalia in 1648. The religious conflicts of the 16th century divided the country as it has remained divided until to-day. Under the influence of Zwingli at Zurich and Calvin at Geneva, large parts of the country abandoned Catholicism. At Basle the Jesuits were in a district that had turned completely Protestant ; the bishop had been expelled and the Catholic worship suppressed.   When they penetrated into the canton of Thorgau, they were still in a district predominantly Protestant, but one whose apostasy had been less complete than that of Basle. About sixteen miles from Constance they put up at an inn. The minister, who had previously been the parish priest but after changing his religion had taken a wife and begotten a family, called on them and invited them to dispute.   Laynez argued with him, and after a time the minister proposed that they should adjourn the discussion and sup with him.   This they refused to do, and when the discussion was resumed afterwards, the minister, whether annoyed at a refusal which he considered churlish and self-righteous, excited with wine or merely irritated at meeting stronger opposition than he had expected, flew into a passion and swore that he would delate them and have them put in prison.   In the temper of the times their danger was, as bystanders warned them, considerable, for the local government was, of course, Protestant.   However, they persisted in spending the night at the inn, and the next morning were conducted by a young German to the road to Constance, which they reached in safety.   As they entered the town a woman, noticing their chaplets, brought to them pieces of crucifixes which the Lutherans had smashed.   These the Jesuits reverently kissed, to the woman's great joy.   From Constance they struck down through the Grisons country into Italy and to Venice, which they reached on January 6th, 1537, where St. Ignatius welcomed them with tears of joy.   " *Gavisi sunt valde omnes,*" records Bobadilla.   They were nineteen days in advance of the promise which they had made at Montmartre two and a half years before.   It was not possible to sail at once for the Holy Land.   They therefore occupied their time in works of charity in the hospitals, St. Francis Xavier offering himself to suck the poisoned blood out of the wounds of the invalids.

It was decided that it would be well before further prosecution of their plans to obtain the Papal approval. St. Ignatius would not go to Rome himself. Paul III. had compelled the Theatines to re-establish their headquarters at Rome, and the fiery Caraffa had therefore returned thither. He was in favour with Paul, and had just been created cardinal at the end of the previous year. He was a good, slashing hater, his temper as uncertain then as it was to be twenty years later when he was himself on the Papal throne, and St. Ignatius fancied that he bore him a grudge either for his refusal to join the Theatines, or for a somewhat frank letter of advice which St. Ignatius seems to have written to Caraffa in favour of a strict interpretation of the vow of poverty, or because St. Ignatius was a Spaniard, and the Neapolitan Caraffa hated all Spaniards ; or indeed for the reason for which the author of the famous little poem bore a grudge against poor Dr. Fell. Ortiz, who had, it will be remembered, been the tutor of de Castro and Peralta at Paris and had thus taken a part in denouncing St. Ignatius to the Inquisition at Paris, was also now at Rome as Charles V.'s Ambassador. St. Ignatius imagined—mistakenly, as it proved—that these men would be his enemies, and he thought the chances of Papal approval greater if he himself did not come to Rome.

In the middle of Lent, therefore, the rest set out under Faber's leadership. They followed the coast down to Ravenna and Ancona, taking with them no money and suffering their usual hardships. One of them had to pawn his breviary at Ancona, and he records of St. Francis Xavier, " When I was passing through the streets of Ancona, begging alms with which I might redeem my breviary, I saw one of my companions, wet and barefooted, asking the market-woman to give him in charity a little fruit or vegetables. I thought of his high birth, his great talents, the riches he had renounced, the eminent learning and virtue which would have given him such influence in the world ; and I felt unworthy to be the associate of such men." And indeed the story of these men must make strange reading to those who make what they are pleased to call " success " the object of their lives.

From Ancona the Jesuits paid a visit to the so-called Santa Casa of Loretto, the story of which had at that time come recently into prominence, and thence they travelled on to Tolentino, where their wants were relieved by a mysterious stranger who came up to them in the street, pressed money into their hands and vanished without a word.   From Tolentino they on the next day reached Rome.

CHAPTER VIII

It is common to say of autocratic governments that the machine is always too strong for the man, and to no government is this judgment more freely applied than to that of the Papacy —especially of the Papacy in the 16th century. "Excellent men," we are told, "full of good intentions, but the environment triumphed over them." Of the career of some of the Popes, Adrian VI., say, the explanation is possibly a just one. But to pretend that the victory of the machine is in accordance with inevitable law is false folly. The machine did not triumph over the one certainly great statesman who sat upon the Papal throne during the 16th century—Paul III.

For fifty years the throne of Peter had been occupied by men who either would not or could not cope with the enormous problems of reform without which the Catholic Church could hardly be saved. At the turn of the century, Alexander VI. was still Pope, " that Simoniac, that Jew," as Julius II. called him. He was to die in 1503, as Guicciardini records, " to the unspeakable joy of all Rome." He was an Italian patriot who might have been the first to take for himself the motto of " *Italia fara da se*," and a statesman of ability, but statesmanship and Italian patriotism are not sufficient qualities for a Pope. Of him the less said the better. After Alexander came Pius III., who reigned only for twenty-six days ; after him, Julius II., less openly infamous than Alexander in his private life, as patriotic and as culpably worldly in his politics, yet deserving honour as the only ne of the early Renaissance Popes who made a real attempt to solve the difficult problem of the relation between the Church and the new art. Legend records that he died with the words " *fuori i barbari* " on his lips. After Julius, Leo X.,

the Medici, a lover of peace and of the arts, a cardinal at the age
of fourteen, the holder of three canonries, six rectories, a priory,
a precentorship, a provostship and sixteen abbacies, nevertheless
of irreproachable private life, a pious Christian in spite of
irresponsible chatter, spread abroad by the unspeakable John
Bale, about his scepticism, a man of much charm but quite
lacking the energy to tackle grave problems, short-sighted both
in policy and in physical fact. " *Multi caeci Cardinales creavere
caecum decimum Leonem,*" jeered the wits. " He would have
made an ideal Pope," gibed Sarpi, after a panegyric on his
virtues, " had he added to these qualities some knowledge of
the things of religion." During his reign came the great
challenge of Luther, and he proved himself unfitted to meet it.

After Leo came Adrian VI., the Fleming, by whom, as has
been described, St. Ignatius was received on his visit to Rome
in 1523, a good man, but, so far as a short pontificate could show,
apparently unequal to the gigantic task required of him.   After
Adrian, Clement VII., cousin of Leo X., a shifty and un-
successful diplomat, whose ineffectual tergiversations were
responsible for the sack of Rome.   In his reign the difficulties
of the English annulment were added to the already existing
difficulties of the Church, and though Clement's refusal to
grant Henry's appalling demands was greatly to his honour, yet
the result was to leave to his successor a problem so greatly
complicated as to seem insoluble.   That successor was the
Farnese Pope, Paul III. : the brother of Giulia Farnese, *belle à
merveille,* the mistress of Alexander VI. ; cardinal at the age of
fourteen owing to this sinister brother-in-lawship with the
Borgia ; as a young man imprisoned in San Angelo for forgery ;
besieged in San Angelo along with Clement VII. in 1527, when,
as will be remembered, Cellini [1] nearly brought his career to an

[1] The mention of Cellini reminds one that many people—all that
very respectable class which reads memoirs, but does not read either
history or theology—will very likely have in their minds no picture
of Paul save that given by Cellini.   It is therefore worth observing
(1) that in spite of John Addington Symonds it is quite absurd to
treat Cellini as a veracious man ; (2) that, if we read Cellini alone,

end by upsetting a cargo of stones on his head; the saviour of
the Church.   Humanly speaking, Paul could never have become
Pope if his sister had not been the mistress of Alexander, nor
the Church been saved if Paul had not been Pope.   It is a
curious reflection.

Whatever may be thought of the positive theology of Martin
Luther or of the character of him and of his supporters, however
much modern research may show that the hoary legends about
Tetzel need revision, there can yet be no denial that, so far as
Luther was in protest against abuses, there were plenty of
abuses against which it was most right to protest.   Honest-
minded Catholics were as convinced of the necessity of protest as was he.   For instance, Rodrigo Nino, the Imperial
Ambassador to the Doge, wrote in 1535 that " there were few
in Venice who were not more Lutheran than Luther himself
with regard to such matters as the reform of the clergy and their
secular state."   The Catholic doctrine of indulgences remains
to-day what it was in Luther's time, but the attachment to the
indulgence of a financial payment, even though it was still
possible to obtain it without such payment, was a practice
susceptible of the gravest scandal.   A man as far removed from
heresy as Cardinal Ximenes had forbidden the practice in his
diocese in Spain.   The financial conditions of the particular

we get the impression that the whole Papal policy was dominated by
the problem of Cellini's imprisonment in San Angelo.   In point of
fact, the period of that imprisonment was one of the most momentous
in the history of Europe, the period during which Paul's great policy
was taking shape, the last preparations being made for the meeting of
Trent and Catholics, under Papal encouragement, reclaiming for
themselves the enormous privilege of a more frequent participation
in the Sacraments.   Suppose for the sake of argument that Cellini
was really as villainously treated as he pretended to be.   That may
be evidence to bring an arraignment against Pier Luigi or some
Vatican officials, but it is nothing but Cellini's vanity which persuaded him that Paul himself can have ever deeply interested
himself in the case.   It is as if the post was late and we ascribed it
to a personal grudge which the Postmaster-General had against us.
We cannot now discover the exact truth, but, as for the story in the
Memoirs, *c'est magnifique, mais ce n'est pas la politique.*

indulgence against which Luther protested were in some ways especially crude, nor was it an isolated scandal. The whole policy of the Papal court was so cankered with money-grubbing worldliness that Adrian VI. himself said, with exaggeration, it is true, but with only too large a grain of truth, that the Curia had been the fountain-head of all the corruptions of the Church. It was the great task of Paul III. to end this evil state of affairs. It was his great glory, the title to that fame which puts him among the first of the figures in our European story, that substantially he succeeded. The measure of his success is this. Since his time there have been foolish Popes and Popes who blundered. Paul himself indeed was guilty of at least one enormous blunder, when he made his nephews and his grandsons cardinals. Yet of no single Pope from Paul's time to our own, save possibly of the disastrous Julius III., can it be fairly said that he has allowed Papal policy to be dominated by the love of money or of the things of this world. Paul restored to Europe an independent spiritual voice. It was high time. As Baldassare Castiglione remarked during one of the Renaissance conclaves, "May it please God to send the Holy Ghost, for there is great need of Him."

Into a general estimate of Paul's great policy this is not the place to enter. What is important for our purpose is his ready recognition of the enormous strength which the vigour of the new Orders could bring to the Church. The Jesuits were not, as is sometimes thought, the only such new Order. We have already seen how Paul summoned the Theatines back to Rome. He was ready to encourage others, the Barnabites, the Capuchins, and, when the Jesuits came to him, they found a man with vision to use the new weapon which God had put into his hands.

When Faber and his companions arrived in Rome, it so happened that the first person to befriend them was that very Ortiz of whose enmity St. Ignatius was so much afraid. He recognised Faber and Xavier, whom he had known at Paris, and procured for them an introduction to the Pope. Paul wished that they should dispute before him as he sat at dinner—which they did—and he called them up to him, saying, "We are exceedingly rejoiced to see so much learning joined with so much humility." He asked if he could in any way assist them. Faber begged for his benediction and for leave to go to Jerusalem. He gave his benediction and said, "I give you leave readily, but I do not think you will go," for the war between Venice and the Turk was still raging. Afterwards Faber preferred to the Pope another request—that he would give authority for any bishop to ordain all the companions priests. Paul gave them money for their journey to the Levant.

When the summer came, they set out for their return to Venice. It was on this journey, while they were at Ravenna, that Rodriguez went into a house to ask for alms and found to his dismay that it was a house of ill-fame. He beat a very hasty retreat, and so moved was he by his mistake that he at once started delivering to the passers-by an impromptu lecture on the horrors of sin. The harlots, somewhat as if they were characters in a Hogarth picture or in some third sequel to the *Beggar's Opera* and *Polly*, all popped their heads out of the window to hear what was going on, but were so moved by Rodriguez' eloquence that at the end they threw themselves on the ground at his feet and promised amendment of life.

When they got back to Venice, all those of the company who were not already priests, including St. Ignatius, were, in accordance with the Pope's promise, ordained by the Bishop of Arba on the Feast of St. John the Baptist, June 24th. They then all dispersed to different places to make retreats, St. Ignatius going with Faber and Laynez to Vicenza. The retreat finished, the others said their first Masses, but St. Ignatius postponed his till Christmas, 1538. St. Ignatius and three of his companions then took up their residence at a ruined and deserted convent near Vicenza, from which they used to issue forth and preach to the people, whom they both edified and amused by their quaint Italian.

Meanwhile the old suspicions had been raised again. This was novelty; therefore it must be heresy. But St. Ignatius was now armed with his certificate from the Inquisitor at Paris.

He took this to the Inquisition of Venice, and had no difficulty in getting from it a similar certificate of orthodoxy.

While St. Ignatius was at Vicenza, Le Jay and Rodriguez were the guests of a certain Antonio, a pious but morbid hermit, who lived near Bassano. Rodriguez fell very ill, and his life was despaired of. St. Ignatius himself was not at all well; nevertheless he and Faber set out across country to visit Rodriguez. St. Ignatius walked much faster than Faber, and had from time to time to wait for Faber to catch him up. Once when Faber came panting up, St. Ignatius said, " Rodriguez will not die," and, when he reached Antonio's cave, he said again, " Brother Simon, you will not die yet." He was quite right, and after a time Rodriguez recovered. Unfortunately, St. Ignatius was unable to exercise over Antonio his usual fascination. The hermit disapproved strongly of one who professed to have dedicated himself to God but mixed so freely with the world. In his view those of the world lived in the world; those who lived the spiritual life withdrew themselves from the world and conversed with God alone. He did not understand that there was a third class, the members of which were in the world but not of it, who lived the spiritual life yet lived it in the world, using the world, to quote the key-phrase of St. Paul, as though they used it not. When Antonio and St. Ignatius parted, their parting was then far from cordial, but afterwards it was revealed to Antonio in prayer that he had presumptuously condemned a saint, and he said with what Stewart Rose calls " great humility," but what seems to me double-edged compliment, that " God had thus taught him how little you can guess the sap of a tree from its bark."

Yet God, Who sends to some souls the vocation to the Pauline or Ignatian life, calls others to the purely contemplative. When Rodriguez was convalescent, they all transferred to a house in the city of Bassano. In the bustle of the city, there began to steal into Rodriguez' heart a greater and a greater longing for the stark solitude of Antonio's cell. At last he persuaded himself that he had received a higher call than that to which he had vowed himself. Telling no one, he crept out and

along the road to the cell.   But, as he walked along, he saw
coming towards him an armed man with a drawn sword in his
hand who barred his way.   Rodriguez tried to advance, but the
man advanced against him.   He was not of this world, and
great terror seized Rodriguez.   He turned and fled back to his
companions.   He had told no one of his design, nor where
he had been, yet St. Ignatius came to meet him as he returned
and said to him with a smile, in the words of Our Lord,
" *Modicae fidei, quare dubitasti ?* "

The winter came on ; war still raged over the Adriatic.   It
was necessary that they should decide what should be done.
They were delayed for a time by the illness of St. Francis Xavier
and one of the others, but on their recovery all agreed that the
time had come to lay down for themselves some rules of life.
There was no tinge of autocracy about this first sketch of a
constitution.   Each was to be in turn superior for a week.
They were to live on alms and in hospitals.   They were to
preach, provided that they preached short sermons (St. Ignatius
could not abide long sermons), to instruct, to perform works of
charity, to do all that it came to their hand to do for the greater
glory of God.   All these rules were settled in general discussion.
Next there arose the question of a name for the Society.   St.
Ignatius spoke.   It had been revealed to him in the cave at
Manresa that the Society should be called after the name of
Jesus.   The others accepted the revelation of God.

The name was to be the occasion of some dispute later, both
during St. Ignatius' lifetime and later during the generalship of
Acquaviva and the pontificate of Sixtus V.   St. Ignatius, when
told of the opposition to the Society's name, was to write in 1554
" that it had a deeper root than the world knew of, and could
not be altered."   More than a hundred years before this St.
Vincent Ferrer, the famous Spanish Dominican, had foreseen a
day when a company would arise, calling itself the company of
Jesus, and consisting of " men carrying humility and charity,
the pure heart and single spirit to perfection ; men who were to
know nothing but in Jesus crucified ; to love, speak and think
of Him only ; to have no care for themselves ; to desire nothing

but Heaven, and death, that they might come to it sooner."
And it had been prophesied of a little Dutch baby, born in the
year in which on the other side of Europe St. Ignatius was
carried wounded from Pampeluna to Loyola, that it would one
day be a priest of a Society that would be known as the Society
of Jesus.   The name of the baby was Peter Canisius.

For the moment it was decided, since the journey to the
Holy Land was clearly impossible, that St. Ignatius and two
others should go to Rome ; the rest should distribute themselves
in twos among the university cities of Northern Italy.   Le Jay
and Rodriguez were chosen to go to Ferrara.   It was still not
at all certain that Protestantism would not gain for itself a
substantial foothold even in Italy, and Ferrara was a key position
in the religious conflicts of the day.   In 1534, Duke Alfonso of
Ferrara had died, and his son, Ercole, had succeeded him.
Ercole's wife was the famous Renée, daughter of Louis XII. of
France.

Renée, patroness of the arts and letters, hater of Italy in which
she felt herself an exile, had learnt from her cousin, Margaret of
Navarre, and from the poetess, Madame de Soubise, the doctrines
of revolt and of sympathy for the new ideas.   Her ambition
was to make in Ferrara a Protestant salon, and to her court
flocked French and Italian intellectuals who had been attracted
by the new doctrines.   The French Ambassador, du Bellay,
had been there, and with him his secretary, François Rabelais,
and the ladies of the court all buzzed about the place at the
rumour that M. Rabelais, too, was a writer.   By God, he was !
In the year before Le Jay's coming, the lion-hunter had succeeded
in attracting her largest lion, and Calvin himself had visited her,
travelling under the name of Espeville, which made it all so
much more romantic.   There had been a blasphemous display
in one of the churches on Holy Saturday, the people were
scandalised, and her husband had been compelled to take up the
question of Renée and her entourage.   Calvin had to flee, and
Renée, for the moment, to conceal her religious sympathies in
public.   She revenged herself by getting Clément Marot to
write poems against her husband, immortalising his unkindness.

The Jesuits were sent with the hope of reconverting her to a more real Catholicism before a declaration of open apostasy; Le Jay was probably selected because he was a Frenchman, and she had a kindness for her countrymen. However, the enterprise was in its main object a failure. The influence of Calvin was too strong. Renée refused to see Le Jay, and three years later, in 1540, openly rejected the Catholic sacraments, for which, as has been mentioned, her husband allowed her to be put on trial before that same Matteo Ori, before whom St. Ignatius had been examined soon after his first arrival in Paris in 1528.

Yet Le Jay's visit was not fruitless. It chanced that that very remarkable woman, Vittoria Colonna, the lady who attracted the deep spiritual affection of Michelangelo, was at that time in Ferrara. She was a friend to all the members of that brilliant circle of reformers whom Paul had collected round him at Rome —Ghiberti, Contarini, Morone, Pole—and she had heard of the new Order at Rome. She chanced to meet either Le Jay or Rodriguez, sought them out in their lodgings, inquired into every detail of their lives, and eventually introduced them to Duke Ercole, to whom Le Jay became confessor.

Le Jay's influence on Vittoria was most timely. Like many mistresses of the salon, she was more fitted to collect brilliant talkers than to estimate the depth of their wisdom. Just at the time she was much under the influence of Ochino, whom she had induced to preach at Ferrara in the preceding Lent. Ochino was not, it is true, at the time a declared heretic, but his mind was already engaged upon strange speculations. The influence of Le Jay upon Vittoria cannot but have been entirely good and was doubtless largely responsible for her subsequent breach with Ochino.

Meanwhile, Hosez and Codure had gone off to Padua. There they had fallen under the suspicion of the clergy, and been cast into prison. They spent the night in rejoicing and praising God Who had thus permitted them to suffer for His sake. But their glad tribulation was short-lived. The next day they were released, and soon afterwards Hosez preached a

sermon in the market-place on the text, " Watch and pray, for
ye know neither the day nor the hour."   He spoke truly, for
hardly had he finished when he was struck down with an attack
of fever.   He was taken back to the hospital, where he soon
afterwards died.   Death had claimed his first victim from the
new Society.   Codure continued the apostolic work in Padua,
and Rodriguez, unable owing to his nationality to do at the
Court of Ferrara so great a work as Le Jay, came to join him
and to take Hosez' place.

Xavier and Bobadilla went to Bologna, but recently brought
under Papal rule as a result of the ambitious and violent policy
of Julius II.   Xavier, before he set out, had been visited in a
vision by St. Jerome, who told him that he would go to Bologna
and that there a cross should be given him whereby his soul
would receive great profit.   This was proved true.   He said
his Mass in the chapel where St. Dominic lies buried, and the
thought of this great privilege so overcame him that he shed
tears of joy.   It is a pleasant little anecdote for those to recall
who are irritated by the incessant chatter about enmity between
Jesuits and Dominicans.   A certain lady, a member of the
Third Order of St. Dominic, was assisting at St. Francis
Xavier's Mass.   She got into conversation with him afterwards,
and edified by his spirituality, persuaded him to come and live
with her uncle, a canon of St. Petronius.   St. Francis did so,
but soon afterwards the cross which St. Jerome had predicted
came to him.   He fell seriously ill of a quartan fever.   However,
through the kindness of his hosts he recovered and was able to
continue his apostolic work in the city, where he won for
himself a reputation that was to survive for many years.

While the others were at their tasks in the towns of Northern
Italy, St. Ignatius, Faber and Laynez were, as we have said,
making their way to Rome.   At La Storta, six miles outside the
city, St. Ignatius had one of the most famous of his visions, in
which—the tale is not intelligible to us—God the Father in
some wonderful way made it clear to him that he had admitted
him to an ineffable nearness to His Son.   " He gave me to
Christ as a portion," said St. Ignatius to Gonzalez, and Our

Lord answered to him, " *Ego tibi Romae propitius ero.*"   St. Ignatius told this experience to his companions, not knowing exactly what it meant, and thinking that perhaps they were all to be martyred at Rome.   He used afterwards to say that in serving God on the altar, he had sometimes the same feelings which he had experienced " when the Eternal Father placed me with His Son."

As they entered Rome, St. Ignatius took the opportunity to give to his companions some advice on their behaviour.   " Let us avoid all relations with women," he said, " unless those of the highest rank."   A few years before, it will be remembered, St. Ignatius had so despised the trappings of rank that he had purposely spoken with a bucolic accent.   That mood had passed.   He no longer honoured the things of the world sufficiently to insult them.   He now so despised them that he was willing to use them.   Yet to us it cannot but come as something of a shock that he should be always so frank in his readiness to take advantage of other people's snobbery. Doubtless it was his strength that he knew just how far it was necessary to take the world as he found it, if he was going to succeed in leaving it better than he found it.   The prince's soul was of no more value than the peasant's soul, but since the prince's favour could make the Catholic things accessible to a whole population, his disfavour make them inaccessible, it was necessary to win the prince's favour.   Snobbery was so utterly alien from his soul and from those of his first followers—with the possible exception of Bobadilla—that there was no danger at all that he and they, while using the great ones of the world, should be corrupted by the standards of the world.   Yet we are not all so heroic, and snobbery is the easiest, the commonest and the vilest of the vices.   Nothing is harder, as every Labour leader knows, than to associate daily with the rich and yet preserve complete the contempt for riches.   It is impossible not to feel that there was a certain lack of discretion in St. Ignatius' so frank statement of his policy.

Immediately on their arrival in Rome, St. Ignatius and his companions were welcomed by Paul III.   Not a moment must be lost, said the great Pope, in utilising the services of such men for the glory of God.   Faber was therefore instructed at once to begin the teaching of the Scriptures, and Laynez that of scholastic theology in the College of Sapienza, while St. Ignatius was put to the more general work of giving the Spiritual Exercises to such as might be prepared to receive them.   The three made from the first a considerable stir in Roman life, and the Marquis d'Aguilar thought it his duty to tell St. Ignatius that his enemies in the world accused him and his followers of hypocrisy, saying that behind their pretences of humility was concealed the careerism of vulgar and ambitious men.   On hearing this, St. Ignatius made at once the famous and solemn vow that neither he nor his followers for ever should accept any ecclesiastical dignities except by the express command of the Pope.

St. Ignatius early won for himself and for his Order the powerful support of Cardinal Contarini.   This eminent Venetian diplomat had two years before been created a cardinal by Paul III., whose policy it was to collect around him all those whose minds were open to the great necessities of reform.   He was made president of a commission for submitting plans for reform in the Roman Curia, and shortly before St. Ignatius' arrival in Rome this commission had issued its report, *Consilium de Emendanda Ecclesia*.   To no reform did Contarini more enthusiastically lend himself than to that of the recognition of St. Ignatius' new Order, of whose good works in his native Venice he had already heard glowing accounts.

Contarini made it his business to speak to Ortiz, of whose enmity St. Ignatius was so much afraid.   Ortiz was converted and agreed to go down to Monte Cassino with St. Ignatius and there make the Exercises under him, which he did with such effect that he begged St. Ignatius for permission to enter his Order, permission which St. Ignatius refused, arguing that Ortiz was too old and, as is added, too fat to make a good Jesuit. At one point during the making of the Exercises, Ortiz' attention began to wander and his keenness to flag.   To restore him, St. Ignatius danced before him one of the old Basque dances—

a performance that we might have expected to hear of from St.
Francis rather than from St. Ignatius.

While St. Ignatius was at Monte Cassino Hosez died at
Padua. Standing on the spot where St. Benedict a thousand and
more years before had seen the soul of Germanus of Capua
ascend to heaven in a globe of fire, St. Ignatius saw the spirit
of Hosez, surrounded by a glorious light, carried up to Paradise
by angels, and some days afterwards in his Mass, when in the
Confiteor, he came to the words, " *Omnibus sanctis*," he saw the
Heavens opened and Hosez sitting among the spirits of the
redeemed.

On his return from Monte Cassino St. Ignatius met Francis
Strada, the new recruit who was to take Hosez' place. Strada,
a young Spaniard whom St. Ignatius had known slightly in
earlier days, was a sort of secretary to the fiery Cardinal Caraffa.
Becoming wearied of a post of such danger, he sighed for the
comparative security of the wars and was just setting out for
Naples to try his luck as a soldier of fortune when St. Ignatius
met him. He persuaded him that a life lived in the mere search
for adventure would certainly be a life of disappointment. The
fruits of this world are desirable only in prospect. Once they
are tasted they cease to be enjoyed. The only true adventure
was the adventure of the Cross ; and Strada, persuaded, joined
the Society. He was a great preacher but much frightened by
his own success, knowing very well that there are none who find
it harder to practise virtue than those who can eloquently praise
it. The words of St. Paul, " Lest, having preached to others, I
should myself be cast away," rang continually in his ears. He
it was who was responsible for the popular belief that the
sardine trade was under the especial protection of the Society
of Jesus, for, when in later years he landed at Corunna on his
way to Coimbra, his landing happened to coincide with that of
an exceptionally heavy haul of sardines, which was confidently
attributed by the fishermen to the sanctity of the holy father.

In Lent, 1538, St. Ignatius summoned all his companions to
join him at Rome. They came, many of them much regretted
by the congregations whom they had left. Especially was this

true of Codure and Rodriguez from Padua. The companions lodged in a vineyard at the foot of Trinita de' Monti and afterwards at Torre de Melangolo. At first their preaching was the admiration of the city, but it was not long before, at Rome as elsewhere, troubles came upon them. Paul III., anxious in face of the Turkish menace to bring to an end the disastrous divisions of Christendom, had gone to Nice in order to try and arrange a peace between Charles V. and Francis I. A certain Augustin, a secret Lutheran, took advantage of his absence from Rome and began to preach to the people. He had already cleverly won their confidence by straightforward discourses upon undisputed doctrines, and now began to insert into his sermons little points of specifically Lutheran teaching. Salmeron and Laynez, who chanced to hear him, perceived what he was teaching. They went privately to remonstrate with him, but he repulsed them with contempt and from that moment saw in the Jesuits his chief enemies. He determined to discredit St. Ignatius by putting about a garbled version of his past troubles. "A wolf, disguised as a shepherd," he called him, "who had committed frightful ravages in several of the first universities of Europe . . . under the mask of sanctity. Rome, though perhaps late, ought not to show herself less prudent than Paris, Salamanca, Venice, where Ignatius, convicted of heresy, escaped death only by flight. . . . But even in Rome there are men of incorruptible faith, belonging to his own nation, who have renounced him. There is one especially who, attracted at first by this man, has left him with horror."

The "one" was that Michel Navarro who had tried to murder St. Ignatius in Paris in anger at his conversion of St. Francis Xavier. Navarro had, it will be remembered, at first professed great penitence for his atrocious project, but he had afterwards slipped back again and had now accepted a sum of money in return for laying an accusation against St. Ignatius before Conversini, the Governor of Rome. Cardinal de Cupis, head of the Sacred College, was won over to the defence of the Jesuits, and with this support St. Ignatius was willing to dare his opponents to try their accusation before Conversini. Before the tribunal Navarro deposed on oath that St. Ignatius had been condemned for heresy by the tribunals of Alcala, Paris and Venice.   St. Ignatius was able to reply by reading a letter of Navarro, written in his days of penitence, in which he had born witness to St. Ignatius' honesty and orthodoxy.   Navarro's case collapsed and he himself was banished for calumny.

St. Ignatius pressed, as was his custom, for formal attestation of his innocence.   It so happened that Figueroa, who had tried him at Alcala, Ori, who had tried him at Paris, and Doces, who had tried him at Venice, were at the moment in Rome.   The opportunity was therefore exceptionally favourable for obtaining a final statement of the true history of all his troubles. Conversini, anxious for peace, wished simply to impose an obligation of silence on all disputants.   This did not satisfy Ignatius, who waited for the Pope's return from Nice and then followed him one day out to his villa at Frascati.   In an interview of an hour he was able to persuade Paul of the justice of his demand, and a sentence was passed that " not only had no fault been found in these persons, either in law or in fact, but the excellence of their life and doctrine was fully shown ; and while their accusers were proved to have uttered only false and empty statements, the best men, on the contrary, had given the strongest testimony in their favour."   Of those accusers Augustin afterwards perished at the hands of the Spanish Inquisition ; Navarro turned in remorse to that charity of St. Ignatius to which none ever turned in vain ; and the rest, it seems, died penitent and confessing the innocence of the saint.

Towards the end of the year Rome was visited by a terrible famine.   So high was the esteem in which the Jesuits now stood that people were willingly ready to entrust to them funds for the famine relief and were able to care for as many as three thousand sufferers.   Their work brought them into contact with another influential patron, Margaret of Austria, the natural daughter of Charles V.   This sad lady, afterwards to have the unhappy post of Regent of the Netherlands during the early years of Queen Elizabeth's reign, was at this time a widow, her first husband, Alessandro de' Medici, the Duke of Florence, having been assassinated in the previous year. A few years later she was to be unhappily married to Pope Paul's grandson, Ottavio Farnese, and the issue of their marriage was to be that great and gallant general, the Duke of Parma, whose task it would have been, had the Armada succeeded, to command the army of the invasion of England. She now took Codure for her spiritual director, and after his death she turned to St. Ignatius himself and the relationship between them continued for life.

This Christmas St. Ignatius at last said his First Mass for which he had so long prepared himself. " I went at Christmas," he wrote to his brother, " to Sta. Maria Maggiore and said there, with the help of God, my first Mass, in the chapel which contains the cradle where the infant Jesus was laid."

The time had now come to see whether the ecclesiastical authorities would agree to the establishment of a new Order. St. Ignatius called his followers together and bade each prepare himself by prayer and fasting and solitary meditation for his share in the decision of future policy. When they assembled again St. Ignatius submitted to them, as the first question, " Should they remain disconnected, independent and disorganised ? " All were opposed. Should they, then, add to their vows of poverty and celibacy a vow of obedience ? Opinion was in favour, but it was decided to proceed " by way of election." That is to say, at the next meeting every one was under obligation to produce any arguments of which he had been able to think against the vow. The three most powerful were, that public opinion was hostile to religious orders and it was therefore folly to choose this moment for the founding of a new one, that an obligation to obedience might repel many who would be glad to join a more free society, that the Pope might refuse. At the next meeting the arguments on the contrary side were brought forward. It was urged that none among the older orders was precisely suited to the needs of the time nor to the especial work to which the new Order would dedicate itself, and that, while some might be repelled by a vow of obedience, others—and in particular the most valuable and energetic of the present members—would be attracted by it. The arguments in favour of the vow were unanimously held to have carried the day, and a declaration in favour of it was drawn up and signed by all present. All the well-known names are there, and, in addition, a mysterious R. Cacres, of whom little else is known.

That was on April 15th, 1539. On May 4th, at another meeting, it was decided that they should add to their other vows a special vow of obedience to the Pope, that every member of the Society should give public instruction in the catechism forty days a year for about an hour at a time, that they should elect a superior for life, and that the affairs of the Society in the future should be determined by the votes of the majority of its members at the time resident in Italy. St. Ignatius was designated to draw up the petition for Papal recognition.

Cardinal Contarini agreed to act as go-between and to present the petition to Paul, supporting it by his own advocacy. Paul gave it to a Dominican, Tommaso Badia, for examination, who reported in its favour, and Paul, on reading the Constitutions which St. Ignatius had drawn up, is said to have exclaimed, " The finger of God is here." Yet official machinery moves slowly. Even the works of God had to be submitted to the regular sub-committee of three before they could receive the honour of Papal approval. And of the three, one, Bartolomeo Giudiccioni, was strongly opposed to the creation of any new religious orders. There were, he very sensibly argued, far too many already. All religious Orders, he said, were founded with the highest of intentions and rapidly degenerated into corruption. It was folly to load the Church up with another of them ; a much better plan would be to abolish some.

Giudiccioni's point of view was so full of common sense that it was impossible to alter it by argument. There was nothing for it but to have recourse to prayer. In the name of himself and all his company St. Ignatius vowed that three thousand Masses of thanksgiving should be offered if Papal approval was secured. Soon after Giudiccioni desired that the Constitutions should be read to him. Hearing them, he at once changed his opinion and joined with his colleagues in recommending Papal approval. There is no reason to doubt that Giudiccioni's conversion was God's direct answer to Ignatius' prayer. As soon as he had received the report of the committee Paul issued the Bull of Establishment, the famous *Regimini Militantis Ecclesiae*, on September 27th, 1540.

It is rarely that much can be made out of the titles of Papal Bulls. As is known, these titles are simply the first words of the Bull—words which by themselves have more often than not no significance whatsoever. Here was an exception. It was with a bold, memorable gesture that the great Pope hurled the light horse of the Church upon the gathering armies of the world with the splendid battle-cry of " For the Government of the Fighting Church." There was to be nothing like it until three hundred years later another great Pope was to call all Christian men to apply to the grave problems of industrial life the eternal principles of ,Christ with the call " Of New Things," or even until in our day the present Pope was to answer the challenge to Christian social morals with the *Casti Connubii*.

For the moment the numbers of the new company were limited to sixty, but three years afterwards, on March 14th, 1543, by a further Bull, *Iniunctum Nobis*, this restriction was removed.

CHAPTER IX

ART AND THE SPIRITUAL EXERCISES

If we are to understand St. Ignatius and the Jesuit movement of the 16th century, it is necessary to interrupt the direct narrative in order to consider two important problems—the spirit of the Renaissance, the age in which St. Ignatius found himself, and that peculiar weapon with which he met the assaults of the world, the Spiritual Exercises.

It is not possible to understand the spirit of the Renaissance unless we delay a little upon the very difficult question of the relation between religion and art. The early years of the 16th century found the Church faced with four grave problems—problems which are sometimes confounded together in all-embracing phrases, but which it is important to keep distinct from one another—the theological, the moral, the political and the æsthetic. The theological question, the question " What is Catholic doctrine ? " was answered at Trent. The moral task, the task of inducing Catholics to live according to Catholic principles, was the task which the Counter-Reformation set itself. The political question, the question how could the Pope avoid being involved in the political problems of the country in which he resided, was a question which of its nature admitted of no final solution. Every plan had, and has, its disadvantages. But at least the purposes of the Church have never again been so largely complicated by the political problems of the Papacy as they were in the 16th century. The hardest, if perhaps not the most important, of the questions was the æsthetic, and to it no solution was found.

The problem was, What should be the relation between the Church and secular art—that is to say, art which has no directly didactic religious purpose ? There are three common answers to this question. There is the answer of Savonarola and, I suppose, of Plato, that all secular art, since it does not directly enforce the truths of religion, is therefore evil. There is the answer of Leo X., that all art, simply because it is art, is therefore good, and that the Church should encourage every activity which boasts itself to be artistic. There is the answer of the modern world that religion has one field and art another, that it is the business of each to go its own way and to interfere with the other neither by suppression nor by patronage.

All these answers are, I think, superficial, for they give us no solution of the fundamental metaphysical problem. That problem I would put, in its simplicity, thus : If God is good and if beauty is good, then the whole scheme of creation must be beautiful. What seems ugly, must seem so only because our vision is partial. We do not see it rightly in relation to the whole. Ultimately beauty must be truth, truth beauty, and beauty and truth not two but one.

From this it follows that a beautiful work of art must be a revelation of things as they truly are, and therefore a revelation of God—and that simply in virtue of its beauty and irrespective of whether its subject be what is commonly called religious or what is commonly called secular. Beauty doubtless is, as St. Thomas tells us, *id quod visum placet*, but this is a description, not an account. The only adequate account of beauty is the mystical. The artist has opened to us a window through which we can get a glimpse of the timeless reality behind the perishing insubstantiality of this world.

" The world and its pageants," Baudelaire tells us in *L'Art Romantique*, quoting, or almost quoting, Poe, " are a glimpse of a correspondence with heaven. The insatiable thirst for everything beyond, which life reveals, is the liveliest proof of our immortality. It is at once by poetry and through poetry, by music and through music, that the soul perceives what splendours shine behind the tomb ; and when an exquisite poem brings tears to the eyes, such tears do not argue an excess of enjoyment, but rather attest an irritation of melancholy, some peremptory need of the nerves, a nature exiled in the imperfect, which would fain possess immediately, even on this earth, a paradise revealed "; which is perhaps the reason why Shakespeare makes Jessica say :

"I am never merry when I hear sweet music."

If what Baudelaire says is true, then it is clearly the business of the Church, the mother of truth, to teach her children the love of beauty, and wherever, as had happened at the Renaissance, the artists have conquered some new province for beauty, the Church ought to welcome and bless the conquest. We are commanded to "worship the Lord in the beauty of holiness." To offer God less than the best—to offer Him what is known as "the art of St. Sulpice"—whether through mere laziness or through the vile notion that tawdry art is necessary to arouse the devotions of the vulgar, is the ultimate blasphemy. God, Who is beauty, is to be worshipped only in beauty.

This necessity imposes on the Church and the leaders of the Church the duty to follow a policy very different from that of Savonarola or of those who argue that religion and art should have nothing to do with one another. It imposes the necessity for a policy as different from the intellectual and æsthetic Epicureanism of the Medici Popes. Only one, I fancy, of the Renaissance Popes fully grasped the philosophic necessity for this alliance between beauty and truth, and he, a man in some other ways by no means admirable, Julius II. The evidence, as the late Professor Kraus truly said, is the Vatican.

He who looks upon the Vatican as an unsystematic collection of very beautiful things does less than justice to the great, unifying mind of Julius. Julius, on his accession to the Papacy, on the one hand formed in his own mind the conception of a great design; on the other hand he had the good fortune to find ready to his hand three of the grandest creative spirits that the world has known—Bramante, Michelangelo, Raffael.

The greatest of Bramante's works, the building of the Basilica of St. Peter's, was never accomplished. Yet we have all the sketches and plans so annotated that it is possible for us to follow the grand design. The classical forms emphasise the lesson of the absolute validity of reason within her own sphere, while the Greek cross that was to surmount the whole teaches how the firm discoveries of the reason lead Man to that Faith which teaches him truths that, unaided, he could never discover and stretches out from the central point of a cross illimitably to heaven above, to hell beneath, and to the farthest corners of the earth.

The lessons that architecture was to have taught in St. Peter's painting was able to teach both in the Vatican and in Julius' own monument. He left instructions to Michelangelo that he himself should be represented there as Moses. The symbolism is obvious. Just as Moses had led the children of Israel from captivity and the wilderness to the vision of the Promised Land, so Julius had led the Christian world to the vision of an alliance between truth and beauty, more complete than had been enjoyed before. The possibilities of this new, liberated life that lay open before mankind, were as yet not fully explored. Julius had been Moses ; a Joshua was yet to come.

The same lesson was to be taught by the famous Sistine roof. Fallen Man was to be shepherded to Christ, to use St. Clement of Alexandria's phrase, to be led gradually back step by step to that life of the full and harmonious enjoyment of all his faculties, his will at union with the will of God—that life of which Adam's sin had deprived him. Very foolish are those critics who point to the presence of Sibyls, along with Patriarchs and Prophets, as the leaders of mankind and laugh at them as evidence of the feebleness of the Christian faith of the Renaissance. Julius had learnt from Marsilio Ficino and Pico della Mirandola—he might have learnt it from St. Augustine—to look on the whole of history as a single and purposive unfolding of God's plan. If the Incarnation was delayed until a certain date, it was delayed for a purpose—in order that unaided Man might first be allowed to see how much he could do for himself and to recognise that it was not enough—and the greatest of pagan souls were, as truly as were the Hebrew prophets, the precursors rather than the enemies of the Faith.

Turn from Michelangelo to Raffael, from the Sistine Chapel

to the Camera della Segnatura. Of the four pictures there, one —the *Parnassus*—represents the attempt of humanity to come to knowledge through beauty—through this window, as I have called it, which God has opened to us. The second—the *School of Athens*—shows us how reason may lead us to the knowledge of God and the study of science to an understanding of His laws. The third—the *Gift of Ecclesiastical and Secular Laws*—shows how law and order, the conditions of progress, are the gifts of God. The fourth—*Theology*—how, when reason has led Man to God, God gives back to him through revelation more than reason could ever have discovered for herself. The lesson of the whole was that, just as St. Paul had taught that the service of God did not necessarily demand obedience to the Jewish law, so now Julius was to teach that the proper use of every faculty was a glory to God and would lead men to a greater knowledge of Him. Man need not confine himself to those inquiries and practices which are known as religious in the narrow sense. As Marsilio Ficino had put it, " *Gratiae et Musae a Deo sunt atque ad Deum referendae.*" If it be true that Julius died with the words " *Fuori i barbari* " on his lips, he was referring to his political rather than his artistic ambitions. But he would have been more nearly justified in boasting of his warfare against the Philistines than of that against the French.

Julius' great dreams were never realised. The Pope quarrelled with Michelangelo. Michelangelo quarrelled with Bramante and was jealous of Raffael, Bramante's young kinsman. No Joshua arose to carry on the work of Moses. The Papacy soon lost its position as the patron of the world's greatest art and has never regained it. Rome never really recovered from the great sack of 1527. Who was to blame for the failure ? There were deficiencies on both sides. It would be absurd to pretend that the failure was entirely a failure of the Papacy. It would be as absurd to pretend that the Papacy was not at all to blame. After Julius came the Medici Popes. Artists congratulated themselves that with their reign there would be born a golden age. They were from Florence, the original home of those speculations upon the relations between pagan and Christian culture which had been so largely the inspirer of all that was noblest in the Renaissance, the Renaissance' "Hellas of Hellas." Raffael had introduced into his *Gift of the Laws* Leo X., then Giovanni de' Medici, standing by the side of Pope Julius.

The artists were not altogether disappointed. They received patronage both from Leo and Clement. Yet these years were the years of the beginning of the decline from greatness. Where Julius' had been a principled patronage, theirs was little more than the indiscriminate patronage of a rich, dilettante nobleman. It was left to Paul IV. finally to shatter those dreams of which the Medici had proved unworthy. Paul hated beauty as if it were a Spaniard. He gave orders that Michelangelo's *Last Judgment* should be effaced, and was only at the last minute induced to revoke his order, and he did actually make Daniele da Volterra dress the figures that had injured his scruples, as he had already made him dress Raffael's *Isaiah*. By setting the Papacy in direct opposition to the ambitions of the Renaissance Paul destroyed for ever all chance of the realisation of Julius' great dream, in which the guardian of truth should be the guardian also of beauty.

Yet, as I have said, there were deficiencies also on the other side. Had the Papacy's attack on the Renaissance not shown itself at all until the reign of Paul IV., we might be inclined to think that the failure was wholly explained by saying that the Papacy was unworthy of its opportunity. Yet, though there was no invective nor violent abuse, we can find signs of the new policy of deliberate Papal abdication of the privileges of artistic patronage in the earlier reign of a much greater Pope, a Pope much more capable of estimating the virtues of the Renaissance at their true value—in the reign of Paul III., the patron of Michelangelo. It was a deliberate abdication. The Medici Popes had perhaps been unworthy to be the patrons of the greatest of the world's artists, but the greatest of the world's artists had also proved themselves unworthy of the patronage of the Vicar of Christ.

Even a school which deserved so well of the world as the great Platonic Academy of Florence soon developed the oddest eccentricities. To rediscover Plato was the noblest of tasks, but, if Plato was merely to be used, as he was used by Gemistos Plethon, as a weapon with which to discredit Aristotle, the world would be the loser rather than the gainer by the discovery. The Platonists, too, fell with amazing rapidity from their high standards of untrammelled scholarship into peculiarly ridiculous forms of superstition. Special rites of initiation were invented ; a taper was kept perpetually burning before the bust of Plato. As a *tertium quid* to infallible Church and infallible Bible there was erected infallible Plato. Of the great figures of antiquity there was none that was less suited for such extravagant treatment. For in Plato noble truth is mingled so inextricably with Manichæan Puritanism that, while of all thinkers he is the most worthy of study, at the same time of all men he is the least worthy of imitation. For it is the simple and dangerous error of Platonism that, rightly insisting that the intellect must judge which pleasures are worth having, it falsely assumes that the intellect will always award the preference to intellectual pleasures.

All heresy is at bottom a revolt against reason, and there was a revolt against reason in the Platonism of Florence every bit as much as in the Lutheranism of Germany. Against the one attack as against the other it was the duty of the Church to defend the Godlike faculty in man. The modern scholar who airily condemns the Church's lack of sympathy with Platonism would, I daresay, have found a trifle dreary the simple, highbrow life of Plato's *Republic* or of the Renaissance counterpart of it, Campanella's *City of the Sun*.

It is most important that this menace to the Christian faith of an exaggerated classicism should be adequately understood, and it is perhaps easiest to bring home that danger to an English reader by an example that will be more readily familiar to him than any that can be drawn from Italy. It is a commonplace that one of the products of the Italian Renaissance was that body of thinkers who are known as the Italian Reformers, and that Milton was afterwards considerably influenced by Ochino and other of these thinkers. Now no study could in itself be more legitimate and valuable than that of comparative religion,

nothing more important than to understand how the best minds
of the Greeks were both in their philosophy and in their mytho-
logy groping out towards the truth, how they were again and
again on particular points expressing in one language essentially
the same truths which the Christian religion was afterwards to
express in another.   A long line of great Christian thinkers
which stretches from St. Augustine, if not from St. John, to
Blessed John Fisher had already enriched apologetics by such
researches.   Yet the language of comparative religion, while
it enriches the mind if it is used to show how the pre-Christians
were searching for those truths which the Christians came afterwards to possess, impoverishes the mind if it is used to argue
that Christians and pre-Christians were *merely* saying the same
thing in different languages.   For this is false.   The Christian
revelation contained ampler truth than any to which pre-
Christian philosophy or religion had come, and it can only be
assimilated to pre-Christian teaching by being robbed of some
of its fullness and balance.   Thus, when Milton in his *Ode on
the Morning of Christ's Nativity*, says of the shepherds watching
their flocks by night :

> " Full little thought they than
>   That the mighty Pan
>   Was kindly come to live with them below,"

one cannot but feel that not only is Milton's suggested identification wholly, not to say blasphemously, false, but also that what
the shepherds did think was a great deal more important than
what Milton says that they did not think.   The poet's mind
has not been enriched, it has been narrowed, by his classical
learning.

Again, art may be—indeed, in a certain sense, certainly is—
amoral.   That is to say, the artist, as artist, is not concerned with
a thesis.   Yet that does not excuse the artist as man for being
immoral.   And immoral the attitude towards life which the
Renaissance developed certainly was—not in the small sense
that it produced naughty men who broke the sixth Commandment, but in the large sense that it was based on a fundamental
denial of Original Sin.   That which was the Renaissance of

Michelangelo was also the Renaissance of Machiavelli and of Cellini. Michelangelo might plead, " I teach nothing. Here is a strong man ; admire the beauty of his form." But with Machiavelli dogma had come in, and with Cellini the divine right of the self-blown trumpet. Machiavelli taught men to worship strength, and from the worship of strength—which is at least an objective quality—they soon sunk to the far more ignoble worship of the mere accident of success. The Renaissance which began by praying God for the survival of the fittest ended by thanking Him for the survival of the survivors.

When in America at the beginning of this century the cry was raised that the Government should keep out of the banking business, William Jennings Bryan very pertinently answered, " Let the banks keep out of the Government business." So with the Popes and the Renaissance. If the Popes of the Counter-Reformation are accused of lack of sympathy with the artistic triumphs of the Renaissance, it can be answered for them that they might have been content to patronise the Renaissance if the Renaissance had been content to remain an artistic movement. But, consciously or unconsciously, it attacked Christian morals. If artists are concerned with morals, then the guardian of morals has a right to criticise them ; if they are not concerned with them, then they have no business with attacking Christian morals.

St. Thomas, in a penetrating phrase, told by anticipation the whole history of the last four hundred years when he said that " all evil is a mistaking of means for ends." Kings, democracy, material progress, humanitarian reforms—all these idols which, one after another, men have set up for themselves, were worthy objects of service but unworthy objects of worship. So, too, with art. " The frenzied passion for art," said Baudelaire, " is a cancer which eats up everything else." The colour of Turner, the strength of Michelangelo, the poetry of Shakespeare, the music of Mozart—these are given to us for our delight, but they only delight us because they are revelations of the Eternal Beauty of Eternal Being. Worship them for themselves, and we are idolaters and are damned.

The first business of the Pope was with the purity of faith

and the reform of morals. To that first business even the great dreams of Julius must be sacrificed, and the sterner, in some ways less lovely, spirit of the Counter-Reformation had to be called in to conquer the vices of degraded Christendom which had shown itself unworthy to receive the full privileges of truth. Julius' was a grand dream, and the day may come when it will be realised. If it be true that the earth is some millions of years old, why, then we live in a time hardly removed at all from the Incarnation. We are the early Church; things are only just beginning. The failures of the past are but the first blunders of a boy who is still learning to ride his bicycle. What triumphs the future may hold none can say.

The problem of the relation between beauty and truth is one of the deepest and most fascinating of all problems, and, in the 16th century particularly, was one of the most pressing and practical of all problems. It may perhaps be asked what place it has in a biography of St. Ignatius. It must be admitted that it played little part in his life. For almost a quarter of a century St. Ignatius resided with hardly a break in Rome. I suppose that he must have heard of the Sistine Chapel, but there is no evidence at all of his having done so. Indeed—to put it frankly —there is, for all intents and purposes, no evidence at all of his ever having heard that there was such a thing as art. Music was the only one of the arts for which he seemed to have cared at all. Of Michelangelo there is, I think, but one mention in all his journals. It was thought that Michelangelo was going to do for St. Francis Borgia the rebuilding of the Church of Santa Maria della Strada. " The most celebrated man now known, Michelangelo, is undertaking the work for mere devotion and without any gain," wrote St. Ignatius. Even that link was never forged, for Borgia's plan failed.

If, then, we would gain a true picture of St. Ignatius, we must understand both what was, if I may call it so, the general air around him, the controversies that were raging, the great opportunities and the great refusals, and also St. Ignatius' own utter indifference to these things which were all life to so many of his contemporaries.

ART AND THE SPIRITUAL EXERCISES   161

It is, I think, true that, just as he who has seen the Creator face to face can never again be satisfied with a creature's love, so he who has seen Absolute Beauty face to face does not need the comfort of those hints of the abiding reality, which are the beautiful things of this world.   There is no reason to think that Our Lord cared much for *objets d'art*.   As no less a man than Michelangelo said, " Painting and sculpture will lose their charm for the soul turned to that Divine Love which opened its arms upon the Cross to welcome us."   Yet in honesty it must be admitted that there was a starkness in St. Ignatius' soul.   Even if he had not been a saint there is no reason to think that he would have cared much for beauty.

There was in St. Ignatius a streak of what some might call Puritanism ; yet it would be false to call it so.   Insensibility to beauty, the lack of ease in the company of happy men or, worse still, the perverted hatred of beauty and joy—it is false to pretend that these disabilities are found only in the inhabitants of Protestant North Europe.   It is easy to rake through Catholic history and show how it is full of men who suffered from these sad instincts every bit as much as a Calvin or a Knox.   The lack of a love of beauty is a disability from which a proportion of the human race is condemned to suffer in every culture and country.   But the difference between the Puritan and the Catholic Philistine is that the Puritan not only is insensible, but worships insensibility.   The Puritan who is not a Philistine—he who loves beauty but is terrified of it—is in a sadder case still. St. Ignatius was insensible and, if he had not been a Catholic, might well have been an iconoclast.   But there was the authority of the Church which, though it could not teach him to love beauty, could at least compel him to respect it.   There is no soul so ample that it can drink up with zest all the joys and beauties of life with which God has filled His world, but, whereas he who relies solely on his private judgment is always tempted to look on his own insensibility as a virtue, he who accepts external authority is compelled daily to listen to a voice which reminds him that his deficiency is a deficiency.

*   *   *   *   *

What, then, was the weapon with which St. Ignatius faced the world? That weapon was the weapon of the Spiritual Exercises. I have no intention of attempting either to paraphrase or to criticise the Exercises, but from time to time in the telling of the story of St. Ignatius' life I have had occasion to refer to them. I shall have occasion to refer to them again, and it would not be possible to present any book that called itself a life of St. Ignatius and did not attempt to explain what they were.

The first rough draft of them was made by St. Ignatius at the time of his experiences at Manresa in 1522, but he was continually altering and rewriting them during the rest of his life. It is not my purpose to indulge in the impudence of a criticism of them. The purpose of the little book—a book so small that, as St. Francis Xavier said, it has converted more souls than it contains letters—is to provide for the anxious soul a method by which he may use profitably a four weeks' retreat so that it may bring him more close to that union with God which should be the soul's desire. The soul is led on from stage to stage of the spiritual life, to each week being assigned its especial purpose— the first, *deformata reformare*; the second, *reformata conformare*; the third, *conformata confirmare*; the fourth, *confirmata transformare*—or, to use another and perhaps more easily intelligible phraselogy, the Exercises deal in turn with each of the three common divisions of the spiritual life—the purgative, the illuminative and the unitive. During the first week the soul learns to purge itself of all desires save the desire to do God's will; during the second and third it comes to the understanding of what God's will is; and during the fourth it enjoys the experience of being at one with God which, in the ultimate and divine paradox, is the reward of the freedom of complete submission to the will of Him, *cui servire regnare est*.

All those who were thinking of joining the Society of Jesus were required to make the Exercises in order to test their vocation. Yet the Exercises were not designed solely for this purpose. They were to be used by any devout soul, in religion or in the world. At the same time, as the story of his life has clearly shown, no one could be more fully aware than St. Ignatius that the direct, conscious, unitive life with God was only offered to the few. Therefore, as the *Constitutiones Societatis Jesu* say, " the Spiritual Exercises should be given in their completeness only to a few, namely, those from whom a large measure of fruit to the glory of God may be hoped." Yet everyone can gain profit from at least a part of the Exercises, and those of the world, whose vocation it is to remain in the world, may with benefit undergo the purgative exercises of the first week in order that they may assure themselves that they are not allowing the loves of this world to hinder them from the love of God.

Those who join an order—whether St. Ignatius' or another—have, of course, to take a vow of poverty. But such a vow is only for the few, nor is it valuable in itself, but only as the best means for certain souls to an end which is obligatory on all souls. The obligatory end is that of the spirit of poverty.

A millionaire may possess the spirit of poverty (though doubtless St. Ignatius would have agreed with the Founder of his religion that in point of fact very few camels do get through the eyes of needles) ; a beggar may lack it. Indeed even a religious who has accepted actual poverty does not necessarily possess the spirit of poverty. He has not necessarily put from himself the desire for wealth. Mr. Longridge, in his book on the Exercises, points to the very pertinent example of Judas Iscariot, and it would be possible to find other examples less notable. By the spirit of poverty St. Ignatius meant a spirit of " indifference " towards wealth. It is wrong to make the acquisition of wealth the object of life. For a man in the world with, let us say, a wife and children and the other responsibilities of the world, the complete Franciscan indifference is obviously not only impossible but wrong. The life of the feckless sponger is as far removed from that of the Franciscan or Ignatian ideal as is that of the rich snob. One of the first concerns of the married man should be to provide for his dependents by honest means the standard of living to which they have been accustomed. But, that task accomplished, he should be done with money and not go chasing round the world for more of it, not surrender to what St. Ignatius in his *Meditation on Two Standards* calls " the lust of riches," or what a foolish and question-begging modern phrase dubs " the desire to better himself." It passes for a virtue in modern England if people save and scrape and work themselves to the bone at silly things in order that their children may go to slightly more expensive and exclusive schools than those to which they went themselves. I doubt if it is a virtue at all, nor is there anything less edifying than the sight of pious people, possessed of an income far above that of the average of the human race, yet complaining loudly of their poverty and announcing that they " will do anything for money."

St. Ignatius did not advise every rich man to sell all that he had and give to the poor. Nor did Our Lord. Our Lord gave the advice to a particular rich man who had found riches an obstacle to the spiritual life, and He showed by His subsequent discourse that, though wealth was one of the largest of obstacles to the good life, it was not an absolutely insuperable obstacle. So, too, St. Ignatius, writing to his brother about this time, says, " For a man to spend all his care and solicitude in building and enlarging houses, increasing his revenue and his state and leaving a great name behind him—it is not for me to condemn him, but neither do I commend him, since, as St. Paul says, we ought to use this world as if we used it not."

The importance of the Spiritual Exercises to one who would understand the history of the Society of Jesus is immense. Towards the Jesuits popular English literature is uncomprehending, even when it is not unfair. Take, for instance, Macaulay's not ungenerous passage upon the Society in the essay on von Ranke's *History of the Popes*. One would gather from that essay that the Society of Jesus was a very heroic and very cunning body for the combating of Protestanism by the energy of its propaganda. There are two important misconceptions in such a view. As we have traced the life of St. Ignatius so far, we have hardly had occasion to mention Protestantism at all, and we shall not have enormous occasion to mention it in the future. At the time of his conversion there is no reason to think that St. Ignatius had ever spoken to a Protestant in his life or ever heard of Protestantism, except perhaps in the way in which we, residents in England, have vaguely heard that there is to-day a civil war in China. His followers were devoted to whatever work the Church might need, and therefore, among many other activities, some among them were brought into contact with Protestantism. But the combat with Protestantism was not at first intended to be, and in fact never was, the main work of the Society. Its main work was, and has ever remained, to arouse the love of Christ in the hearts of Catholics, to convert Catholics to Catholicism.

Macaulay's more serious error is to give the impression that the spiritual life of the Jesuit, such as it was, was merely concerned with shaping his character in such a way as to make him more efficiently able to perform certain tasks, as a soldier's drill trains him to obedience in the day of battle.[1] The parallel is constantly in people's mouths, but it is a false parallel. To the soldier the battle is the important thing, the drill only justifiable so long as it makes the soldier more fitted for battle. To the Jesuit the spiritual life is the supremely important thing, and practical activities only valuable so long as they lead people to the spiritual life. What was the special lesson which St. Ignatius had to teach? Like all great lessons it was an old lesson, and it can perhaps best be put thus. It is often thought a very sensible thing to say, " Let the monk stay in his cloister and let the affairs of the world be run by men of the world." The dichotomy sounds glibly satisfactory, but in practice it is quite impossible thus to divide this world from the next, for, if there is not another world or if we know nothing of it, there is no reason whatever for troubling very much about this, provided only that we can somehow or other patch it up well enough to last out our time. St. Ignatius saw—and it has been seen in every other age by those who care to see things, and can be seen again to-day—that " men of the world " have very notably

---

[1] A similar criticism might be made of Herr Fülop-Miller's *Power and Secret of the Jesuits*.

proved themselves unfitted to manage the affairs of the world. They may be the most diverting company in the bar or the smoking-room, but it is too risky a luxury to entrust them with positions of real responsibility. As Canon Lyttelton says of our times, " The less we think about the next world, the more hideous do we make this one." The only solution is that the affairs of this world should be managed by those who have gained an intense and vivid grasp of its transitoriness—not necessarily by Jesuits or even by priests—that is another question altogether—but by people, lay or clerical, to whom the spiritual values are the supreme values. Other qualities, the ordinary practical qualities, are obviously also requisite, but it is this quality which is all-important. It is unsafe to entrust power to those who have not learnt to be indifferent to it.

Thus described, the Ignatian Republic can be seen to have much in common with the Platonic Republic, except that the philosopher-king, in the Ignatian view, must be endowed not only with lucid intellect but also with the spiritual quality of the love of God. For Ignatius, as for Plato, the difficulty is that, the more complete his grasp of truth, the less willing a man is to mix himself up in the affairs of men. For this reason, I suppose, foreseeing that there would necessarily be some to whom such intense spiritual experience would reveal that God was calling them to a purely contemplative life, St. Ignatius laid it down from the first that any Jesuit who wished could always exchange his obedience for that of the Carthusian Order. Yet the Ignatian plan was more competent to cope with that difficulty of reluctance than the Platonic, for St. Ignatius taught a truth that was not only good but lovely. The saint could be found to suffer for the greater glory of God what the philosopher was unwilling to suffer for the reality of an absolute value. Ignatius provided just that purpose for life which Plato from the accident of his date inevitably lacked. When all is said and done, it is a dreary business just sitting down and thinking. But Ignatius can offer an adventure where Plato can only offer a day-dream.

The unitive life with God was not then, to St. Ignatius, a mere disciplinary means—it is a grotesque parody to speak of it as such. And yet at the same time, valuable in itself, it was also valuable as a means. The Macaulayesque view is only false as a half-truth is false. For it was the Ignatian discipline which sent men forth, as Macaulay says, " in spite of oceans and deserts, hunger and pestilence, spies and penal laws, dungeons and racks, gibbets and quartering blocks . . . arguing, instructing, consoling, stealing away the hearts of the young, animating the courage of the timid, holding up the crucifix before the eyes of the dying." For it is a paradox of faith that the Gospel which tells us that the world is but dust and ashes and a foolish toy is also the one gospel which provided us with a sufficient motive for unselfish action in that world. The spiritual vision was both the end, desirable in itself ; it was also a comforting strength, through the grace of which he who had enjoyed it was able to go back into the world, like a rescuer returning to the stranded ship, and bring back others to share with him in his felicity. Or, if one may put the same difficult truth in simpler and nobler phraseology, Christ Who was the Truth and the Life was also the Way.

CHAPTER X

EIGHT days before Paul issued his Bull, St. Ignatius was sitting in the house at the Torre di Melangolo one evening when there came a ring at the front-door bell. The saint went to answer it himself and found there a young boy, aged about fourteen and dressed in the livery worn by the pages of the great Roman lords. He begged for admission and St. Ignatius let him in.

His name was, it was found, Pedro di Ribadaneira, and he was of a noble family of Toledo. Earlier in that same year Cardinal Alessandro Farnese, Paul III.'s grandson and eldest brother of that Ottavio Farnese who, as we have said, married Margaret of Austria, had come to Toledo to convey Paul's condolences to Charles V. on the death of his wife, Isabella. The Nunciature was, as it happened, just opposite Ribadaneira's mother's house, and the young boy used to run in and out. He caught the attention of stern Giudiccioni, as yet unconverted to Jesuits, who was in Farnese's train, and Giudiccioni persuaded Farnese to take him as a page. The boy was delighted at the prospect of seeing the world, and his mother, falsely imagining that a certain tinge of sanctity would hang round even the grandson of a Pope, consented to the plan.

Alessandro soon found that he had got more than he bargained for. Paul III. gave a great entertainment to all the princes of the Church. Behind each Cardinal stood a page with lighted flambeau. Suddenly, in the midst, where all was dignity, Ribadaneira threw his torch at a neighbouring page on the ground that he had made faces at him. On another occasion he kissed the Pope's hand when he was supposed to kiss his toe, and there was no end of trouble. In general, he was a great nuisance, and

on this particular day, the day of his call on St. Ignatius, having
been ordered to accompany Alessandro Farnese into the country
and not being in the mood for obedience, he had absconded and
spent the day in the town.   Now evening was coming and the
Cardinal was returning.   Suddenly Pedro had lost his nerve.   He
did not dare meet Alessandro and, remembering that Ortiz had
told him to go one day and visit St. Ignatius, he thought the
present the best of days and went and threw himself on St. Ignatius' mercy.

Rarely in history has anyone jumped more completely out
of the frying-pan into the fire than did poor little Ribadaneira.
Alessandro Farnese was not a man of deep virtue but he was
tolerant and kindly, with the kindliness of a lazy gentleman.
The follies of etiquette were too flagrant for him to be angry at
its violation, and the life of a courtier so empty anyway that it
mattered little whether he did what was right or what was
wrong.   He forgave his enemies because it was too much trouble
not to.   St. Ignatius, on the other hand, was a kind man, but no
one could call him an easy-going one.   Ribadaneira's conduct
seemed much more grievous to St. Ignatius than it did to
Alessandro.

The Jesuits kept him that night, but the next day he must go
back to his master and receive the beating which, they presumed,
awaited him.   St. Ignatius himself led him by the hand.   They
found Farnese, but the Cardinal only laughed, and Ribadaneira
was to be received back without punishment.   All seemed settled,
and would have been settled had not Ribadaneira confused the
issue by announcing loudly that he would not go back to the
Cardinal.   He was going to become a Jesuit.

We must never forget that the Southern boy matures at a
much earlier age than the Northern.   Ribadaneira at fourteen
was probably as fully developed as the English boy is at eighteen
—the age at which it is usual to enter the Jesuit novitiate.   Still
his conversion had been too sudden to be altogether trust-
worthy.   He had not at the time even made his first Communion.   St. Ignatius compelled him to remain a little longer
with Alessandro and to take the advice of friends.   However, he

persisted in his desire, so after a time St. Ignatius received him into his house and, a little later, formally admitted him to the novitiate.

No quality in a boy is more embarrassing to his superiors than that of unvarying, docile and conscientious obedience. It is not in itself very attractive nor very valuable and is the product rather of a lack than of strength of character. It has little of the purgative value of the reasoned obedience of the grown man. The superior, unless he is a fool, would greatly prefer a more natural, turbulent, noisy schoolboy. At the same time, these habits are an immediate convenience, and the stupid fellow, who sees duty solely in terms of this wooden obedience, will be bewildered if such an obedience should not win for him the highest praise and will probably abandon all standards altogether. Ribadaneira presented no such problem. His piety was not a piety of dull conscientiousness. From the moment of his entrance the place was in pandemonium. He banged doors, whistled, shouted, did not get up in the morning, filled the room with dust, spoiled St. Ignatius' food, smudged and miscopied his letters. All the other Fathers were for packing him out of the place, but St. Ignatius, who remembered his own youth and had no love for the mentality which sees a cardinal virtue in low spirits, bade them bear with him. His effervescence, though a nuisance to others, was yet a good quality. Vitality is not in itself a virtue, but it at least gives promise that, when the will is trained and virtue acquired, that virtue will be most useful. St. Ignatius hated mere obstinate self-will. When an eccentric Father insisted on walking about the house in a nightcap instead of a birreta and replied to the saint's remonstrance by saying, " I can judge what is decorous myself," St. Ignatius packed him off at once. Yet on the other hand he always preferred those who in youth found it difficult to control their high spirits. So Ribadaneira was allowed to persist. He lived to become not perhaps a wholly satisfactory member of the Society, but at least a loyal and devout priest, the biographer of St. Ignatius and, as those who are competent to judge affirm, one of the greatest of all masters of Castilian prose.

It has been shown how most of those who had previously opposed St. Ignatius had afterwards been converted to him. Among these was Govea, who had tried to birch him in Paris. Govea had by now returned to Lisbon, and John III., the King of Portugal, asked him his advice on the best method of Christianising the Portuguese Indian colony of Goa, which had been conquered by Albuquerque in 1510. A few Dominican friars had gone out there first, but in 1517 the Franciscans had set up their Indian headquarters there, and in 1534 Paul III. established a bishopric under a Franciscan bishop.

More workers for the mission field were wanted, and Govea advised King John to apply to St. Ignatius for some of the Fathers of the new Society. King John ordered his Ambassador in Rome to make the request. The Ambassador asked for six missionaries. This was too much, but St. Ignatius offered him two, and Rodriguez and Bobadilla were selected. However, before Bobadilla could start he was struck down with rheumatism. St. Francis Xavier was therefore chosen to fill his place. On March 16th, 1540, the great missioner set out for Portugal on the first stage of his journey. "*Ite, omnia incendite et inflammate*," said St. Ignatius in bidding him farewell. When Rodriguez and St. Francis reached Portugal the King was so charmed with them that he changed his mind and begged that they might be ordered to remain in Portugal. A compromise was arranged. Rodriguez remained at home to live out a busy and contentious life; Xavier sailed for Goa and the East to tasks among the greatest and most heroic that have as yet been accomplished by any among the sons of men. What an amazing thing is Christian energy! At the very moment at which the very existence of the Church was in most deadly peril at her centre, she was sending out her astounding, divine counter-attack to the ultimate corners of the earth. In ten years he was to preach from Goa to Malacca, from Malacca to Japan. Even the conversion of the great Empire of China was to stir his ambition and he was to set out upon his last voyage in 1552 with the words on his lips, "If any way is opened to me you shall find me either in a prison in Canton, or in the Emperor's palace in Pekin." It is not surprising that his letters in which he recounted his exploits should have circulated rapidly from hand to hand throughout Rome, and that copies of them should have found eager readers in every country in Europe. For I do not know that in all the annals of history there is record of a greater man. The adventures of his companions in India were always of enthralling interest to St. Ignatius. He could not be told enough about them. "Oh, dear," he once cried, "how much I should like to know how many fleas bite them at night!"

Others found tasks nearer to hand, Laynez and Faber in Parma, Le Jay in Tuscany, where Brouet joined him on his return from a somewhat ineffective visit to Ireland; but perhaps the most interesting work during these years was that which fell to Bobadilla. Already before his selection for the Indian mission Bobadilla had been at work in Naples, and after recovery from his rheumatism he returned thither. Naples at this time was a part of the Spanish Empire and was ruled by a viceroy. Until 1532 the viceroy had been Cardinal Pompeo Colonna, an unspiritual, and indeed unedifying, cleric who had been created Cardinal on account of his family name by Leo X., but who had supported Charles V. in his quarrel with Clement VII. and had taken part along with the Constable Bourbon in the assault on Rome in 1527. His reward was the viceroyalty which he held until his death in 1532.

He did not look on the enforcement either of sound morals or of sound learning as a part of his duty. The result was that the clergy had sunk to a condition almost incredible even for the 16th century, and among the educated classes fashions of speculation of a very doubtful orthodoxy were beginning to grow up. Not only did the clergy, from bishops down to curates, openly keep mistresses in their houses, but these mistresses even had the amazing impudence to claim benefit of clergy in the law courts. "Wonderful to hear," says Giannone, "some such exemptions were granted."

Even more serious were the intellectual problems of the unhappy people, and Colonna's successor, Pedro di Toledo, a harsh military man to whom orthodoxy was the duty of a loyal

Spanish soldier, found himself faced with problems which he was quite incompetent to solve. Things were not made any easier by a flying visit paid to Naples by Charles V. in 1536, and a savage edict which was issued threatening death and confiscation to anyone who held communication with a heretic or any who were suspected of heresy. The leader of Neapolitan intellectual society during these years was a most interesting and attractive man of the name of Juan Valdez. There were two twin Valdez brothers. The elder, Antonio, was secretary to Charles V. and author of some clever *Colloquies*, in which a certain Lactantio and an archdeacon are made to discuss the corruptions of the time in the spirit perhaps of an Erasmus but not in that of a heretic. The younger, Juan, is often said to have gone further on the road of heresy. It is hard to prove it. In emulation of his brother he published in 1529 a *Dialogo de Mercurio y Caron*, in which the souls of the departed are made to discuss the affairs of this world and the next. Perhaps its highest claim to fame is that Cervantes seems to have been indebted to it for the advice which Don Quixote gave to Sancho Panza on his appointment to a governorship. From 1533 to his death in 1541 Juan lived in Naples, producing a number of works but occupied chiefly in Biblical study.

It is true that in one place he condemns prayers to Our Lady, in another seems to show sympathy with the Lutheran doctrine of justification by faith. But it is not fair to hunt microscopically through the works of a prolific and popular writer for the discovery of heresy. It was a fluid and speculative age, in which none but the very wisest and most careful were able to avoid the occasional lapse. Contarini, for instance, if one cared to use these minute tests, could be proved a heretic half a dozen times over. The only fair test of orthodoxy was that of the acceptance of Papal authority. The question that we should ask is not " What did such a man say ? " but " Was he prepared to maintain his doctrine if the Pope declared against it ? " It was neither good charity nor good theology, when the accusers at Carnesecchi's trial in 1566 tried to throw aspersions on the orthodoxy of thinkers who had held opinions that were subse-

quently condemned but had not been condemned at the time of
their holding them. It was a scandal, too, when in 1571 Damiao
de Goes, the Portuguese, was condemned because he had held
prior to the Council of Trent certain opinions which the Council
afterwards condemned, although it could not be shown that he
had continued to hold them after the Council had spoken. Such
a policy of repression was a discourager not of falsehood but of
inquiry, and, though individual Catholics were guilty of it, it
was quite unjustifiable by Catholic principles. Defiance of
authority is the only ultimate test of heresy, and the very
existence of a defining Voice argues that no one can be in heresy
until the Voice has spoken. His opinions may be temerarious,
but they are not yet heretical.

The question then is, " Was Valdez anxious for such defiance ? " There is no reason at all to think that he was, even
though Bobadilla in one place speaks with characteristic exuber-
ance of him as " vomiting forth blasphemies." " His disciples,"
writes Niccolo Balbini, the Protestant historian of the Italian
Reformation, " did not cease to frequent the churches, to resort
to Mass like other people and to share in the current idolatry."
It is clear that those who consorted with him did not imagine
that they were committing an offence against Charles V.'s edict
of 1536.

Yet, if not a heretic himself, Valdez certainly suggested ideas
which more obstinate disciples might carry to heretical conclu-
sions. Ochino, whose influence Le Jay had to counteract at
Ferrara, was his disciple, and the Italian Protestant, Benedetto of
Mantua, author of the *Beneficio della Morte di Cristo*, wrote
under his influence. At the trial of Carnesecchi in 1566 the
influence of Valdez was held responsible for Carnesecchi's apostasy. His was not necessarily a bad influence, but it was certainly a dangerous influence. To follow him was a fashion in
Neapolitan society, and it was never certain whither he would
lead. The habit of historians is only too often to discuss the
opinions of such a man from a too exclusively intellectual point
of view. We know, of ourselves and of our contemporaries, how
much larger a part snobbery, of one sort or another, plays in

the formation of our opinions than reason, and it was certainly
no different in the 16th century, whether among leaders or among
disciples.   People of a certain wit and no real learning might, if
the problem was mishandled, find themselves slipping into a
heresy through a desire to be in the latest movement.   The situation was not unlike that which Le Jay had found at Ferrara a
few years before.   Indeed not only was the play the same ; in
one important respect the caste was also the same.   Vittoria
Colonna was at Naples, just as she had been at Ferrara.   With
her was her cousin, Constanza d'Avalos, and her other cousin,
Giulia Gonzaga, whom Hayradin Barbarossa, sweeping down
from Algiers, had tried to kidnap—which made all the rest
green with envy—and Bobadilla was sent down to Naples with
his work cut out.

Meanwhile St. Ignatius remained at Rome.   There were still
battles to be fought even after the issue of the Papal Bull.   First
there was the attack of Dominic Soto, the Dominican, who
objected to the establishment of an Order free from the obligation of singing the office.   " It could not have any right to call
itself a religious Order at all," said this shocked conservative.

Up to now the Order had had no head.   After the Papal
approval it was clearly necessary to elect a regular superior.
At Easter, 1541, therefore all of the Fathers who were able were
bidden to come to Rome for the election of a General.   Only
five were able to come, but Xavier and Rodriguez had deposited
their written votes in sealed envelopes before they left for Portugal, and the other absentees now sent theirs in writing to
Rome.   On April 7th the papers were opened, and it was found
that every vote had been given for St. Ignatius except his own,
which he had given to no one, contenting himself with an expression of readiness to serve under anyone whom his companions
might select.   St. Ignatius received the news with a dismay which
only those who understand very little his character will venture
to think insincere, and begged those present to reconsider their
decision with prayer and to hold a fresh election.   They consented, but when on April 10th they once more cast their votes,
it was found that again every vote had been given for St. Igna-

tius. The saint then said that he must consult his confessor, Father Theodoric, of the Convent of San Pietro. He went to spend three days in quiet meditation at Father Theodoric's convent, and while he was there he was able to cast a devil out of one of the lay brothers. It was said that the Devil in revenge came to him in the night and tried to stifle him by pressing his two jaws together. St. Ignatius routed him by repeating the Holy Name of Jesus, but the next morning the tenderness of his jaws bore witness to the struggle through which he had passed.

Father Theodoric, having listened to all St. Ignatius' arguments, agreed to think the matter over and then to lay his opinion before the other Fathers. A day or two afterwards he sent down his opinion. It was opened in the presence of all and read, and was found to say that in Theodoric's opinion it was St. Ignatius' duty to accept the responsibility for which he had been selected. On hearing this St. Ignatius at last reluctantly withdrew his opposition and submitted.

On Friday, April 22nd, the members who were present all met together at the Church of St. Paul-beyond-the-Walls for the taking of their last vows. St. Ignatius said Mass, and, before communicating, he stood before his brethren, holding the Body of Our Lord in the one hand and the text of his vow of obedience in the other. He then read out his vow and afterwards communicated. One by one the other five read out their vows and received communion from St. Ignatius, St. Ignatius vowing his obedience to the Pope and the others theirs to St. Ignatius.

To all who were present the ceremony was as impressive as that somewhat similar one which had taken place seven years before at Montmartre. But no one, it was noticed, seemed so wholly filled with joy as was Codure. Codure was at the time waiting in Rome, expecting at any time to be sent on a mission to Ireland. But soon afterwards, the mission having to be postponed owing to the political troubles in the British Isles, St. Ignatius, in order to keep him occupied, appointed Codure his *socius*, or secretary. Six months later he was seized with a dangerous illness. It will be remembered that St. Ignatius possessed the curious and not altogether convenient gift of knowing what was going to happen in the future, and what happened at a distance.   He set out across Rome one day to say Mass for Codure at the Church of San Pietro in Montorio, where Bramante's little round temple perpetuates a very doubtful tradition of the spot of Peter's crucifixion.   When he came to the Sistine bridge, he stopped in his walk and, turning to his companions, said, " Let us return to Rome ; Codure is dead." It proved to be so.   The second of the Companions had gone.

St. Ignatius inaugurated his generalship by performing in turn all the humblest and most menial tasks which fell to the lot of any of the members of the Society.   He served for some days in the kitchen.   He taught catechism in the little church which then stood where the Gesù now stands.   His Italian was so bad that a translator of his letters has said with wit and justice, " The liberties taken with the language and the grammar are such as only a saint can expect to see forgiven either in this world or in the next."   And when Ribadaneira, speaking as only sixteen can speak to venerable middle-age, told " the holy old man," as he calls him when he recounts the incident, that he should try to free it from some of its more atrocious blemishes, St. Ignatius replied, " You are right," and bade Ribadaneira tell him of his faults.   When we recollect that Ribadaneira was himself a Spaniard to whom Italian was a foreign language just as much as it was to St. Ignatius, we are amazed at the impudence of the boy and the humility of the man.   But St. Ignatius was no linguist, and even with little Ribadaneira's coaching there was little improvement.   " My Pietro, what can we do against God ? " he asked.

A steady dribble of recruits came into the Society.   Laynez' brother came to Rome, full of suspicion of the company which Diego was keeping, but instead became himself converted.   He went through the Exercises, joined the Society and died young after an edifying life.   Two nephews of St. Ignatius also joined, of whom one, Antonio Araoz, was sent by St. Ignatius to Spain. The Viceroy of Catalonia, the Marquis of Lambay, of whom we have already written twice, heard of his fame, and sent for him. He was curious to learn all that he could about this new Society, was pleased with what he heard of it and promised his protection. Four years later his wife was dead and he himself prepared to give up all for the love of Christ and the Company of Jesus.

St. Ignatius drew up a code of nine provisional rules to guide the conduct of the Fathers until the full Constitutions were ready. They were—

1. The Fathers are constantly to occupy their hearts with God; whether in their cells or in the world, they are never to leave His Divine presence. The life of Jesus is to be their example. His Divine model must be impressed upon their souls.

2. They are to see in their Superiors the image of God Himself, assured that obedience is a guide which cannot deceive; to reveal all their thoughts as well as actions to those appointed over them, knowing that we must ever mistrust our own judgment.

3. When they converse with their sinful fellow-creatures they should use such precautions as would be reasonable in regard to a drowning man, so that two may not perish together. But the sinner should be dear to every one of the Society; not only as the child of their common Father, but he should love him as himself. In argument the greatest vigilance must be used to avert the desire of triumph. There is but one rational end to be proposed in discussion, the establishing of truth; the spirit as well as words must be guided by this only.

4. They are to keep silence when necessity does not compel them to speak; then neither worldly nor vainglorious nor idle talk must in any way mix with their conversation.

5. If it please God to operate great things through their means they must count themselves as nothing but a worthless instrument, as was the hand of Samson. To be satisfied with our judgment, or wisdom, or prudence would be folly. A religious must consider himself best rewarded for what he

does for his neighbour when he receives reproach and contumely, such as the world gave to the labours of the Divine Lord.

6. If any Father should fall into an obvious error, likely to diminish the esteem in which they were held, they ought not to be discouraged, but thank God for having shown their weakness, so that they may walk humbly and carefully in future, and that their brethren may take warning that all are formed from the same clay, and pray earnestly for the sinner.

7. During the recreation they must observe the moderation which the Apostle requires at all times, neither mirthful to excess nor too grave.

8. They must never neglect an opportunity of doing good for the sake of some greater future good; for this is an artifice of the Devil to turn our minds from the common works they might have performed.

9. Let each remain firm in his vocation, as if the roots were laid deep in the foundations of the Lord's house. For as the enemy often inspires the solitary with the desire of living in a community, he frequently makes those who are called to convert souls desire solitude, leading them to a path contrary to that which it is their duty to follow.

The only points in these rules upon which any will feel inclined to comment are the stress, which will seem to some excessive, laid on the virtue of obedience, and the harshness with which the pleasures of conversation are condemned. As for obedience, it is true, the objector might say, that, to quote St. Ignatius, " we must ever mistrust our own judgment;" Man is fallible. But are not Superiors men? By all means submit yourself entirely to the Will of God, but how can you be sure that your Superior's will is the will of God? Grossly as the drill-sergeant side of his character has been exaggerated, yet there is no question that St. Ignatius was a lover of discipline. Discipline is a soldier's virtue, and ours which is, if not a peace-loving, at least a war-fearing generation, is apt to be antagonistic to the soldier's virtues. Perhaps St. Ignatius sometimes exaggerated in the opposite direction. " *Volo et nolo non habitant in hac domo*," he made a poor novice chant, when he had been shy about taking a message to a prostitute and had got somebody else to take it for him.   He imposed obedience on others and accepted it for himself.   It is true that the famous phrases of the constitution, in which obedience is demanded from the inferior as if he were a corpse or as if he were an old man's staff, did not originate with St. Ignatius.   Yet it is certain that, though he may have found the metaphors in St. Francis, he welcomed and adopted them as his own, because they very exactly expressed the notions of his own mind.

Yet at the same time it must be remembered by the sigher after liberty that St. Ignatius was not laying down a general ethical code.   He was prescribing rules for a small company— at the time of these provisional rules still limited to sixty members—called to a very special vocation.   In order to teach a careless world the superiority of spiritual to worldly things, it was essential that they should deny themselves not only the bad but also the good things of this world; should submit themselves to rigorous discipline simply because freedom is a lovely thing; should deny themselves what is perhaps the greatest of all the natural pleasures of this world, the pleasure of the meandering, idle gossip which " tires the sun with talking and sends him down the sky."

It is not demanded of us that we become Jesuits; it is only demanded of us that we try to understand.   We who enjoy the freedom of the Abbey of Thelême enjoy it because others accepted the discipline of Manresa and the similar disciplines of the other Orders.   It was the discipline of the Jesuit—for of that we are speaking at the moment—which repelled the attack on the free Christian life in the 16th century, just as in the time of war it is the soldier's discipline which alone preserves the liberties of life for the civil population.   And it is not generous if, after the battle is done, the saved civilians can find nothing better to say to their preservers than to jeer at them because they form fours when they are told to.

The Church in St. Ignatius' day was under siege.   For this

reason St. Ignatius thought it an imperfection in his followers even to wish to be ordered to one field of work rather than another.   When Laynez said that he longed to be sent to the Indian mission, St. Ignatius answered, "If I felt such a wish arising in my mind I would tear it out."   He always used to ask of the Fathers three questions.   " Were they ready to obey in whatever occupation he chose for them ?   Did they think themselves better fitted for one occupation than another ?   Would they prefer one occupation to another ? "   They were expected to answer truthfully, but. he was always best pleased when a Father could answer the third question in the negative.

Shortly before his death he wrote out and left to the Society a paper containing eleven maxims on obedience.   They are perhaps worth quoting in order that we may understand clearly his mind.

1. On my first entrance into religion, and at all times after, I ought to resign myself into the hands of the Lord my God and of him who governs me.

2. I ought to desire to be ruled by a Superior who endeavours to subjugate my judgment and subdue my understanding.

3. In all things except sin I ought to do the will of my Superior, and not my own.

4. There are three sorts of obedience ; the first, when a strict obligation is imposed upon me—and this is good ; the second, when the simple command of the Superior, without any addition suffices for me—and this is better ; the third, when I do a thing without waiting for an express command because I know that it will please him—and this is best of all.

5. I ought not to regard him who gives the order, whether he be the Superior, a deputy or a subordinate, but God alone, in Whose place he stands, otherwise the merit of obedience is diminished.

6. When it seems to me that I am commanded by my Superior to do a thing which my conscience revolts against as sinful, and my Superior judges otherwise, it is my duty to

yield my doubts to him, unless I am otherwise constrained by evident reasons. If submission does not appease my conscience, I must impart my doubts to two or three persons of discretion and abide by their decision. If this does not content me I am very far from having attained the perfection required by a religious life.

7. In a word I ought not to be my own, but His Who created me, and his, too, by whose means He governs me, yielding myself to be moulded in his hands like so much wax; and whether in writing and receiving letters, conversing with one another and other like things, placing all my devotion in doing whatever is required of me.

8. I ought to be like a corpse, which has neither will nor understanding; or like a little crucifix which is turned about at the will of him who holds it; or like a staff in the hands of an old man who uses it as may assist or please him. So ought I to be under my religious rule, doing whatever service is judged best.

9. I must not petition the Superior to send me to any place or appoint me to any office. I am permitted to acquaint him with my intentions or desires, but with entire abandonment of myself to him and a disposition to approve whatever he determines.

10. Nevertheless, in unimportant matters such as going to the stations or prayers for any particular grace and such like, it is well not to ask for permission, if only I am ready to consider it best whether I am permitted or refused.

11. So with regard to poverty, I must depend on my Superior and possess nothing which I esteem my own. I should be like a statue, which makes no resistance to him that takes aught away from it, whatever the occasion may be.

These maxims bear the stamp of St. Ignatius' personality, but, to tell the truth, the obligation of obedience among the Jesuits does not differ greatly from that of the older Orders. Indeed, if we examine the maxims closely, we shall see that in many ways they are more remarkable for the reservations upon absolute obedience than for their insistence on it. As Genelli said, " In no case have so many precautions been taken that the mediation of reason should intervene between the command and obedience, in order that in the occupations, the orders, the commissions that are given to the religious, superiors may always consult not only the strength, the talents and the disposition, but also the taste of the individual. Moreover, St. Ignatius desires that for the good of the individual and of the whole Society the religious who has received any command should not merely be allowed without violating obedience, but be obliged, to set forth, after having consulted God in prayer, any doubts that he may have concerning the opportuneness of the order or commission that is given him."

At the same time, in an anxiety to refute exaggeration, it must not be forgotten that it was the teaching of St. Ignatius, as it is the teaching of the Church at large, that obedience is in itself a virtue as well as a practical convenience. The will is the source of all corruption, and virtue is the free subordination of our will to the will of God. A man who has tamed his will, even if he has only tamed it by obedience, if you like, to the foolish commands of others, is the more easily able clearly to consider what is the will of God with a judgment unclouded by inordinate and selfish desires.

Again, without submission there cannot be humility, and humility has its economic as well as its moral advantages. I do not know what proportion of our income we spend on pride— that is to say, on things that we do not really care for in themselves but which we should be ashamed to lack because of what other people might think. But clearly the proportion is very considerable. You have but to make a person indifferent to the contempt of others, and not only does he escape hell in the next world, but he escapes an overdraft in this.

In framing the Constitutions St. Ignatius proceeded, as was only reasonable, with the greatest deliberation. His plan was to write out what came into his head, then to lay it upon the altar and to offer his Mass over it until God helped him to a decision. He knew well that the ultimate responsibility was the Superior's, and he did not seek to shirk it.   Yet he was not of the type which refuses to take advice.   He was continually consulting whichever of the other Fathers might happen to be within reach.   It was the vocation of the Jesuits to serve God both in their own spiritual life and in the world.   From the first—indeed, as we have seen, from a time long before the foundation of the Society—St. Ignatius had understood the importance of education.   The Catholic life is a full life not only at each particular moment, but also throughout its duration. The Faith has its message for every stage of life.   There is a Catholicism of the child and a Catholicism of adolescence, a Catholicism of manhood and a Catholicism of old age, just as we can love as a child and love as a youth, love as a man and love as an old man.   The soul which, either through conversion after a non-Catholic upbringing or after an upbringing by careless Catholic parents, comes late to the full Catholic life has lost something which can never be recaptured.   No sanctity of middle life, however heroic, nor devotion, however intense, can ever fill the gap which the lack of Catholic schooldays must necessarily leave in the fullness of a convert's life.

People cannot free themselves from this notion of St. Ignatius as a recruiting sergeant and a propagandist, and his anxiety to get hold of the children is ascribed to an anxiety to get hold of future propagandists.   The ascription is a false and crude confusion of secondary and primary purposes.   The first object of the Jesuits was, as it has remained, to enable the children to live full Catholic lives.   It was characteristic of St. Ignatius' common sense that he soon saw that the Jesuits could not hope to attract pupils if they only gave instruction in catechism and religious doctrine.   It was necessary that, while providing the religious instruction, they should also provide instruction in secular subjects at least as good as that of any other school.

According to the Constitutions the members of the Society were to be divided into four classes—the lay brothers, who were people of little education and whose duty it was to act as servants to the rest ; the scholastics, or those in preparation for the priesthood ; the ordinary Fathers ; and the professed

Fathers, who were compelled to take a fourth vow of special fidelity to the Constitutions and to whom the posts of especial responsibility in the Society were to be entrusted.   Rules were laid down governing the conditions of admission of novices. Only under the most especial circumstances were only sons to be admitted, and those of illegitimate birth and any who had worn the dress of another order for even a day were also excluded. If such applied they could only be admitted by dispensation.   Novices on their admission were divided into three classes—those destined for the priesthood, those destined to be lay brothers, and those who were willing to enter either state according to the judgment of their superiors.

The novice on admission was to spend a month in retirement, occupied with the Spiritual Exercises, and after that to make a general confession of his sins.   Then followed a novitiate of two years, during which he abstained entirely from all secular study.   For a month he served the sick in hospital, for another month made a pilgrimage to some holy spot; the rest of the time he spent in the directly spiritual life.   After that came a three or four years' juniorate, during which he began to prepare himself for that work in the world for which his Superior should judge him to be best suited.   St. Ignatius remembered how he himself had misspent his time at Alcala through lack of system, and detailed regulations were laid down to ensure that the time was used to the best advantage.   His juniorate and his course in philosophy completed, the Jesuit, as he had by now become, was free to devote the rest of his life to the direct service of his fellows, with the exception of one year—known as that of the tertianship—in which he returned and lived again the life of the novitiate, and thus renewed those emotions with which he had first set out on his dedicated life.

The General, who was to reside at Rome, was to be elected for life by the assembled Society. He appointed provincials, who were to be superiors over each province of the Society, the heads of the professed houses and the rectors of colleges. Every country was to consist of one or more provinces.   Every Superior was to write to the General on the affairs of his house

every week, if it were possible.   Every year every provincial
had to send to the General a full report on the affairs of his
province.

Besides the General the congregation of the professed Fathers
was to elect four assistants and a *socius*, who were to reside in
Rome and advise the General on policy.   In case of grave
scandal these assistants were to have the right to summon a
meeting of the congregation in spite of the General's opposition,
and even to propose to it his deposition.

In every house only the language of the country in which it
was situated was to be spoken.

I mention only those points in which the Constitutions
most notably differ from those of other Orders.   These are the
chief.   But St. Ignatius was the last person to worship rules
for their own sake.   They were but means to the end of God's
greater glory.   And from the first the new Society took the
whole world as its parish.   Before even the Constitutions were
completed, while Xavier was ploughing his way to the splendid
adventures of the East, two of his colleagues were facing the
risks of martyrdom in Christ's ultimate island of the northern
sea.   The blind Archbishop of Armagh, the remarkable
Wauchope, who had fled to Rome rather than admit Henry
VIII.'s supremacy in the Church, appealed to Paul III. to send
an apostolic nuncio to Ireland to fortify the people in their
persecuted faith.   At first Codure, as it will be remembered,
had been selected for this perilous task.   After his death
Salmeron and Brouet were chosen in his place.   They set out
in September, 1541, accompanied by a young nobleman called
Francis Zapata, who was anxious to enter the Society and to
prove the sincerity of his wish by sharing the most arduous
labours of those whom he desired for his companions.

Francis I. had just taken advantage of the failure of Charles
V.'s expedition against Algiers to recommence war with the
Emperor, and the warlike preparations made the journey from
Italy to France no easier than that from France to Italy had
been, when the companions first left Paris in the winter of 1536.
However, they at last reached the Channel coast and crossed

thence to Scotland, where they presented letters of introduction from the Pope to James V.

Twenty-nine years before another James had gone down to death before Henry's army at Flodden, and this James had inherited from the memory of that disgrace an undying distrust of all the policies of his uncle of England—a distrust through which his devotion to the Church grew greater with every act of defiance of the Pope of which the news from England told—a distrust which before this very year was out was to bring Scotland to Solway Moss and James to a grave far less honourable than that of his father, and to leave upon the throne of Scotland a little baby girl whose sorrows and whose laughter still inspire mankind with a romance that has lasted across three hundred years.

James received the guests kindly and sent them on their way. They reached Ireland at the beginning of Lent. The rumour of their coming had got abroad, and there was a price on their head. It was death to harbour them. For thirty-four days they travelled through the country, bringing consolation where they could. But persecution can only be avoided by skilful organisation. To allow them to remain longer, until better preparations had been made, would, Paul saw, be merely to waste valuable lives. He therefore ordered them to return. They obeyed, recrossing to Scotland. It had been their intention to travel down into England and there seek an interview with Henry VIII., confident that they would be able to convince him of the error of his ways. But in Scotland those who were better acquainted with the situation and with Henry's character were able to persuade them how naive was such a hope. They therefore sailed instead for Dieppe. They left Zapata at Paris, where he had decided to take the course at the university, and, after the adventure of being arrested as Spanish spies at Lyons, got back to Rome in November.

Xavier was, of course, in the East, and Rodriguez in Portugal. But with these exceptions the rest of the Fathers were, after the return of the Irish expedition, all occupied in evangelical work at one town and another in Italy. Perhaps the most interesting task was that of Brouet, who attempted the reconversion of the apostate Ochino, of whose sincerity and intelligence both he and St. Ignatius entertained a high opinion.   The attempt, as is known, ended in failure.   Ochino left Italy for England and Switzerland, and in his later years became the victim of wilder and yet wilder extremes of speculation.   For the most part in these early years the Jesuits seem to have aroused comparatively little hostility.   The only exception was that of Salmeron at Modena.   Enemies denounced both his morals and his orthodoxy to the Pope, and St. Ignatius, conscious of his innocence, insisted on his returning to Rome and vindicating himself before Paul, which he did with complete success.

Meanwhile under Rodriguez the Society was making large headway in Portugal, and he it was who was responsible for the inauguration of a new policy, when in 1546 he opened at Coimbra a college whose pupils were not confined to those who were intended for the priesthood.   It was the first of the great Jesuit colleges.   Rodriguez ruled it in Coimbra with an eccentric but on the whole successful policy, to a consideration of which we shall have to return in a later chapter.

CHAPTER XI

ST. IGNATIUS IN ROME AND THE GERMAN TROUBLES

For St. Ignatius himself the days of travel and of adventure were now at an end. Only three times more did he leave Rome. The first time was to confer with Paul III. at Montefiascone, the second to arbitrate between the inhabitants of Tivoli and those of San Angelo, where a petty quarrel seemed likely to lead to bloodshed. St. Ignatius' friend, Margaret of Austria, by now the wife of Ottavio Farnese, was the lady of the manor of San Angelo, a certain Luigi Mendozze lord of the manor of Tivoli. St. Ignatius persuaded both parties to lay aside their arms and to accept the arbitration of the Cardinal of Cueva. In thanks for his services Mendozze presented the Society with a house at Tivoli, where a college was opened and carried on successfully, in spite of the somewhat obstreperous conduct of the bishop.

St. Ignatius' third journey was in 1553 to Alirto in Naples. It was the Colonnas this time, and his mission was to reconcile Ascanio Colonna, Vittoria's brother, with his wife, Joanna of Aragon, with whom he was quarrelling. He succeeded for the moment, but the reconciliation was not lasting.

For the rest he remained at Rome very adequately occupied. The routine of the day varied little in sickness or in health. It began with a meditation, then followed Mass, the saying of which he never missed until Paul III. was persuaded to inhibit him lest he should injure his sight by attempting to use his eyes when they were filled with tears, as they always were when he was at the altar. His Mass occupied him for an hour, although —it is an interesting example of the way in which he tried to dissuade others from the extremities in which he felt compelled himself to indulge—he thought half an hour quite long enough for anybody else. In the same way, when a too scrupulous priest called Brugelman spent the whole day in the saying of his office, St. Ignatius bade him give only half an hour to the task, and dispensed him from whatever might be still unsaid at the end of that time.

After Mass he spent two hours in thanksgiving. Then, if business compelled him to do so, he went out, accompanied by one of the other Fathers, probably Ribadaneira, or else received those who wished to see him at home, making it a rule to refuse himself to no one. Dinner was at twelve. After dinner the whole community went to another room, where an hour was spent in recreation. He then went to his room and either wrote himself or dictated to his secretary until supper time. After supper all those who had positions of responsibility in the house came to make to him their daily report. He was especially keen in his questioning of the infirmarian, for he was untiring in his solicitude for the sick. If he found that the minister had neglected to provide for them anything that should have been provided he would send him out in the middle of the night to make a purchase or to fetch a doctor. Once when funds were short and only three pauls remained, St. Ignatius said, " Spend them on the sick man ; we will dine on bread." The doctor once forbade Ribadaneira to fast in Lent on account of his poor health. It came to St. Ignatius' ears that some of the community at Toledo had either grumbled or sneered at this relaxation. St. Ignatius wrote to them a stinging letter which he commanded to be read in the refectory, threatening with instant dismissal anyone who should repeat such an offence against charity.

After the reports had been made, St. Ignatius would talk a little while more with his secretary. After the secretary departed he would walk up and down the room with a stick, praying aloud. What happened during these mysterious hours is a matter of conjecture. Giovan Paolo, who at one time lived in the next room to St. Ignatius, used to hear sounds and blows, and once went to see what was the matter. But there was nothing to be seen, and St. Ignatius forbade him ever to

return.   It was conjectured that he used to wrestle through the
night with evil spirits, but he never told anybody of these
experiences, whatever they may have been.   At length he went
to bed, allowing himself but four hours of sleep.   At intervals
throughout the whole day he was continually examining and
re-examining his conscience—a habit which he imposed both on
himself and on all other members of the Society.

St. Ignatius believed with St. Paul that "*radix malorum
omnium est cupiditas !*"   Her own worldly wealth has throughout all the ages been the Church's greatest enemy.   He was
therefore especially diligent that in his Society neither the vow
nor the spirit of poverty should be in any way relaxed.   He
was always displeased when any member of the Society showed
any concern for creature comforts.   Once when Bobadilla asked
for a larger room, St. Ignatius commanded him instead to share
his room with two others.   When a certain Landini grumbled
much at the sufferings which he was compelled to bear in illness,
St. Ignatius had him most tenderly cared for as long as the
illness lasted, but ruthlessly dismissed him from the house the
moment that he was well, and was only with great difficulty
persuaded to take him back again.

The colleges were allowed to accept within limits of prudence
whatever gifts might be made to them, but on the houses of the
professed, such as that in which he himself lived, he imposed a
much stricter discipline.   These houses were to receive their
daily bread as an alms, and the bread of alms was often
insufficient and unappetising.   "*Modicum venenum non nocet,*"
said Bobadilla one day with a wry face on seeing his horrid
little portion.   Not even an image or picture in a room was to
be moved without permission.   The houses of the professed
were not to receive any gift, however trivial, from the super-
fluities of the colleges.   It was forbidden to a professed Father
even to pick up a fallen apple from the ground or to pluck a
flower as he walked along, and St. Ignatius allowed to himself
no delicacy nor comfort which he refused to his subordinates.
At the same time he was no friend of dirt or slovenliness.   He
it was, perhaps, who taught St. Philip Neri so often to repeat

the saying of St. Bernard, " *Paupertas mihi semper placuit ; sordes vero nunquam.*" And he insisted that the Fathers and Brothers should present themselves as attractively as means would allow, and approved of those who ate with a hearty appetite. "Now continue to nourish yourself and grow strong to serve God and our Society," he once said to a voracious novice. He punished one whose room was disorderly by making him put all his possessions into a sack and carry it through the house on his shoulder, telling all whom he met of his fault.

Similarly he had a keen, if somewhat mediæval, sense of humour, loving a joke himself and loving to see others enjoying one. " *Qui in eius cubiculo laetissimi semper ac risibundi,*" says Nadal. " Francis, I see that you are always laughing," he said to a Flemish novice. " I am glad of it." His own favourite joke was to send defaulters as a penance to pray before the Blessed Sacrament until he should tell them to desist. If they asked what they should pray about, he answered, " Pray that I may not forget it."

To some his strict concern for poverty may seem exaggerated. But if one looks at the world and sees the enormous hold which the lust for possessions easily gets upon all people, men and women, priest and layman, Catholic and non-Catholic, unless it is most brutally controlled, how there is no limit of baseness of which people cannot be guilty for money, how at the last it come even to make the financial profitableness of an activity the test of its virtue, it must be agreed that St. Ignatius was quite right in feeling that it was not possible to be too keen or too careful in the combat with such an enemy. This greed, which we find in all men, was especially rife in the Catholic world of the 16th century, in which we are tempted to say that men would do anything for money except work for it, and most of the corruptions of which can be traced in some way or other, as the report of Paul III.'s own commission very truly asserted, to the greed for money.

To others the rule by which no Jesuit might ever visit a woman alone may seem prudish, and the severity with which he punished breaches of that rule excessive. A poor old man who had violated it without any suspicion of an evil motive—he had indeed been to hear her confession, and had only not taken a companion because there was no one about—was yet made to flog himself while eight of the Fathers stood round him, reciting penitential Psalms. Yet when we consider the incredible laxity of the lives of so many of the clergy of that day, we can see how vitally important it was that the Jesuits should be guarded not only from opportunity for transgression but also from the possible reproaches of lying scandal. It is less easy to sympathise with his sudden dismissal for the making of a Rabelaisian jest of a poor infirmarian whom he turned out to travel twelve hundred miles home without either money or habit.

St. Ignatius, as I have already said, was always ready to take the advice of others. He disliked those who came to rapid decisions without having fully weighed the issues. It was rare to hear him speak any evil of another or be guilty of any indiscretion. He said rather that " there was not in all the house one who did not in some thing give him an example to imitate or some cause to humble himself by comparison." Indeed he went further in one of his letters and wrote, " When I associate with anyone, even if he be a great sinner, to discourse about the things of God Our Lord, I am the one to gain, and I find great advantage for myself." Once, having spoken of a slight fault in a lay brother to three people, and on reflection having reached the conclusion that it would have sufficed to have spoken to two, he at once rushed off and confessed his fault with much contrition. When he made a promise of assistance which on further reflection he did not think that he could fulfil, he said to Gonzales, " I do not think such a thing has happened to me these eleven or twelve years past."

He hated any untruthfulness, direct or indirect. It was the Jesuit teaching, as stated afterwards by Suarez, that God Himself cannot excuse a lie. When a Father simulated a sympathy which he did not feel with a society known as the Priscillianists (an obscure and ancient sect who held some half-magical, half-Manichæan doctrines), in order to discover their practices, St. Ignatius disgraced him. "*Suspensa, vel ambigua, vel obscura verba, perplexum de industria incertumque sermonem, uti barbaras artes, et subdola mendacii tegumenta, fideique ac societatis humanae perniciem, semper est detestatus.*" "Let Truth and Simplicity be and remain our colours," was the grand advice which Canisius gave to his colleagues of Germany.

*   *   *   *   *

I have not dwelt at length on any of the merely vulgar accusations against Jesuitism, nor is it here necessary to say more than one thing concerning them. For the most part they are attributable to pure malice. So far as they have any more honourable origin, that origin is to be found in St. Ignatius' utter lack of capacity for acting on any principle which he did not explicitly confess. It is but a pale shadow of the truth to say that there was no realm of conduct in which St. Ignatius was not enormously more scrupulous than the average man. He was indeed so scrupulous that he was unable to act without formulating the principle on which he was acting. We all of us think ourselves justified in saying to our hostess that we have so enjoyed ourselves, even though in truth we have been greatly bored. St. Ignatius would not have thought himself justified in so acting, unless he stopped to make a note of the fact that there were occasions upon which it was not one's duty to adhere to strict verbal accuracy. Thus Herr Fülop-Miller, in his *Power and Secret of the Jesuits*, somewhat naively says of St. Ignatius, "Was he not the inventor of that dubious method of correspondence which distinguished between ' main letters ' with a definite edifying content which could be ' used for show,' and ' enclosures ' which contained the real and strictly confidential instructions ? " Yet surely even a Quaker's scrupulosity could not deny that sometimes there might be things which one might wish to say to a trusted subordinate, and not wish to have published to the world or communicated to the other party with whom one was negotiating. That in the age of Machiavelli and Ferdinand of Aragon and Henry VIII. nobody had ever thought of the use of such a very mild little bit of strategy, that it was left to St. Ignatius to " invent " it, is a proposition that can hardly be treated with grave seriousness. But what is possible is that St. Ignatius was the first person definitely to lay down in so many words the principle that there were occasions when this strategem might be adopted.

St. Ignatius had a great hatred for laziness. " Dear brother, for whom are you doing that ? " he once asked a lay-brother who was loitering at his task. " For the love of God," answered the brother. " Then I assure you," said St. Ignatius, " if you do no better hereafter I shall give you a heavy penance ; if you were working for men, it might be no great fault to do it with so little pains ; working for God so carelessly is without excuse."

There is no point of view of which history has record more wholly contemptible than that of the worship of energy for its own sake, no quality in the world that is less of a virtue than a mere incapacity to sit still. This worship of the entrail is merely the combination of a deification of the means with a feeling that it is unpractical to think about the end at all. It is important to clear St. Ignatius of any suspicion of being associated with such a belief. He proved himself by results to be at least as efficient as any successful business man. Indeed, not only was he efficient; he also effected things. Yet, as the anecdote shows, he never at all fell into the error of worshipping means, that general error which the penetrating intellect of Aquinas showed to be the root of all particular error. If the end was not worthy, then it was not worth troubling much about the means—and, in spite of the absurd maxim of the nursery, there are many things which are worth doing and yet not worth doing well. When, on the other hand, the end was worthy, then it became important to strive for it with energy. Probably the two most irritating qualities in the world are, on the one hand, a mad, rabid worship of efficiency, on the other, a feckless incompetence about engagements and the necessary business of life. St. Ignatius struck admirably the mean between these two evil extremes.

What must undoubtedly seem to some a less attractive trait

in his character was his opposition to particular friendships among members of the Society. To the northern temperament it may seem neither strange nor undesirable to discountenance the kiss between males, but to the southerner the kiss was the mere symbol of friendship, and it was friendship itself which St. Ignatius was really anxious to discountenance. "If anyone were to say, 'This man is my friend,'" writes one of the early Fathers, "or 'such an one loves me,' such worldly language would be regarded as strange, and heard with astonishment, for, where all love each other as themselves, all are friends." We must remember, as we have already insisted in considering his attitude towards the family, that St. Ignatius was not laying down rules for the generality of mankind but for those called to a very special vocation. To those for whom the true love of Christ was so unutterably real, a special friendship would perhaps truly be an obstacle to the full spiritual life. It would be an impudence for one in, and of, the world to attempt to dictate on such a policy. It was also most reasonable that St. Ignatius himself, as a Superior, should be careful not to betray any preference for one over another of his subordinates, showing if anything a greater harshness to those whom he most loved. Yet it is only honest to add that as the Society grew in numbers it continued to attract some of the greatest and holiest of mankind, but also it inevitably had to include among its members some who were not so noticeably more spiritual, more capable of the love of God than the rest of us. For such souls St. Ignatius' policy was full of dangers. Not truly capable of the higher love, forbidden the lower, they were likely to fall between the two stools into a horrible aridity. And as we look through the grand history of the Society it is not honestly possible to refrain from saying of a proportion of its members that, since they were clearly not going to love God in this very especial sense anyway, it would have been better if they had been allowed to love another just a little more. Such a phrase as "Where all love each other all are friends" is little more than words. We can have charity towards all, but it is not in nature to have equal fondness for all. Nor, to speak with frankness, is there anything so detestably "worldly" in preferring the company of one person to that of another. Our Lord Himself was not ashamed to have a favourite disciple.

*   *   *   *   *

Germany was the central battle-ground of the new religious warfare, and, although none of its original members were of German blood or speech, yet it would have been surprising had the new Society long succeeded in keeping itself free from the German controversies. Anxious to heal the religious divisions of the Empire in order that Germany might present an undivided front to the menace of the Turk, Charles in 1540 convened a Diet to meet at Worms on the site of its more famous predecessor of twenty years before. He sent to Paul and Ignatius and asked them to lend him a theologian of spotless integrity, of eloquence and ability, who might act there as the spokesman for the Catholic cause. Faber was selected.

We have the letters which he sent back to St. Ignatius in report upon the situation in Germany as he found it. He was quick to see that the difference between Catholic and Lutheran had by now grown into something much larger than a difference of misunderstanding to be adjusted by sympathetic explanation. Yet he thought with Erasmus that here, as often, the Church's most dangerous enemy was not the enemy without but the enemy within. He writes :

"I wonder there are not twice or three times as many heretics as there are, because nothing leads to errors in belief so rapidly as a disordered life. It is not the false interpretations of Scripture nor the sophistry which the Lutherans introduce into their sermons and disputes that have caused so many nations to apostatise and so many towns and provinces to revolt against religion. All the mischief is done by the scandalous lives of the clergy."

And again :

"Would there were in this city of Worms only two or three churchmen who were not living openly with women, or guilty of some other notorious crime, and who had a little

zeal for the salvation of souls. . . . That part of the flock
which is bound to lead the faithless into the fold is precisely
that which drives Catholics to become Lutherans by the
spectacle of their dissolute lives."

It was the opinion of Erasmus, and even of a Catholic as
exemplary as Bishop Pflug of Naumburg, that experience had
proved that only the most exceptional of men were capable of
continence, and that therefore the wisest policy for the Church
would be to avoid recurring scandal by the frank abandonment
of the attempt at a celibate clergy.   Such letters and from such
a man as Faber teach us how very plausible such an opinion
must have seemed.   To the men of that time the level of
morality among the clergy of to-day would doubtless seem a
thing incredible and quite beyond the capacity of human nature.

Faber, in alliance with the one priest in the town who was of
unimpeachable morals, was just able to save the town from a
universal apostacy.

In the next year, 1541, another Diet was held at Ratisbon.
Faber was again present.   Contarini was Paul's legate, and care
had been taken that both sides should be represented only by
their most moderate and conciliatory spokesmen.   The menace
of the Turk and of France made it of importance to Charles to
restore the unity of Germany if it should be in any way possible
to do so.   The story of the failure of all attempts at compromise,
after some early appearances of success, belongs to a larger
history than that of this book.   The Jesuit policy was to hold
aloof from these political schemes, to expound Catholic doctrine,
to preach the reformation of morals, and then to leave the event
in the hands of God.   At Ratisbon first, and afterwards in
Nuremberg, Faber carried out this policy, which proved in the
end to be wiser and more fruitful than that of the arranging
diplomatists.   And afterwards, when the Pope and St. Ignatius
had sent Faber with Ortiz for a year's mission to Spain, Le Jay
and Bobadilla came to carry on the work which Faber had
begun.   At Ratisbon the enraged people at one time threatened
to throw Le Jay into the Danube, but he contented himself with

saying to them, as Oliver Mallard had said under similar circumstances once before, " What does it matter to me whether I enter heaven from earth or water ? " The religious divisions of Germany were not healed, but the tide was turned. The Church began to recover ground which she had lost, and the cause of Christ was preached as a spiritual cause, and one which did not stand or fall with the political fortunes of His adherents of this world.

Faber returned to Germany in October, 1542, and went first to Speyer. Thenceforward he was continuously occupied in apostolic work, first in one town and then in another, as also were all of his companions. One among the results of their work was a steady stream of new recruits to the Society's novitiate. It would neither be possible nor interesting to attempt a full list, yet at least one among the most remarkable must be mentioned.

In January, 1543, Faber was preaching at Mainz, summoned thither by the Archbishop, Albert of Brandenburg. Thither large crowds flocked to hear him, and among others, a young Dutchman of the name of Peter Canisius. This young man, now twenty-three years of age, having been born in the year in which St. Ignatius was wounded at Pampeluna, was the son of wealthy and worldly parents. It had, as has already been said, been prophesied of him, when he was but a baby, that one day he would belong to a society which should be called the Society of Jesus. Whether for this reason or for another, the young man, now a brilliant graduate of the universities of Cologne and of Louvain, made his way to Mainz to hear Faber's sermons. " Never have I known or listened to a more learned man," was his verdict, " or one of more eminent virtue—if indeed he be a man and not rather an angel from heaven."

Canisius attached himself to Faber, and, when soon afterwards the troubles into which Archbishop Herman had plunged his electorate of Cologne called Faber from Mainz to Cologne, Canisius went with him. Thither one day came news that Canisius' father was dangerously ill in Holland. He was just able to reach the bedside in time for a last farewell, but the father's death left the son in great anxiety, for the old man had lived a worldly, though not a wicked, life.   However, that night Peter had a vision in which he learnt (so he believed) that his father and his mother, also dead, were both saved.   In gratitude he determined at once wholly to renounce the world.   He distributed his ample inheritance to the poor, and at once set out for Cologne to seek from Faber admission into the Jesuit novitiate.   Such was his zeal that he even persuaded three chance travelling-companions also to try their vocations, and one became a Jesuit and the other two Carthusians.

Archbishop Herman of Wied, a man of stupidity so intense that it shines like a beacon-light across the blackness of four hundred years, thought that it was necessary to reform the morals of his diocese—as indeed it was.   Yet reform might well have begun with the Archbishop himself, for according to Charles V., he was " so ignorant that he could not even say Mass."   Charles had heard him, and he could not read the Introit. The reform began instead with Gropper, his archdeacon, who, returning one morning from Matins and finding a woman making his bed, tore off the bedclothes and threw them out of the window, lest he should lay his body upon material defiled by the feminine touch.   Finding such tactics not wholly effectual, Herman next called in the Protestant leader, Martin Bucer, explaining to those who protested that he wished to use Bucer's moral influence though he did not approve his doctrines, among which was in fact a theory of marriage so revolutionary as to provide the argument for Milton's sonnets on Divorce. Bucer did no more good than throwing bedclothes out of windows, and in panic Faber was sent for to put things right.

Faber effected something and Herman promised him that he would be obedient to Rome.   The promise obtained, St. Ignatius ordered Faber to repair to Spain.   He went first to Louvain, where the Jesuits had established a college that was carrying out under much difficulty work of the highest importance.   There he fell seriously ill.   After his recovery he had, in January, 1544, to pay a second visit to Cologne, where he found to his dismay that the egregious Herman had invited back not only Bucer but also Melanchthon and Pistorius. Faber indulged in controversy with them, first laying down for himself the following rules to be observed. " All who desire to do them good," he noted, " should show them the greatest charity, love them truly, and disperse all prejudices that might lower us in their esteem. We should seek their good-will and confidence by a friendly intercourse, conversing of the matters on which we are agreed, and shunning altercation. We teach them first what they ought to practise, then what they ought to believe ; not as was the custom of the early Church in those times when men's minds were first of all to receive the faith which comes from hearing and then be led by degrees to the practice of good works. Therefore we should endeavour to win them from evil ways before we attack their evil doctrine. If Luther himself could be brought to a virtuous life, it would be easy to draw him back into the true Church."

As for Herman, Paul III. very properly deposed him and excommunicated him, and soon afterwards he died.

Faber meanwhile had departed for Spain, leaving behind him Le Jay as the most prominent of the Jesuits in Germany. Le Jay had less belief in mild and courteous measures than Faber, and continually urged the Emperor to attack heresy with a vigorous policy. One effect of this more aggressive policy was to bring into unpopularity Canisius and the other Jesuits, whom Faber had left behind in Cologne. The magistrates closed down their house on the excuse that the law did not permit new establishments. But the Carthusians, as ever the allies of the Jesuits, offered them hospitality, and they continued with their work, using the Chartreuse as their headquarters. Hamontan, the Superior of the Carthusians, took advantage of this opportunity of kindness to propose to the General Assembly of his Order in 1544, to admit the Society of Jesus to a participation in their prayers and works, and St. Ignatius replied by admitting all Carthusians to a similar participation in the prayers and works of the Jesuits.

St. Ignatius meanwhile at Rome was devoting what attention could be spared from the business of direction of the Society to the organisation of charitable institutions.   Of these many were inevitably of a conventional type, but two, at any rate, are worth mentioning.

He founded a refuge-house for fallen women who were willing to make the arduous effort of a return to virtue.   This brought down upon his head the anger of the vicious, who with a gross brutality accused St. Ignatius of contracting the market and thus raising the price of pleasure.   It also brought down upon him the no less brutal contempt of some of those who ranked themselves among the virtuous, and who proclaimed from their worldly wisdom that the confirmed sinner was beyond reclamation, and trouble taken on her behalf was certainly wasted.

The vicious contented themselves with collecting in front of the refuge, breaking the windows and shouting out obscene remarks—with the conduct, that is, of good, honest, straight-forward swine.   The virtuous preferred to sneer.   How incredible in every age of history has been the callousness of some among those who pass for virtuous through the accident that they lack any temptation to vice !   St. Ignatius was content scornfully to answer to such people, " If I can prevent even one sin against God, I think it is worth all the trouble I can take."

The dangers of such work are deeper than those of which the shallow think.   The emotions of pity and of love are so closely allied that none but the saint can greatly pity and yet be sure of holding himself quite free of any desire for the object of his pity.   And, if he does hold himself free, he can never be sure that the object of his pity will not misunderstand his motives.   And he who tries to help others must be prepared to endure again and again that most aching, desolated, abandoned of all sorrows when the soul sees how to help and yearns to help another, and through some intolerable misunderstanding the help is rejected by the person who needs it.   Philanthropists are the last people who ought to try and help men and women ; the effort will break their hearts.   It is the work for saints. For the lover of men and women there will be compensations— sudden and incredibly welcome acts of gratitude and tokens of remembrance, coming often at the most unexpected moments—

but, human nature being what it is, the compensations are not likely to be as many as the disappointments.

Women were received into this refuge and there kept, living a religious life. They were only allowed to go out in order to return to their husbands, if they were married, or to enter a convent if they were not. Father Diego d'Eguia was made their confessor, St. Ignatius thus breaking for the only time his rule that Jesuits were not to accept the spiritual directorship of women.

St. Ignatius also established a house for converted Jews, and made arrangements to prevent them being deprived of their property by their ex-co-religionists. The synagogue was to support them during their period of instruction.

At the beginning of the year 1542, a quarrel broke out which looked as if it might have consequences most inconvenient for St. Ignatius and his rising Society. The Society had no two more faithful friends than the Pope, Paul III., and King John III. of Portugal. It was therefore most unfortunate for St. Ignatius when Paul nominated Michel da Silva, the Portuguese ambassador in Rome, to the see of Viseux without consultation with the King, and John angrily protested against what he looked upon as an insult to his rights and his *amour propre*. John sequestered the revenues of the see, and peace was only secured by St. Ignatius' mediation, a compromise being effected by which Cardinal Farnese was appointed to the see, and agreed to leave the duties and make over the revenue to da Silva as his deputy.

The result of St. Ignatius' mediation was not altogether fortunate. From motives that were doubtless mixed, but among which one of the most prominent certainly was, as Cardinal Pucci roundly said, a desire to fleece the Jews, King John III. had long been pressing the Pope to give authority for the establishment of a Portuguese Inquisition. Lobbying, accompanied by lavish corruption, had been carried on by both the King and the Jews at Rome. Clement VII. had not been at all enthusiastic about the shady project, and Paul on his accession was little more favourable. He eventually agreed by a Bull of

May 23rd, 1536, to the establishment, but insisted that "new Christians," who had received baptism by compulsion, were not subject to the laws of the Church. This exception, ruling out from his jurisdiction, as it did, all the rich money-lenders, did not at all suit John's purposes. He tried to enlist St. Ignatius' assistance in getting Paul to withdraw, and St. Ignatius, doubtless not wholly understanding what was afoot, seems to have agreed to help. Fortunately Paul refused to make any considerable concession.

St. Ignatius' next activity was one in which it is not honestly possible to pretend that he appears in an attractive light. Innocent III. had in 1215 forbidden physicians to attend a patient who was dangerously ill until he had first received a priest and made confession. The command, though not repealed, had fallen into desuetude. St. Ignatius made it his business to obtain its reinforcement. Paul III. was absent from Rome, having gone to meet Charles V. at Buseto. In face of the opposition of the physicians, St. Ignatius wrote to Cardinal Carpi, the Papal legate :

"Many die without the help of religion, either not confessing at all or imperfectly. They ought to be warned to do it as soon as the malady begins to seem dangerous, so that they may not wait until they have not the strength necessary for a sufficient confession, or for any at all, and the urging it may hasten their death. These evils would be avoided if they confessed at the beginning, for this not only saves the soul, but gives relief to the body and much contributes to its recovery. And this has been your Eminence's motive in restoring, as you have done, the observance of the decree of Lateran, with this relaxation that the physicians may visit once or twice but not oftener persons who have not confessed. In spite of this concession many physicians have done all they could to oppose this holy intention, while some have upheld it. They who oppose pretend that it is contrary to charity to let a man die because he refuses obstinately to confess ; for, they say, if he lives he may repent. But all reasonable persons answer that laws are made for the general benefit, and must not be set aside even if they cause damage to particular persons. . . . If this objection had any value, we might say of Ananias and Sapphira that if they had lived they might have repented."

Doubtless the awful horror of sin oppressed St. Ignatius with a vividness incomprehensible to lesser men. Yet for all that it is impossible not to feel that the physicians had the better of it. Ananias and Sapphira were struck dead by the inscrutable wisdom of God. God knows when the moment has come to snatch a soul from the world, but Man has no right to forestall that decision. The duty of Man is to do all that he can to keep alive his fellow-man, saint or sinner, in mortal sin or in state of grace. If we all treated one another as God treated Ananias and Sapphira the depopulation of the world would be somewhat accelerated.

It is very easy, when one reads such a story as this, to let slip into the mind a picture of St. Ignatius during these years as a cold, hard, controlled, efficient organiser. The great struggles of Manresa, we feel, are behind him. He is master of himself. All that he does is done doubtless for the greater glory of God, but there is a certain coldness and ruthlessness in the application of the principle. Men and women have now easily become to him but pawns, and it is no longer a suffering to him to see them suffer, so long as all is for the benefit of the great cause. Now it is true that he was an organiser of an almost incredible efficiency, that he was by now the master of a will that could never be turned from its purpose by any inordinate affection, that where he loved he loved only for Christ's sake, but any who imagine that competence and business, or organisation and success, in any way dried up the powers of love in his soul, as they dry them up in those of lesser men, can have formed but a very little picture of this great saint. If you would understand how this iron ruler—the greatest perhaps among all the rulers of men—yet governed his subjects by the power of love, turn from some vulgar, legendary stuff to the writings of Pedro

Ribadaneira, of whose entrance into the novitiate I have already spoken.

St. Ignatius was above us, the companion and the friend of God. He is free from our question, a Shakespeare among saints, sparing only his clouded border to our foiled searchings. But Ribadaneira—I speak as a fool—was of our clay. He loved noise and laughter and many men and the happy things of a lovely world, enjoyed without philosophy but simply because it is lovely. He could have drunk up life with all the great gusto of a Rabelais. He persevered in the straighter way, but he never was able to subdue in him those obstinate questionings, which are just the questionings which we of the world must always be tempted to ask as we read the great story of St. Ignatius. For all of us, unless we are either exceptionally priggish or exceptionally blessed, must often feel with Voltaire that

" Je ne suis né pour célébrer les saints."

So Ribadaneira was continually saying to himself, " What is the sense of all this ? Is it worth it ? Is it not rather an insult to God to deny all the joy and laughter and good living which He has so bountifully offered ? " As for rules, he loathed them as much as every intelligent Jesuit has always loathed those necessary evils, nor is his character the less attractive to us because he, alone among the early Jesuits, refused to follow the general custom of the Society and break off all relations with his family. There was but one power which stood between him and the return to the world—the power of St. Ignatius' love.

During the time that these great policies were shaping themselves in Germany and Rome, Ribadaneira was in France. He was not well when he set out from Rome in April, 1542, to complete a course of studies at the University of Paris, and his companions asked that he should be allowed to ride while they walked. St. Ignatius answered, " Pedro may do as he pleases, but if he be a son of mine he will travel on foot like the others." To Ribadaneira this was more than a command. He went on foot.

At Viterbo they halted for the night and Ribadaneira, wandering round the town, strayed into a church and climbed up into the pulpit. The sacristan, by way of a joke, rang the bell and some people trooped in. Nothing would content them but that Ribadaneira should preach a sermon. Nothing loath, he repeated a sermon which he had preached a little time before for practice in the novitiate at Rome. So great was its effect on at least one member of his casual congregation that an old man came up to him and told him that he had long avoided the altar and the confessional because he was meditating a great act of revenge. He had determined to abandon his project and return to his duties. Ribadaneira was able to hand him on to a priest-companion of his.

From Viterbo they crossed the Alps to Avignon, where they parted from some companions who were going to Coimbra. Ribadaneira and one companion, named Diaz, went on to Barberousse, where they were met with rumours of a new war between Francis I. and Charles V. As Spaniards, they were likely to be ill-treated by the French authorites, and under the circumstances Diaz was for abandoning the attempt to reach Paris and for catching up their companions instead and going with them to Coimbra. Ribadaneira insisted on adherence to orders, and after two months of difficulty and danger they reached Paris in June.

Hardly had they established themselvès in the Jesuit college there when an order came for the expulsion of all subjects of the Emperor. The Rector of the college, Jerome Domenech, was a Spaniard, and the college looked upon as a centre of Imperialist influence. Besides, the first rumblings of the quarrel between the Society and the Sorbonne were beginning to be heard. Therefore, in spite of the efforts of their friends, Francis I. insisted on the expulsion. Diaz and Ribadaneira were to go along with the rest. Diaz, in disgust, abandoned the Society altogether and soon afterwards was killed in a duel. Ribadaneira accepted and obeyed. The party set out for the Spanish Netherlands. At Amiens they had great difficulty in persuading the Governor that the period of grace allowed them to get out of the country had not elapsed. At Arras they were on Spanish territory, and they went on thence to Brussels, where the Franciscans gave them hospitality. Louvain was their destination, but owing to an invading army it was some time before they could proceed thither.

When they at last reached Louvain Ribadaneira tried to settle down to his studies there. But after such excitements the drudgery of text-book cramming and exam-passing seemed to him an idiot's life, intolerable to his love of incident, adventure and movement and murderous of his very real intellectual and artistic interests. He fell into a listless melancholy, asking hopelessly what was the purpose of the nonsense.

Domenech saw that he could do nothing with him. Therefore, being himself recalled to Rome, he determined to take Ribadaneira with him to visit St. Ignatius. They travelled first to Mainz, where Faber showed them kindness. Thence over the hills to Venice and Laynez. At Ravenna Domenech fell ill, but he bade Ribadaneira go on alone. At Loreto Ribadaneira himself fainted, but at Tolentino he found Salmeron and Brouet, who cared for him, and he at last reached Rome on April 20th, 1543, after just a year of this ceaseless journeying. It was early in the morning. He went straight to the Gesù and found St. Ignatius just vesting himself for Mass. He threw himself on his feet before the master whom he loved and begged for the blessing without which he had not strength to continue in his dedicated life. St. Ignatius gave it to him and the disease of the soul was cured.

Take, as another illustration, the story of Michel Torrez. Torrez, the prefect of the University of Alcala, had conceived a prejudice against the Society. When, therefore, some business brought him to Rome, at first he would by no means listen to the proposal of the Spanish Ambassador to introduce him to Salmeron. At last he was persuaded to see him secretly and by night. Salmeron entreated him to meet St. Ignatius, but he only answered, " Do you suppose I would speak to such a man ? " Yet a second time his reluctance was in the end overcome. A meeting was arranged in the garden of the Jesuit house, and so powerful was the impression which St. Ignatius made on him that Torrez at the end threw himself into his arms, crying, "Do with me what you please." Torrez went through the Spiritual Exercises and, when his business was concluded, he resigned a worldly position of some consideration and entered the Society. St. Ignatius made him Rector of the new Jesuit college at Salamanca.

In the coldness of print such stories may not sound very impressive to the unimaginative. The secret of St. Ignatius' magic we can never hope to recapture any more than we can recapture the secret of the oratory of a Demosthenes or the acting of a Garrick. It is unanalysable and indescribable. We can but record the fact that he had about him a charm of personality of which people of every sort were willing to testify that they had never met with it in any other.

Michel Torrez went, as I have said, to Salamanca, and there he soon had the misfortune to fall foul of the Dominican preacher, Melchior Cano, who attacked both him in particular and the Jesuits in general, finding in them the marks of anti-Christ, calling them *illuminati*, visionaries and heretics, and accusing them of under-flagellation.

"In My Father's house are many mansions." There are as many separate types of excellence as there are separate souls. God calls one to work of one sort, another to another. There is room for all. As St. Ignatius very sensibly said, in answer to the request of the Barnabites to be allowed to join his Society, "each order had its particular character and aim, and it was for God's greater glory that each should serve Him in its own way." Throughout the whole history of the Church there is no spirit that has been her more deadly enemy than that of what I may call "Order *esprit de corps*." It is admirable that a man should love his own Order for the work which it is doing for Christ's sake—should love it as Xavier loved the Society, when he said, "*Si oblitus unquam fuero tui, Societas Jesu, oblivioni detur dextera mea*," or Blessed Robert Southwell, when he spoke of the Society as a "*corpus in quo posita sunt mea vita, meus amor, totum cor meum, omnesque affectus*," but it is horrible if he cannot love it without a petty envy of those who are doing Christ's work in some different way. In the underworld of every religious Order are to be found small-minded men who are for ever sneering at what they call " rival Orders." Debarred by their vocations from the normal competitions of the world, they find a refuge in this far more dangerous competitiveness. Cano, a Thomist of learning and distinction, was a man whose talents should have raised him far above this low class; it was his tragedy that they were not able to do so, and he devoted only too large a proportion of time that might have been so much better spent to petty rivalry, both with the priests of other Orders and with those of his own, who chanced to have won fame for themselves—in particular with Bartolomé de Carranza, the Archbishop of Toledo, whom he at last brought with sorrow to his grave. Such men as Cano little understand how great is the scandal which their petty rivalries can give.

People sometimes speak loosely as if the whole history of the Church were dominated by these rivalries between Orders. It is far from true—and nowhere is it less true than in the history of the early years of the Society of Jesus. In the composition of the Exercises St. Ignatius borrowed much from the understanding of many members of other Orders, and, in particular, from that of the Benedictine, Cisneros. It was a Benedictine, Jean Chanones, who first encouraged St. Ignatius to his great project; a Carthusian, de Castro, who gave to him the fortitude to persist in it. It was the Franciscans who gave a refuge to the Jesuits, expelled from France, and now it was the Dominicans who rallied to their vindication against one of their own members. The great Pinna at once defended them against Cano, and before long the General of the Dominicans himself, Romée de Châtillon, wrote on December 10th, 1548:

" In these calamitous times a new Order of priests, under the name of Jesus, has been sent by divine goodness from Rome as a battalion of reserve, which for the good it has done the Church by teaching and preaching in public, exhortations in private, assiduously hearing confessions and the offices of the Church and its example of a saintly life, has been approved and confirmed by our Most Holy Father. . . . And this we desire to ratify to you, lest some, misled by the recent date of this institute, might ignorantly attack our companions in arms who have the same objects with ourselves . . . and thereby calumniate the proceedings of these priests; whereas we should rather applaud their success and imitate their piety."

And Luis of Grenada wrote to one of the Fathers, " This new opposition, striving to destroy the Company, is forced to become an occasion to exercise it in humility, make it more and more pious, exemplary, circumspect, devoted, and thence rise to greater credit and higher favour with the world. So the means invented by this monk to oppress your Reverences will be used by God to lift you up; and instead of proving as he says, that you are working for anti-Christ, he will prove to have been working for you."

It is hardly necessary to add that St. Ignatius was as nobly free of this detestable preference of his Order to his Church as was the great de Châtillon himself. In his illness in 1551 he lay wondering if there was any misfortune at which he could possibly feel sorry, and he thought that he would be sorry if the Society were suddenly to fail. " But even then," he said, " I think in a quarter of an hour I should be quite comforted." When the Archbishop of Florence wrote an eulogy of the Society in 1555 he selected as one of their especial virtues " that the Jesuits are greatly disposed towards all Orders recognised by Holy Church and strive, as far as possible, to keep peace and true unity among them."

*   *   *   *   *

This book tells the life of St. Ignatius and not the history of the early years of the Society of Jesus. It is not therefore possible even to attempt to trace the developing story of the Society's activities. Deeds of heroism, the evangelisation of a nation, were under St. Ignatius' generalship matters almost of routine. We can only concern ourselves with his own major decisions. It has already been mentioned that, partly for good

and partly for bad, St. Ignatius had particularly close relations
with King John III. of Portugal. In 1546 King John, moved
by the amazing success of Xavier in India, asked St. Ignatius to
send a mission to convert the nominal Christians of Ethiopia.
This strange nation, one of the earliest in the world to turn to
Christianity, had preserved a faith of a sort throughout the
Middle Ages, but, living as it did completely cut off from Rome
and from the rest of the Christian world, it had developed strange
practices and beliefs of questionable orthodoxy. In 1442 the
Emperor Zera-Jacob had sent messengers to the Council of
Florence asking that Abyssinia might be reunited to the Universal Church. The request was granted, but the messengers,
who were taking back the good news, were set upon and killed
by Coptic Christians when passing through Egypt. Meanwhile,
as so often happens, the poor Abyssinians, denied the Christianity of the missionary, were beginning to suffer from the less
pure Christianity of the trader. King John asked Ignatius for
an Abyssinian Xavier. It was exactly the sort of need to supply
which the Society was formed, and St. Ignatius leapt excitedly
at the suggestion. He thought of Brouet as the best man.

As it happened there was considerable interval between suggestion and accomplishment. It was not until 1553 that the
Jesuits actually departed and Brouet, for some reason or other,
was not in the end selected for the mission. Nunez was sent
out as patriarch, but, when he reached Goa whither he was
ordered to go first, he found there a certain John Bermudes who
claimed that he had been appointed to the patriarchate by
Paul III. At the same time it appeared that the disposition of
Prester John towards Catholicism was not as friendly as it had
been represented to be, and he was not at all minded to give a
welcome either to the one patriarch or the other. Before the
unsatisfactory dispute could be settled Nunez was dead.

Death and sickness had from the first, as we have shown, been
busy among the members of the new Society, and even young
Ribadaneira had been seriously ill throughout all the winter of
1544, St. Ignatius himself gladly undertaking the task of ministering to him. But as yet St. Ignatius had lost none among the

most prominent of his companions. In 1546 died the first of these, Faber. It was to be the year of the great Council of Trent, so long clamoured for, so eagerly awaited. But the Council was not destined to meet without the loss by each of the religious parties of one of its most outstanding leaders. Early in the year poor Luther died and, as the summer wore on, Faber followed him. Faber, as we have seen, had been sent from Germany to Spain, but, with the Council coming on, Paul chose him as one of his theologians. He had come to Rome on the way to Trent to receive his instructions and to consult. He was in reality too ill even to have made the journey to Rome, and St. Ignatius, hearing of his condition, wrote to excuse him. " It is necessary to obey but not to live," Faber answered, and a few days after reaching Rome he died at the Gesù. Gentle, charitable, the lover of angels, a man of great learning but humble and avid to accept authority, as are all such when they are great in the quality and not merely in the quantity of their knowledge, a lover of poverty the more fervent because of his addiction to the good things of life in his student days, he would have asked for no higher panegyric than that it should be said of him that he was not unworthy to be the second of the Jesuits.

As can be imagined, St. Ignatius had during these years suc-ceeded in establishing for himself a very considerable position in the life of Rome. For some years now he had been free from those campaigns by which at first he used to be so continuously troubled. Yet it was his prayer that his Society should never for long remain unharassed by the enmity of the world, and he did not wish that he himself should escape that enmity which he desired for his companions. As it happened, the year 1546 saw three bitter personal attacks on him. The first came from a certain Mattia, postmaster of San Cassiano. Mattia had run away with another man's wife, with whom he lived. This woman, having heard one of St. Ignatius' sermons, repented and sought refuge in his hostel. So furious was Mattia that he first made a nocturnal attack on the hostel and then, when this failed, started a campaign of calumny against St. Ignatius, charging him with every crime of which imagination could con-

ceive. So persistent was he that St. Ignatius thought it necessary to follow his usual policy of demanding an investigation.
He applied to Paul III. At the moment an investigation was
not possible, as Paul's vicar, Archinti, was ill, but on his recovery
Paul allowed the machinery to be put into operation. Foreseeing exposure, Mattia in a panic went about everywhere con-
tradicting what he had previously said and speaking in praise
of St. Ignatius. Thus he hoped to induce St. Ignatius not to
bring the matter into court. However, Ignatius thought it
necessary for the reputation of the Society that he should do so,
and Archinti, after investigation, gave judgment "That the
accusations are false, lying and malicious. That these priests
and their congregation are of such ways of life, purity of morals,
piety and strict Catholic doctrine, they have brought now for
many years such rich cultivation into the Lord's vineyard, they
stand in such good favour and repute with all men, that they are
placed out of reach of all calumnies and imputations, but most
of all their Superior, the honourable Don Ignatius of Loyola."
St. Ignatius had no wish to see Mattia punished and, indeed, so
grateful was the libeller at his light escape that he afterwards
became a benefactor of the Society.

The second attack was of a similar nature, and from a secular
priest, Giovanni di Torano, Superior of St. Ignatius' house of
Jewish proselytes. St. Ignatius did not think it necessary to
demand a second investigation so shortly after his vindication
at the first, and therefore kept silence. Foolishly taking silence
for a confession of embarrassment, di Torano pressed his charges
and demanded an investigation from his side. The investigation
took place and revealed such defects of hypocrisy and baseness
in di Torano's own life that he was suspended from his priestly
functions and banished.

The third attack came from a Spanish monk called Barberan,
who accused St. Ignatius of wishing to have all the faithless
wives in Rome put to death. The motive for this strange and,
of course, quite baseless piece of nonsense has never been discovered. The incident is only interesting because of a letter
which it drew from St. Ignatius.

"Senor, say to the Father Brother Barberan, you say you wish that as many of our people as are in Spain, from Perpignan to Seville, might be burnt; but I say I wish this, that you and your friends and all that belong to you, not only from Perpignan to Seville but all over the earth, may be inflamed by the Holy Spirit and burn so well that they may reach the summit of perfection and make themselves shining lights, to the glory of the Divine Majesty. Further will you say to him that our business will be investigated by the governor and vicar of his Holiness, that a sentence may be given. If therefore he has any complaint to make of me he may address it to these judges, that, if I be guilty in anything, I may atone for it; and much rather would I make amends with my own body (which would be very acceptable to me) than that all the others between Perpignan and Seville should be burned without the least fault on their part."

Genelli, quoting Döllinger's *Reform*, humorously prints side by side with this letter of St. Ignatius concerning his enemy a letter written three years before by Luther in reply to a certain Schwenkfeld, who had made him a proposal for the reconciliation of their grievances.

"MY DEAR SIR,

"You will tell your master, Gaspar Schwenkfeld, that I have received the books and the letter which you brought me. May it please God that he should drop his underhand tricks, for he has lighted against the Eucharist in Silesia a veritable conflagration, which is not yet extinguished and which will indeed burn for ever. Besides that he continues to propagate his eutychian doctrines and to bring confusion into the churches without authority or vocation to do so. The old fool is possessed by the devil and does not understand a word that he is talking about. If he is not willing to hold his tongue and to cease to plague me with his books, may the Devil spit on him and excrete over him. Here is my last word, 'May God punish the Satan that is in you, and the mind which has brought you to such things, and the life

which you lead, and all those who have anything in common
with you, sacramentaries, eutychians and the rest; may He
confound you, you and your blasphemies, as it is written,
'They have run, and it is not I that have sent them; they
have spoken without my orders.'"

As has already been mentioned, St. Ignatius thought that, if
the spirit of his Order was to survive, it was absolutely necessary
that two peculiarities should be preserved—that no Jesuits
should accept ecclesiastical dignities and that they should not be
the spiritual directors of women. Against the acceptance of
dignities St. Ignatius had already taken an oath on behalf of
himself and the Society. Difficulties could only arise if this
prohibition should conflict with the supreme duty of obedience
to the Pope, but this, St. Ignatius felt, was only too likely to
happen if care was not taken to prevent it. So many of the
Jesuits were so eminently fitted for posts of high command that
inevitably it would not be long before temporal sovereigns
began to petition the Pope to issue his special injunction. This
happened. Ferdinand, King of the Romans, wanted Bobadilla
to accept the Bishopric of Trieste. Bobadilla refused, and
Ferdinand then fixed on Le Jay, and this time would not take
"No" for an answer. The Imperial Ambassador at Rome was
instructed to press Paul for an injunction and Paul was inclined
to agree to the issue of one. St. Ignatius, however, employed
Margaret of Austria as intermediary, and she was able to persuade Ferdinand to withdraw his petition, while he himself was
able in the end to persuade Paul that his rule was vital to the
welfare of the Society and that the Pope should only force
dignities upon Jesuits when there most literally was no other
person at all capable of performing the duties of the dignity.
"Holy Father," he said, using a famous and important illustration, "I consider the other Orders in the army of the Church
Militant as squadrons of soldiers who remain on the ground
assigned, keep their ranks, stand firm against the enemy and do
not change their position or mode of combat. But we are like
the light horse who are always to be ready, night or day, in

times of alarm and surprise—who attack or support according
to circumstances, go everywhere and skirmish on all sides.
Therefore being obliged to remove constantly from one town
or province to another and even from one end of the earth to
the other at the least intimation from the Vicar of Christ, they
cannot rightly be fixed anywhere." Paul agreed to St. Ignatius'
request, remarking, "It is the first time that any sovereign has
heard such a request as this."

As strict was St. Ignatius in the enforcement of the Order's
other peculiarity. A number of women at one time and another
urged both St. Ignatius and others of the Fathers to accept their
spiritual direction. He refused them all except Isabel Roser, his
benefactress of Barcelona, who had by now followed him to
Rome and with three companions established herself in a little
community of her own. The direction of that little community
he accepted at Paul's special request, but he soon found, as he
said, that it was more trouble to him than the direction of his
whole Society, and, after breaking the news with all gentleness
to Isabel, he petitioned Paul absolutely to forbid to him or to
his Society the acceptance of any such tasks. Paul was persuaded and agreed.

As far as can be judged, St. Ignatius, once he had made up
his mind that the change was necessary, took trouble to treat
Isabel Roser with all the tact that was possible. Yet pious
women are a touchy lot, and she either could not or would not
see that St. Ignatius had done what he had done solely from the
necessities of a general policy. She listened to a nephew, a
Doctor Ferrar, and allowed him to persuade her to commence
a suit for the recovery of some money which she had either given
or lent to the Society. The facts of the case are obscure, but St.
Ignatius certainly maintained that this money was not due. He
suggested that the dispute be submitted to two arbitrators, one
chosen by each side. Roser preferred to carry it before the Pope's
Vicar-substitute, who was at first well disposed towards her,
but, after looking into the case, decided against her and enjoined
upon her silence from her slanders against St. Ignatius. She
obeyed, and it is believed that in later years some correspondence

again passed between them. Yet the old friendship was not renewed. St. Ignatius had, it seems, nothing with which to reproach himself in the dispute, yet, though he nowhere tells us of the secret feelings with which it afflicted him, he must have been among those to whom no unkindness is so hard to bear as that which comes from those to whom we are anxious to show nothing but kindness.

CHAPTER XII

THE COUNCIL OF TRENT

WHAT an extraordinary life was that which St. Ignatius lived at Rome ! We find there the record of days filled with little, petty, wearing disputes, touching but tiny acts of charity such as fill the life of a Breton curé, and, sandwiched between them, come other days, given to the taking of grand decisions by which the life of Europe and of more than Europe is still affected to this day. While St. Ignatius was pleading with Isabel Roser, the delegates were gathering together at the little Alpine town of Trent for the beginnings of that Council at which the whole policy of the Counter-Reformation was to be given its form. St. Ignatius himself remained at Rome, but even from Rome he played his part in the policies of Trent.

Ever since the religious troubles had begun to affect Europe and since the scandals of the times had begun to cause a cry for reform, there had been a steady demand for the submission of Christendom's difficulties to a General Council. The secular princes were loud in the demand, and the Popes were neither able nor willing wholly to refuse it. Yet there were many detailed difficulties in the granting of the demand. As the history of England had so tragically shown, Catholics of the day were not well instructed in the nature of the Papal headship of the Church, and yet, if Europe should lose the authority of that headship, she must certainly fall into chaos. In the evil days of the Great Schism General Councils had put forward inordinate claims of superiority to the Pope. Could a Pope be quite certain that a General Council now would not revive such claims ? If revived, might not the consequence be disastrous for desperate Christendom ?

Again, a Council must meet in some place. That place must

be within the territory of some temporal ruler. Is it possible to be quite certain that other temporal rulers will not be piqued if preference be given to a rival ? or that he who is preferred will not dominate the Council and use the Church for the furtherance of his own secular purposes ?

Old-fashioned books used to lay the whole blame for the delay of the summoning of the Council on the Popes and to ascribe the policy of the Popes entirely to unworthy, dishonest and selfish motives. I have made no attempt to pretend that the characters of the early 16th-century Popes were of at all a spot-less integrity. Yet such sweeping charges cannot be at all sup-ported. There were plenty of difficulties about the summoning of a General Council other than those of the Popes' creation. Anyway, during Paul's pontificate and after the failure of the colloquy between German Catholics and Protestants at Ratisbon in 1541, the difficulties were in a measure overcome. Paul and Charles met at Lucca, and it was agreed between them that Paul should summon a General Council to meet at Trent on Novem-ber 1st, 1542. The Papal legates attended at the agreed date, but Francis and Charles were by that time once more disturbing Europe with war. None but a few Italians were able to appear. The Assembly had clearly no ecumenical nature and had to be adjourned.

Paul, having once agreed to the summoning of a Council, was determined that a Council there should be, whether Charles wished it or not. For he was justly nervous lest Charles, in his anxiety to preserve the political unity of the Empire, might make some inadmissible concessions to the Lutherans. He sent Ales-sandro Farnese to arrange things with Charles. Charles begged Paul to defer the summoning of the Council until Charles' nego-tiations with the Protestants were concluded. It was just these negotiations of which Paul was nervous. He therefore refused and threatened, if Charles was obstinate, that he would transfer the Council from Imperial territory to Bologna or Rome. Charles capitulated and agreed that the Council should be summoned for 1545.

Paul wisely determined not to preside in person. He sent as

his representative legates Giovanni Maria del Monte, Marcello Cervini and Reginald Pole. Of these the two Italians were the real masters of the Council's business. They were destined to be Paul's two successors on the Pontifical throne. Del Monte, the first, entered the Council with no prejudice of good will in favour of Charles or the Imperial cause, for at the sack of Rome in 1527 he had been one of the hostages given by Clement VII. to the Imperialists and would have been murdered by the Landsneckhte in the Campo di Fiori, had not Pompeo Colonna arranged a secret escape for him. Though a strong Papalist, he was a man who brought but little credit to the cause which he served and, when after Paul's death he emerged from the conclave as Julius III., there was little doubt that he had gained the dignity by a very questionable bargain with the Farnese faction. His rule was certainly disgraced by shameless nepotism, while the indiscretion of his flagrant favouritism of the seventeen-year-old Innocenzo del Monte was such that the Pope had only himself to blame for the interpretation which gossip put on their relationship. It was not reasonable to expect much serious effort for reform from such a man.

Cervini, who was to succeed Julius III. as Marcellus II. and who is to-day mainly remembered for the *Missa Papae Marcelli* which Palestrina composed in his honour, was a far better man. The uncle—it is no small claim to fame in itself—of no less a man than Robert Bellarmine, a conservative like del Monte, yet he differed from del Monte as a Huskisson differed from a Sidmouth. It was probably a misfortune for the Church that he, a master of diplomacy, a sincere believer in the urgent necessity for reform of the moral abuses of the Church, was only to survive his elevation to the Papacy twenty-two days.

Reginald Pole, the third of the legates, is well known to all readers of English history. It was to be the tragedy throughout life of this sad, unfortunate man that, while temperament had made him for the cloister, circumstances were to compel him to attempt to ride the whirlwind of the affairs of men—a task for which he was not well-suited and in which he was as little successful at Trent as he was afterwards to be in England. He was a friend of Contarini and had been called to Rome and raised to the purple by Paul III. in pursuance of the Pope's policy of surrounding himself with friends of reform. By temperament he was more inclined to conciliation than either del Monte or Cervini, and for that reason doubtless Paul associated him with them. His personality was also less repugnant to Charles V. But he was greatly the inferior of his colleagues in knowledge of the world and in the arts of the management of men, and his influence at Trent counted for but little. His ill-health soon compelled him to withdraw from a stage on which he had but little opportunity of playing a part of usefulness.

On March 13th, 1545, the legates made their entry into Trent, but the arrangements between Charles and Paul were not finally concluded, and it was not possible to open the Council until December 13th. Even then attendance was by no means as full as had been hoped, especially meagre being the representation of the Empire of which Cardinal Madruzzo, the Bishop of Trent, was the only person who could properly be called a representative. The only members of the Society of Jesus present at the beginning of the Council were Le Jay, representing Otto Truchses, the Cardinal-Archbishop of Augsburg, and a new Father called Corvillon, who was theologian for the Duke of Bavaria.

From the first it was clear that difficulties would arise owing to the two meanings with which people had come to use the word " reform." It was used indifferently to mean a reform of morals, which was desired by the most ardent Catholics, and a reform, or alteration, of doctrine—the object of the Protestants. It was necessary to make it clear that the Council, while anxious for reform in the former sense, would have none of it in the latter. As Carnesecchi put it in his Catholic days, " The Catholic religion is ours already ; all that we desire is that it should be better preached."

All was not easy. The tradition of Conciliar superiority was still alive. Controversy arose even over the very name which the Council should give itself. Some were for a form of words which should hint at the Council's superiority to the Pope.

The legates opposed this and were able to carry the day. Then arose the question whether voting should be by head or, as it had been at Constance, by nations. Paul, ever since his accession, had clearly seen that the new religion of nationalism was the most dangerous of the enemies of the Church—that her future must be a future of relentless war against that vile vice, whether found within or without her fold. The Italians supported Paul, partly from his own lofty motive, partly perhaps because there were many more of their nation than of any other and voting by nation would therefore deprive them of a great advantage. Paul was again victorious.

It was the Spanish bishops of whom the Papal legates had most reason to be afraid. Utterly unsympathetic to reform in the Protestant sense, they were yet firmly and rightly determined to enforce moral reforms upon those countries where standards were laxer than the standards of Spain. The presence of del Monte in the legatine chair was in itself an argument for the necessity of reform as eloquent as any that could be wished. But combined with this spirit, that was admirable, was another that was less admirable. Since the reforms of Ximenes the Spanish clergy had been the best in Christendom, both in morals and learning. Spain, at any rate to a superficial judgment, was the first of nations, and there had grown up among Spaniards a feeling that she was the essentially Catholic nation, that a Catholic who was not a Spaniard was only half a Catholic, and that Spain had a God-given right to the leadership of Catholic Europe. This feeling, found as it was in the breasts of men, able and honourable, though abominably proud, was played upon by Charles V. for his less lofty political purposes.

Paul, in his instructions to the Council, had laid it down with his customary lucidity that the first business of the Council was to be the definition of Catholic dogma, wherever that dogma was in dispute, its second business the reform of abuses. This was but common sense. The enunciation of principle must clearly come first, the application of it second. However, a party under Cardinal Madruzzo argued with that muddle-headed sentimentality which too often passes for practical common sense, that the reform of abuses was more urgent than dogma, and that, when the Church had been purified, then the time would come for the discussion of dogma. This sentimental opposition had the advantage of the support of Charles, who was afraid that clear-cut definitions would force him to an open breach with his Lutheran subjects, while Paul's policy suffered from the disadvantage that among its supporters were people like del Monte, who cared very little either for dogma or for reform, and who were only anxious that the discussions on the one should precede those on the other from the hope of being able to postpone reform until the Greek calends. It was found necessary, against Paul's better judgment, to accept a compromise, suggested by Thomas Campeggio, according to which the discussions on dogma and on reform should proceed simultaneously before different commissions. The rules of procedure were then prepared, and the dogmatic discussions began on April 8th, 1546. The first question to be considered was that of the rule of faith.

Six weeks later, before the discussions had progressed very far—on May 18th—Laynez and Salmeron arrived at Trent as the special theologians of the Holy See—posts which imposed upon them the duty of speaking first and last in all discussions. They came armed with full instructions from St. Ignatius, the text of which is worth quoting.

" As we may glorify God by His favour assisting us, when we strive for the good of souls in our intercourse with a large number of persons, all having a spiritual object; so also if we do not watch over ourselves and if we are not helped by Him, we shall lose much and do harm to those with whom we converse. But since the way of life to which we have bound ourselves obliges us not to shun such intercourse, we shall find it profitable in the Lord in proportion as we are prepared beforehand and follow an exact rule. Therefore I will give you some counsels which may be useful in the Lord, whether you follow them literally or retrench them in some sense. Generally speaking, I earnestly desire that in the exercise of this new employment you should never lose sight of these three principal points.

" 1. In the Council, the greater glory of God and the welfare of the whole Church.

" 2. Out of the Council, your original rule and method of saving souls, which is the object I have principally proposed to myself in this mission.

" 3. The especial care of your own souls, that you may not forget and neglect yourselves, but on the contrary strive, by assiduous watchfulness, to make yourselves daily more worthy of your vocation.

" In the Council you must be slow, rather than prompt, in speaking, considerate and charitable in your opinions of what is done or intended, attentive and calm in listening, taking pains to seize the spirit, desires and intentions of those who speak, so that you may better see when to speak or be silent. In the matters which will be discussed you must state the reasons on both sides so as not to appear attached to your own opinion. You must always, as far as you can, contrive that no one shall be less disposed to peace after hearing your discourses than he was before. If the points controverted are such as oblige you to speak, express your opinions modestly and calmly ; conclude always ' with deference to better judgments ' or some such phrase. Lastly, be well persuaded of this, that to treat worthily of really important subjects, whether human or divine, it is very necessary to discuss them with composure and deliberation, not in haste or in a cursory manner. You should therefore not make the order and time of the discussion suit your leisure and convenience but accommodate the person who wishes to argue with you so that he may the more easily be guided whither God would lead him.

" Out of the Council neglect no means of doing good to your neighbour. Rather seek occasions of hearing confessions, preaching, giving the Exercises, instructing children, visiting the poor in the hospitals, so that the grace of the Holy Spirit may descend more abundantly on the Fathers of the Council, as you will call it down in these acts of humility and charity. In your sermons avoid the points controverted by the heretics, but aim always at moral reform and enforce obedience to the Catholic Church. You must also speak often of the Council and exhort people to pray for its fortunate result. In hearing confessions think that all you say to your penitents may be heard upon the house-tops. For penance desire them to say prayers for the Council. In giving the Exercises at all times speak as you would in public. You will visit the hospitals alternately every four days, that is to say, each of you once a week, at times that will not be inconvenient for the sick. You will comfort them as far as you can, not by words only but also by little gifts. Though in answering questions it is needful to use concise and well-considered language, it is on the contrary desirable to speak with some amplification and with a show of benevolence when you want to excite in your hearers a spirit of piety.

" As to the last point which concerns your own selves and your protection from the evils to which you will be exposed, although you must never neglect what belongs especially to the Institute, you must remember beyond all things to preserve the most perfect union and entire agreement in thought and opinion. Let neither of you trust in his own prudence exclusively ; and, as Claude Le Jay, whom the Cardinal of Augsburg sends to the Council as procurator, will join you in a few days, you will fix a time every evening to confer on what you have done during the day and what you have to do to-morrow. You will decide on the subject of your consultations either by vote or in some other way. In the morning you will deliberate together on the plan of action for the day. You will also twice a day make your examination of conscience. You will put this into execution at latest on the fifth day after your arrival at Trent."

Those who imagine that the Society of Jesus grew through a system of inhuman obedience to the lightest word of a Superior will do well to notice the phrase, " whether you follow them literally or retrench them in some sense." Now, as at all times,

St. Ignatius was willing to grant sensible discretion in the letter of obedience to trusted subordinates.

Salmeron was only thirty-one and Laynez thirty-four. They must, therefore, have been among the youngest of the delegates. They disported themselves with the humility proper to youth rather than with the dignity that might be expected of Papal theologians. Their clothes were at first clean but patched, though they later accepted some new suits which the Spanish bishops offered to them. Outside the Council they were diligent in the performance of those works of charity which St. Ignatius had recommended.

The entertainment that was provided for their creature comforts was not such as to tempt them to forget their vows of poverty. I quote from Mr. Sedgwick's translation the long and amusing letter which Laynez sent to St. Ignatius about it.

"TRENT, *August* 11, 1551.

To FATHER IGNATIUS LOYOLA,

"We will inform your reverence about what has happened to us since we came here and about our lodgings, not to find fault with anybody, unless it be ourselves, but to let you know the facts lest they may be reported in Rome after another fashion.

"When we arrived here, the Very Reverend Legate (Cardinal Marcello Crescenzi) received us, as far as we could judge, with great cordiality, for even before we had got here he had spoken of our coming to many prelates, saying he was glad to have us; and they said nice things about us, as we know both from him and from them. He said he would lodge us both in a room in his house and that an inn should be at once looked up, which he hoped would be near-by in order the better to enjoy our society, and he also hoped that we would regularly dine with him, but if we preferred to dine in our own room dinner should be served there. We kissed his hands and took our leave.

"Our expectation was that he would speak to the Secretary of the Council and tell him to take charge of us until an inn was found. The Secretary took us to his own house and said that, as we were not lodged at an inn, we should come there for just that one night; and he gave us all three, for our joint apartment, a little, tiny, smoky oven of a room with a bed in it and a trucklebed (which when pulled out did not leave space to take two steps in the room). There was no table for us to study at, or write a letter, and as for chairs only one footstool, but there were lots of boots, belonging to him and his valet, and a big wallet, an old harp and the valet's sword, which were kept in our oven. I said to Master Salmeron, ' See here, this is a little more than we bargained for; let's stay at the inn and to-morrow on my way to the palace I will tell the Secretary that, in order not to go changing inns and as long as he said we were to be here only for one night, we had decided to stay at the inn.' But Salmeron thought it was better to come to the oven in spite of the heat in order not to show any signs of discontent with the room or any dissatisfaction. So Salmeron slept that night upon a chest, and John and I upon the beds; but the next day Salmeron betook himself to the house of the Bishop of Verona, which was near-by, to sleep, but though I was offered the same, in order that we should not all leave the apartment, John and I continued to sleep in the oven. One day the legate's Secretary came and asked if we lacked anything; and I answered, with my usual freedom or foolishness, ' You can see, we lack everything.' And he said, ' That's so, but at the present moment what do you need ? ' So I answered, ' At least we need a candle to go to bed by.' Then he asked, ' What more ? ' And I said, laughing all the time, ' A candle-stick to put it in.' However the keeper of the store-closet was out, so we couldn't have a candle that night; nevertheless we were the gainers, for we got a torch to go to bed by.

" After about a week, having paid visits upon almost everybody, we went to the Cardinal to beg him to give us a room; for everybody was asking us where we lodged, and a good many people wanted to come and see us, but we did not think that we could receive visitors where we were. He told us that they would surely give us a room; however, the owner of the house where he wished to lodge us was away, but that, as soon as he came back, he would take us in. The owner did return in three or four days and offered us rooms; but, as the house was new and still unfinished, and as there were neither doors nor windows, he asked for an advance of ten ducats on the rent in order to complete the rooms. When we went to ask the Secretary of the Council for the ducats—I was present—the Secretary answered sharply, that he was a dreadful man, etc. After the landlord had gone I said to the Secretary, ' It would have been a good thing if you had given him those ducats for in the end they come out of the rent and it makes little difference.' To which he said: ' What rent do you think that we shall have to pay for those rooms per month, anyhow, that you increase the cost that we shall have to bear in hiring them?' I answered a little indignantly, ' Well, there is some expense for everyone that comes to the Council; do you think you spend much for us? Don't you know that we don't eat our bread for nothing? but that we work as hard as the others? The Pope knows that, and that is why he sent us; and you have done a thing that has neither head nor tail, in putting two priests, sent by the Pope, into your servant's room, and such a room, that I am astonished at you. And since you are not spending your own money you ought to spend according to the orders you receive from the Pope and not keep us all the time where you do; Salmeron had to sleep on a chest the first night and hasn't been willing to sleep there again; and I should have liked to do the same if it had not been that I didn't want to show your shortcomings. But I promise you I shall tell the Cardinal how we are situated, and that I shall write it to Rome.'

"That's the whole story and the full extent of my bad temper. The good man was scandalised, and (so I have heard) told the Cardinal; and I, quite without anger, rather to please Master Angelo, Secretary of the Council, and the Cardinal, told the Cardinal after supper, laughing in the presence of Master Angelo at all that had passed. I didn't blame Master

Angelo but rather my own bad temper and freedom, although at the time it seemed to me right, and seems to me so now, and that's why I told the Cardinal. His Reverence, fore-warned by Master Angelo, said that our having no rooms was from no lack of good-will on his part but because of the chance absence of the houseowner; and he excused Master Angelo, saying that as we were in the habit of preaching patience we must also practise it. And I told him truthfully that I had not done this in order to escape discomfort, for the year before I had passed three months in Africa under a sheet, suffering from heat by day and from cold by night, and that in the oven I could laugh and be content, but that I had spoken out be-cause it was not fit and proper for us to have no conveniences for study, whether to prepare to preach, to read or anything else, nor towards those that sent us, nor towards His Emin-ence, nor for any members of the Council who might wish to come and see us. And I told him truthfully that I had not expressed any discontent to anyone except to His Eminence and to Master Angelo, and that he should take this freedom on my part as in the line of my duty; and that if I had done wrong in any way he should impose penance upon me and I would perform it very gladly, provided that he would har-bour no ill feeling against the Society or against us, and that in time, if the Council continued, he would see our fidelity and our wish to serve him in every good thing that we could. In this way we remain good friends; and I at least had the satisfaction of telling him what was on my mind. And next day, seeing that the matter of the house dragged, for the owner had gone away again and the greater part of it was full of the Cardinal's retinue and there was no place for religious services, and it was expensive for Master Angelo, we went to see our old host of last time and got from him the same rooms we had had before, for so much a month, and he did it most willingly, offering them to us at once and, as he needs the money and gives us three rooms, washing and cooking and what else we need, we have agreed to give him three crowns a month. And so, as the Cardinal is satisfied, we have come here with his permission and on the understanding that we shall dine with him once a week. And His Eminence supplies us from his own house with a generous portion of bread and wine and ten crowns a month, at the Pope's charges, which we asked for, three for our lodgings and seven for other expenses, as Trent is dearer than last time. The Cardinal is to give us also all we need for clothes, etc.; for he does not wish us to take anything from anybody else. We made the same arrangement last time with the Cardinal of Santa Cruz that we do now.

" We have been four days at this inn after having spent eleven or twelve in the oven. . . . We have wanted to write this to Your Reverence, not to make a complaint of anyone, for we certainly have none, but in order that, in case complaints may have been written from here (but we don't think so) you may know the facts and be able to make use of them. And also because, in accordance with my character, I should not be at peace if I had not advised you of this fault so that you might correct me. . . .

"LAYNEZ."

Trent at Council time was clearly very much like Liverpool in Grand National Week, and hotel-keepers and the owners of rooms saw a chance of quick enrichment which they did not think that they could afford to neglect.

Laynez was the possessor of two qualities, not very commonly found together—great learning and great intellectual ability. He had a phenomenal memory, and had assigned to him the duty of every day giving a résumé of the previous discussions, and, in order that all might hear him, a special seat was assigned to him among the bishops.

They had not been there a week when they found themselves prominent in the discussion on the Immaculate Conception of Our Lady. The Jesuits defended it and furnished Bishop Paceco of Jaen with arguments in its favour. Melchior Cano, the Dominican, their enemy, opposed, arguing that, though Our Lady was unstained, yet She could only be said to be Immaculate from

Her birth, not from Her conception. The question was for the moment adjourned.

Meanwhile it was decided that the Nicene Creed was the "*Symbolum fidei quo sancta Romana ecclesia utitur.*" Scripture and tradition were declared to be of equal authority, and it was claimed that the Church alone had the right to expound Scripture. Nacchianti, the Bishop of Chioggia, maintained that Scripture was the sole rule of Faith, but only six could be found to support him in such a patent defiance of Catholic teaching.

At the same time the discussions on discipline had aroused the high tempers of many—especially the debate whether the residence of Bishops in their sees was necessary *iure divino* or only *lege ecclesiastica*—whether, in other words, Bishops had their powers directly from God or from the Pope. Nacchianti was again among the obstreperous. But the real fun was to come when in June the Council took up the discussion of the question of Justification. The Neapolitan Bishop of La Cava was for Justification by Faith Alone, and, in order to enforce his argument, took hold of the beard of the Greek Bishop of Chiron and pulled it out. When Greek meets Neapolitan then comes the tug of beard. Seripando, the General of the Augustinians, attempted to preserve the peace by advocating a mediatory view, which had first been put forward by Contarini in his *Tractatus de Justificatione*. He distinguished between an " inherent " and an " imputed " righteousness : the " inherent " righteousness, the righteousness of works, was by itself of no avail ; our hope lay in the imputed righteousness of Christ. It was in their opposition to this view that Laynez and Salmeron were for the first time able to play a dominating part in the Council. Laynez answered to Seripando that the imputed righteousness became involved in the inherent. We must rely on the merits of Christ not because in themselves they complete our justification but because they produce good works in us. Good works in us are necessary for our salvation. The Jesuits won a sufficient victory to free Catholic theology from any taint of the Lutheran theory of Justification, though the decree that was passed was sufficiently ambiguous to require the further Jansenist controversy before the Catholic doctrine was to be defined with unmistakable clearness.

It has been well said that " if we would understand Roman Catholicism as an organisation between 1520 and 1700 we must study the Council of Trent ; if we would understand it as a religion we must study the Spiritual Exercises of St. Ignatius." This is true, and it would be hard to exaggerate the importance of the great Council. Yet we must not allow its historical importance to give us a false notion of the dignity of its actual meetings. They often resembled an Irish election meeting more nearly than that restrained and distinguished gathering of which we gain an impression from the memory of Titian's great canvas at the Louvre. Personal quarrels had not gone out with the Bishop of Chiron's beard. Cardinal Madruzzo was spokesman for the Imperial interests, and relations between him and del Monte became more and more strained. Paceco took Madruzzo's side, accusing del Monte—falsely, as it proved—of falsifying the votes, until at last del Monte told them that he would no longer have them sitting near him. There was a great tantrum of tempers on all sides, which were only at last quieted by the Archbishop of Palermo, who knelt before the legates and with tears in his eyes besought them for the love of Christ to suppress their resentment. Paceco was induced to apologise to del Monte, who, however, only acknowledged the apology with a curt nod. When Madruzzo followed and received the same treatment, he lost his temper and burst out into a torrent of abuse. Del Monte was able to give as good as he got, and he finished by a threat to transfer the Council to Italy. He managed to persuade Paul to support his threats. " The Council continued to sit at Trent, till the said Paul for certain reasons (Heaven grant that they were good ones) wished to transfer it to Bologna," wrote the disgusted Charles V.

St. Ignatius spoke of recalling Laynez to Florence, but Cervini wrote that his presence at Trent was indispensable and St. Ignatius gave way.

Thus the debates on Justification drew to their end. Before any further questions could be tackled a new and yet more potent argument in favour of the transfer of the Council had arisen. The plague had broken out at Trent and carried off the General of the Friars Minor and the Bishop of Cappaccio. Thus influenced, the Council by thirty-eight votes to fourteen, with four abstentions, on March 11th, 1547, decided to transfer itself to Bologna. Paceco and the other Spanish Bishops remained sulkily at Trent, and Paul was displeased that del Monte should have acted so precipitately.

At the same time the general political situation was modified in three ways. First, Henry VIII. of England had died in January. Second, three weeks after the vote for the transfer, Francis I. died and was succeeded by the more papalistic Henry II., who agreed to affiance his daughter, Diana, to Orazio Farnese. Third, when Salmeron, who had caught the fever at Trent and suffered from it at Verona, arrived in convalescence at Bologna in April, he heard the news that John Frederick, the rebel Protestant Elector of Saxony, had been broken by the Imperialists at the great battle of Muhlberg in Northern Germany.

While they were at Bologna Laynez received from St. Ignatius a letter in which he expressed his wish to resign the generalship in favour of Laynez or some other Father. From deference to St. Ignatius' wish the Fathers met and voted on the proposal, but it was rejected unanimously. St. Ignatius, accepting the decision as from God, prepared himself for a further term of office. The first problem that he had to deal with was that of Bobadilla. Bobadilla had been with the Imperial army at Muhlberg, having been sent thither in company with Ottavio Farnese, and remaining after Farnese's return. Looking upon the war, I suppose, as a crusade, he threw himself into it with great enthusiasm and even managed to get himself slightly wounded in the battle. He was up again at once, preaching and disputing throughout Germany with enormous energy. So strong was the position which he built up for himself that, when in 1548 Charles published the decree known as the Interim of Augsburg, by which permission was given to the Protestants to have the cup in communion and a married clergy, and certain modifications in doctrine were hinted at, Bobadilla violently attacked it. Charles dismissed him from the Court, though without any offensiveness. But Paul III., who was by now on thoroughly bad terms with Charles and had withdrawn his troops from Germany—who indeed suspected Charles, possibly with justice, of connivance at the murder of his son, Pier Luigi, at Piacenza on September 10th, 1547—condemned the Interim. Although himself prepared to make considerable disciplinary concessions to the German Protestants, yet he denied to Charles any right whatsoever to decide questions of Catholic doctrine and refused to censure Bobadilla. Germany, Paul thought, was going the way of England. Charles, as secular ruler, had the right to decide what practices should be permitted, but he had no right to decide what practices were Catholic.

St. Ignatius, however, was furious and would not allow Bobadilla into the Jesuit house at Rome. For Ignatius' orthodoxy was such as to make him constitutionally antipathetic to those who were "*plus Catholique que le Pape.*" "How many Popes are there?" he once asked Otelli, when that preacher had said in a sermon that the Pope "ought to undertake a campaign against the vices of the people of Rome," and on being told "One," had continued, "How, then, do you presume to make mention from the pulpit of a person so exalted and even speak of his conduct as if you could judge what he ought to do?" The Pope had the right, in St. Ignatius' view, to condemn Charles, but Bobadilla had no such right. He had no more business than Charles himself to anticipate the decisions of the Church, and St. Ignatius, always ready to defy the great ones of the earth if they should defy the Church, had far too keen a sense both of tactics and of policy to allow his subordinates to indulge in private heresy-hunts of their own. The fact that Bobadilla was eventually proved to be right as a theologian did not at all, in St. Ignatius' eyes, lessen his guilt and folly in inserting himself and the Society into a controversy in which it was not necessary for them to involve themselves.

CHAPTER XIII

THE DYING OF PAUL III

THE conflict between Paul and Charles was working itself out to a sad and tragic end. As has been said, it had led to the assassination of Paul's son, Pier Luigi, on September 10th, 1547. Mendoza, the Spanish Ambassador in Rome, has left us the story of how the news came to Rome. Paul came down to the Consistory in more than his usual good spirits, " talking of his good fortune and comparing himself to the Emperor Tiberius "—I cannot imagine why. During the morning news came in from Piacenza. Gonzaga, Charles' governor of Milan, was certainly guilty of plotting the murder. Possibly Charles himself had a hand in it.

Paul was an old man now, too old to travel far or fast along the paths of adventure. He toyed with the idea of a grand alliance with France and the Venetians against the prince who was believed to be the murderer of his favourite son. The marriage of Orazio Farnese with the French princess, Diana, was to be hurried on. Paul's contemporaries assumed that he would allow the desire for vengeance to be the dominator of his policies.

The Interim of Augsburg was published, and Paul, as I have said, condemned it. For a few angry months the plans for the punishment of Charles were pushed eagerly forward. Then more and more persistently the whispers began to go round that Paul was losing interest in the grand political projects. He was an old man ; he was a very intelligent man ; he was a pious man, and after the first blaze of his anger had subsided he began to wonder whether the devotion of his closing years to a family blood-feud was in truth the best commemoration of the murder of his son. Had not the great sorrow perhaps been sent to him by the mercy of God in order to call him, before it was too late, to repentance for his great sin of nepotism by which he had so foully blotted an escutcheon that would otherwise have been so nearly untarnished ?   He turned to God.

The Farnese grandsons had little sympathy with any such train of theological speculation.   The possession of Parma and Piacenza was in their eyes of very much more importance than the state of their grandfather's soul, and the murder of their uncle, Pier Luigi, for whose unpleasant character there is more evidence than that so readily produced by Benvenuto Cellini, not wholly a disadvantage, since it meant that there was one less to share the cake.   The two lessons that they learnt from the troubles of Paul's conscience were, that the old man was break-ing up and that it was best to make hay while the sun still shone. They got into negotiations with Charles to see if a bargain could be struck, and Cardinal Gambara, who was in the gang, secretly proposed to Mendoza, Charles' Ambassador, that Charles should cede Siena to the Farnese.   In return " the Pope must re-establish the Council in Trent, and not only proceed in other respects according to the Emperor's desire (as, for example, by acknow-ledging his right to Burgundy), but also declare Charles his successor on the Papal throne."   In support of this singular proposal Gambara adduced the most delicious argument that can ever have been adduced in favour of any candidate's Papal claims.   " The climate of Germany," he says, " is cold, that of Italy is warm ; and, for a man who suffers from gout, as the Emperor does, warm countries were healthful."   Such con-sideration !

Such proposals were more easily made than implemented. Paul, even in the eighties, was not a man who allowed others to do his promising for him.   And the news soon came that, far from agreeing to some bargain with the Emperor, Paul was actually proposing to procure Piacenza to the Church to whom it belonged.   The Farnese could hardly believe their ears.   They had not realised that the old man was as bad as all that.

At first they tried to dissuade him.   They played on those astrological superstitions which Paul shared with most of his contemporaries.   The day fixed for the Consistory at which the new policy was to be announced was St. Roque's Day, notoriously, they said, a most unlucky day for announcing anything.   Then they tried arguments.   They professed concern for the true welfare of the Church.   Would the Church really be the gainer from the exchange of Camerino for Piacenza ?   Was there not a danger in the accumulations of temporal power ?   My kingdom, after all, they ventured to remind his Holiness, is not of this world.

The old man was contemptuous and adamant.   He sent word to Camillo Orsino, the Governor of Parma, bidding him hold that city for the Church and for her alone.   To the Farnese there remained but one weapon, the weapon of rebellion against their Pope, their grandfather and their benefactor.   This they did not scruple to use.   Ottavio Farnese made an attempt to take Parma from Orsino by force, and when his enterprise failed he wrote to Paul that unless Parma were delivered to him he would make an alliance with the Imperialists and call in the aid of Gonzaga, the suspected murderer of Pier Luigi.

There was a rumour abroad that the quarrel between Ottavio and Paul was a staged quarrel, arranged so that the grandfather might be saved from the reproach of having alienated the Church's lands, while the grandson might be able to continue to enjoy the possession of those lands.   This rumour was certainly false.   There is abundant evidence—particularly that of the conversation of Cardinal Este—that Paul was both sincere and heartbroken.   The ingratitude of Ottavio had taken from him all but one of the natural consolations of life.   He could only comfort himself with the thought that at least his favourite grandson, Alessandro, was still innocent of treachery, and devoted to his interests.

Then, as the autumn of 1549 drew out into cold winter, gradually the knowledge was forced into his shrewd, unwilling mind that Alessandro, too, was with his enemies, and was using his confidence only to betray him.   On All Souls' Day, November 2nd, we have the record of the Venetian Ambassador that Paul confessed to him that he now knew the worst.   On the next day the old man left Rome and the Romans whom he loved, and went up into the hills to his country house on Monte Cavallo. He sent for Alessandro. I do not fancy that Alessandro was glad to go, for there was something that was hardly of the world in the power of this old man's wrath, nor was the interview at all less terrible than can have been expected. He tore Alessandro's red hat from his head and stamped it on the ground.

Everyone waited for the next developments—the dismissal of Alessandro, the vigorous counter-measures. They were not to be. So great had been his grief and the power of his anger that the old man's strength could not stand it. On November 10th he was dead. He was eighty-three, but there was no senile decay. "Internally," reported the physicians, "he was found in the most healthy state, and as one likely to live some years; but there were three drops of coagulated blood in his heart, judged to have been caused by the movements of anger."

The people of Rome at least had always appreciated the merits of Paul, one of the greatest of all Roman citizens, and it was through sorrowing crowds, elbowing each other to kiss his toe, that they brought his body home, the body of a great man to whom the modern world owes more than it has ever cared to recognise. The Conclave met. Pole was at first within a vote or two of election; five Cardinals, it was said, voted for Ignatius, but in the end, del Monte, as has been told, struck a bargain with the Farnese that they be allowed to keep Parma, and emerged from it as Julius III. Charles' gout did not have the opportunity of trying that Vatican cure which Gambara had recommended for it.

Moses was not allowed to enter the Promised Land. It was better that he should meet God, having paid the atonement for his one great sin. Perhaps it was the same with Paul. He was so great a man that it would be an insult to attempt to excuse his nepotism with pleas that might well do for lesser men. It is true that he but sinned according to the customs of the age— but then it is the business of such men as Paul Farnese to rise above the customs of their age. It is best to say of his nepotism that it was shameless, it was inexcusable and it was punished.

But it was his only large fault. In his hostility to Charles and Charles' perilous approaches to the favour of the German Protestants, in his superstition, in that quality which von Ranke with somewhat priggish stupidity calls his " worldliness," but which I should prefer to call his love of the colour and beauty of life, in his, perhaps, inordinate love of the pageant—in all these he may not have been wholly free from blame, but at least the issues are confused, the count against him not clear. All the tales about the irregularity of his normal regimen are ridiculous, as, for instance, Cellini's story about his solemnly getting drunk and going out and vomiting once every week.[1] From the time of his ordination to the priesthood there is no reason at all to doubt that he abstained wholly from sexual sin. He had a right to the boastful contrition with which he quoted from the Psalms on his death-bed, " *Si mei non fuerint dominati, tunc immaculatus ero, et emundabor a delicto maximo.*"

So Paul died, and his grandsons did not survive him so very long—neither any of the others, nor Alessandro,whose household according to Ribadaneira who had, it will be remembered, been a member of it, was " a bog, a quagmire, an abyss of hell," but who, it is only fair to say, did at least continue his grandfather's great tradition of support of the Society of Jesus and in 1568 began the building of the present Church of the Gesu. There remained, however, of Paul's seed a strange and vigorous race that ruled in Parma for a hundred and fifty years. One gallant and able captain came of his blood—he who would have been the invader of England, had the Armada succeeded—and at last with the 18th century the line that had thus strangely begun, ended with that wild woman, " the termagant of Europe," Elizabeth Farnese. Spanish Bourbons became the descendants of Paul, and of all the strange jokes which heredity has played there is none stranger than that which decreed that the blood of

---

[1] How could Cellini have known of such a habit as this save through some fourth-hand gossip ? Paul, as a rule, ate and drank, and, *a fortiori* one may presume, vomited alone.

the two great rivals of Europe of the 16th century, Paul Farnese and Charles V., should in the end be mingled in the veins of the wretched Charles IV. and his poltroon son, Ferdinand, who trembled before Napoleon, who betrayed their country and who lost their Empire.

CHAPTER XIV

BORGIA, RODRIGUEZ AND LAYNEZ

"WE have," Sadoleto wrote in pessimism to Contarini on March 13th, 1536, "in our Pope an eminent ruler of the Church who only thinks and wishes what is worthy of him; but he is not stronger than the perversity of the age." It is Paul's glory that substantially he refuted this prediction. The Pope who urged the faithful to a more frequent communion, the summoner of Trent, the patron of Michelangelo, the patron of Copernicus, the patron of Ignatius Loyola, he was the triumpher over "the perversity of the age." Before the record of so great a man it is hard to decide which is the largest of his many claims to fame, but perhaps on the whole he was greatest in that work with which we are concerned in this book, in his discerning patronage of St. Ignatius and his Society. Ignatius well understood how great a friend he had lost in him. For the moment he said no more about resigning the Generalship. All questions of future policy were postponed till the general meeting of the Fathers of the Society, to take place in celebration of the Jubilee in the next year, 1550. Before that meeting he laid the Constitutions which he had drawn up—those Constitutions which, with a few further alterations so as to make them more easily applicable to variety of time and circumstance, were afterwards to be approved by Paul IV., and of which Laynez, St. Ignatius' successor, was to say, "The Constitutions of Father Ignatius would alone suffice to reform and govern all the religious orders in the Church."

In many ways the most interesting pages in the life of St. Ignatius during these years are those which record his growing intimacy with St. Francis Borgia. At the time of Faber's death, St. Ignatius said that God had intimated that the Society was soon to receive a new recruit who was to make good the great loss.   At the same time, Francis Borgia in Spain had taken a vow that if he survived Eleanor, his wife, he would devote himself wholly to God.   In 1548 Eleanor died.   Ever since the day when Francis and Ignatius had passed one another in the street of Alcala, Francis had been in touch with the activities of the Society.   He now wrote to St. Ignatius, begging to be allowed to enter the Society's novitiate.   Though overjoyed, yet St. Ignatius did not at all relax his usual circumspection even in the reception of such a recruit.   He wrote back a letter full of the highest prudence, of the completest knowledge of the world and of the difficulties which Francis must overcome :

" Most Illustrious Senor,

          " The resolution you have taken, which is inspired by Divine grace, gives me great joy.   May the angels and all the blessed spirits eternally thank God for this in Heaven, for we cannot sufficiently praise Him on earth for the favour He has shown this small Society in calling you to enter it.   I hope that His Divine Providence will make your admission very advantageous to your spiritual advancement, and that of many who will profit by your example.   For us who are already members of the company of Jesus, excited by your fervour, we shall begin anew to serve the Divine Father Who has sent us such a brother and chosen such a labourer for this new vineyard, whereof He has willed, unworthy that I am, that I should have the charge.   Therefore I receive you at once, in the Lord's name, for our brother, and in this relation you will always be very dear to me, as one ought to be who enters into the House of God with such generosity as you have shown, in order to serve Him perfectly.   As to what you ask me respecting the time and manner of your public reception, after having much recommended the matter to God both by myself and others, it appears to me that in order to acquit yourself of all obligations, the change should be made leisurely and cautiously, to the greater glory of Our Lord. So that you may gradually arrange your affairs in such a manner that without any secular interference you may before long find yourself free from all impediments to your holy wishes. To explain further and with more detail, I think that, as your daughters are old enough to marry, you should seek to dispose of them according to their quality, and that you should also affiance the Marquis if a suitable person can be found. For your other sons it is not sufficient that they have the protection of their elder brother who will possess the dukedom ; you must also leave them enough to complete their studies in one of the universities, and to live suitably in the world. No doubt if they are such characters as they should be and as I hope, the Emperor will favour them in proportion to your services, and the friendship he has always shown you. Moreover, you ought to push on the buildings you have begun, for I wish all your family affairs to be terminated when your change is made known. But as you are well grounded in letters, I would have you apply diligently to the study of theology, and I hope this science will be useful to you for the service of God. I should even like, if possible, that you should take a Doctor's degree in your University of Gandia. But as the world cannot understand actions like this, I would have it done privately and remain a secret till time and circumstances, by the grace of God, set us at liberty. Other things may be arranged from day to day as they occur, and as I shall write you regularly I need say no more now. I wait for a speedy answer, and I pray the Supreme Goodness to bestow on you more and more of His Divine mercies."

Special leave was given, and Araoz, St. Ignatius' nephew, received Francis' first vows privately in the ducal chapel at Gandia. He was now Brother Francis in the eyes of the Church ; to the world he was still the Duke of Gandia, the manager of the great affairs of his estate. St. Ignatius was one of the few who were admitted into the secret of his interior life of devotion and asceticism. He sent to him advice full of that deep wisdom which experience had brought to him. As always, he was the enemy of a too rigid asceticism.

" When I learnt your practices in spiritual things, as well as in external, for the profit of your soul, I found truly a new cause for rejoicing in the Lord. . . . Yet as I remark in Our Lord that some of these are needful at one time and not at another and . . . even become useless, I wish to tell you, in the presence of the Divine Majesty, what I think on this subject, since your lordship asks my opinion.   First, for the time you have fixed for exercise, either interior or external, I think you might abridge half. . . . For as you no longer want so many arms to conquer the enemy, I think, in Our Lord, that you would do better if you devote half this time to governing your estate, to profitable conversation and to study. . . . But keep your soul at the same time in peace and repose, ready to receive the communications of Our Lord, for it is a great virtue and grace when we can enjoy Him in many employments and places.   Secondly, as to fasting and abstinence, I think it more for the glory of God to preserve and strengthen the digestion and natural powers than to weaken them. . . . I desire then that you will consider that, as soul and body are given you by God, your Creator and Master, you will have to give account of both, and for His sake you should not weaken your bodily nature because the spiritual could not (then) act with the same energy.   If I was pleased once to see you fast . . . rigorously, I cannot be so in the future, because I see that this fasting and abstinence prevent the stomach from . . . even digesting the simple aliments necessary to sustain life.   I rather advise you to eat of all permitted food, and, as often as you are hungry, giving no offence to your neighbour, for we ought to love the body and wish it well when it obeys and assists the soul ; and thus the soul has . . . more strength and energy to serve and glorify our Creator and Master.

" As to the third point—of personal penances—I desire you for Our Lord's sake to avoid drawing the smallest drop of blood.   And if hitherto you have received, as I believe, a special grace and attraction for this and all the penances I have spoken of, I do not hesitate to assert, without giving proofs of it, that you will do better to omit these things in future."

" A sound mind in a sound body," he concludes, in language which the supporters of the English public school system are apt to look upon as their own exclusive monopoly, " is the most useful instrument wherewith to serve God."

Once during these years Francis was even so unfortunate as to incur St. Ignatius' displeasure. Two of the Jesuits stationed at Gandia conceived the desire of throwing up their responsibilities and of retiring into the solitude of the desert. St. Ignatius thought that Francis had at least not done as much as he should have done to dissuade them from this, which he looked on as a betrayal of their vocation. He was angry. However, the Fathers in the end consented to be obedient, and the trouble blew over. In the next year, 1550, the attempt to impose upon Francis the dignity of the Cardinalate for the first time revealed to the world the secret step which he had taken.

During these same years we find St. Ignatius actively forwarding the work of the Society in Germany. The lesson that he had learnt from the civil war and from the fiasco of Trent was that the problems of Germany could be solved neither by arms nor by political arrangements. The only hope lay in the provision of adequate Catholic teaching—a provision that was more pitifully wanting in Germany than in any other country of Europe. Therefore when Duke Wilhelm of Bavaria asked for two Jesuit professors for the University of Ingolstadt, St. Ignatius replied by commending to the Duke the example of John III. of Portugal, and by urging him to establish a Jesuit seminary. Duke Wilhelm agreed, and there were sent Le Jay, who had already taught at Ingolstadt, Salmeron and Canisius— " the incomparable Canisius," the archives of the town describe him. Duke Wilhelm, however, was unable to fulfil his promise, and the Jesuits had to be transferred to other places in Germany. A little later Ignatius sent further missions to Vienna and other German towns at the request of Ferdinand, King of the Romans, while in town after town of Italy a work was being carried on similar to that in Vienna. In 1552, St. Ignatius, working in co-operation with Cardinal Morone, established a German college at Rome, destined to an existence of the greatest difficulty.

In Africa work of a different nature had fallen to the Jesuits. As we have already said, life on the Mediterranean coast during these years was robbed of all its security by the devastating raids of North African pirates. Hayradin Barbarossa in his day had been the scourge of the Christians, and there had now come as his successor Dragut, who, sailing out from the Tunisian port of Mehedia, swept the seas with a broom at his mast-head, like Van Tromp a hundred years later. Up till now Charles V.'s efforts to suppress this piracy had not met with much success. It was determined to make a further attempt, which should not, like its predecessors, fail through the fault of underrating the enemy. A formidable expedition was prepared, and Juan de Vega, Viceroy of Naples, was put at its head. Laynez accompanied it as its chaplain.

To the credit of Julius III. it must be recorded that he was at least an ardent supporter of the works of the Society in all parts of the world, and St. Ignatius was able to procure from him a participation for the army in the privileges of the Jubilee of 1550. The announcement of this concession, contained in a letter sent by St. Ignatius to Laynez, was read out to the army, and Laynez followed it by an address in which he said :

"It is fit that you should remember, soldiers, how different our weapons are from those of the enemy. They fight for plunder and vainglory and wider dominions; we take up arms for the pure love of Christ, ready to brave all dangers and spill our blood to defend our altars and our homes. Great things are done by courage and strength ; but we must confide not in them only, but in the protection of God, on Whom victory depends. You must fight indeed, and bravely, but in camp you must behave as pious Christians, for it would be wicked indeed if, while fighting against the enemy, you were also to wage war against Omnipotent God.

You will make Him propitious to you, if you add goodness and piety to your valour in war. Therefore it is not for wealth and plunder that you should fight, but for the greater glory of God, which should be always before your eyes, so that the pacification of the world and the general safety of our people may be effected by your arms."

The menace of the Mahommedan was still real enough to justify such language.

The expedition was immediately successful, though it involved Charles in trouble with the Sultan, who looked upon Dragut as his vassal. Tunis was captured on August 10th, and Laynez was able to say Mass in a converted mosque.

There was further work for Laynez to do as soon as the African expedition was over.

He returned to Italy, and soon afterwards St. Ignatius fell seriously ill. It looked as if it would be necessary for the Society to elect its second General. While saying his Mass on Christmas Day, 1550, St. Ignatius had a seizure. At first it was thought that the end had come, and even in convalescence he did not think that he would be again fit for the responsibilities of the Generalship. He wrote to the other Fathers:

" To my dearest Brothers in Our Lord, of the company of Jesus,—What I have considered and judged best for the greater praise and glory of the Divine Majesty, being moved neither by any inward nor outward emotion and after pondering for many months and years, I will now declare as in the presence of my Creator and Lord Who will one day judge me for eternity—according to truth and free from all disquiet. When I regard my many sins and failings, my many weaknesses of soul and body, I have often arrived at the full conviction that I want infinitely, so to speak, the force necessary to bear this burden of the Society which they have laid upon me. Therefore I wish the matter to be well considered in Our Lord and another chosen who may fill this place of governing the Society better, or at least less ill, than I, and that I may make over this charge to him. And not only is this my wish, but I have also sufficient reason to judge that it ought to be made over even to one who will do only as well as I, not only to one who would do better, or not so ill.   After considering all this, I now lay down my charge and renounce it, without reserve or condition, in the name of the Father and the Son and the Holy Ghost, One God and my Creator.   I pray and conjure the professed with all my soul, in the Lord's name, and also those whom they may think proper to join to themselves in this consultation, that they will accept this, my proposal, which is so justified in the presence of the Divine Majesty.   And if among those who have to decide on this there should arise any difference of opinion, I pray them for the love of God Our Lord that they will earnestly recommend the matter to the Divine Majesty, that His most holy will may be done to His greater honour and the general good of souls and of the whole company, so that all may be for ever directed for His greater and Divine praise and glory."

One, Oviedo, was for taking him at his word.   The others refused.   St. Ignatius bowed to their will.

Laynez, in the end to be St. Ignatius' successor, was for the moment free to continue in the great work he had begun. Paul III. had put himself into a position where it would have been hard for him, without loss of dignity, to have agreed to the reconstitution of the Council at Trent.   But Julius III. inherited no responsibility for his predecessor's *amour propre*. Besides, quarrelling with Charles V. was hard work, and Julius was not very fond of hard work.   He therefore agreed that the Council should meet again at Trent.

Even now there were difficulties.   The good that Paul III. had done had certainly not been interred in his bones, but nevertheless the evil lived after him.   The problem of Parma and Piacenza remained to trouble Europe and the Church. Henry II. demanded Parma for his son-in-law, Orazio Farnese, and announced that, until it was given, he would boycott the Council.   Nevertheless, the Council met and held its first public session on September 1st, 1551. The organisation was different from that which had been adopted at the first meeting. Instead of the three Papal delegates, there was now only one, Cardinal Crescenzio. He was assisted by two nuncios, Pighini, Archbishop of Manfredonia, and Lippomano, Bishop of Verona. Lippomano's brother, a knight of the Teutonic Order, had given lodging to Laynez in Venice twelve years before, and had made liberal benefactions to the Society both in Venice and Padua. Among the emissaries whom Charles sent to the Council was that Martin de Olave who, as has been mentioned, had given alms to the begging Ignatius when he came to Alcala to undergo his course of studies in the university there. Fortune had smiled on him in the meanwhile. He was now the Emperor's chaplain, but though Polanco, St. Ignatius' secretary, was his friend, he in general bore no love to the new Society. He flattered himself that they had cunning plots to get him to Rome and make a Jesuit of him. At Trent for the first time he came across Laynez and Salmeron, and he accepted for himself that vocation into which he had so suspected others of entrapping him. He resigned all and became a Jesuit.

As at the first meeting, Laynez and Salmeron were present as Papal theologians. The doctrine of the Eucharist was the first to be discussed, and from the very beginning it was clear that the Jesuits were going to play a part in the Council even more prominent than that which they played at the first meeting. Laynez in particular seems to have astonished all by feats that were barely credible. As Papal theologian, he had the doubtful privileges of speaking for three hours and speaking first. He began by expressing his regret at having to speak before he had heard the opinion of so many eminent and learned men. He then went on to ridicule the Protestant claim to find in the Bible the sole authority and to oppose to this unbalanced view the full Catholic doctrine. He would not, he said, quote any author the entire works of whom he had not read. He then proceeded to quote thirty-six authors at great length, from memory and without, it was said, a fault of a single word. " The Fathers Laynez and Salmeron," wrote the Bishop of

Modena, " have splendidly supported our side against the Protestants, respecting the Eucharist. I think myself fortunate in living in an age when I can see and hear these Fathers who are as learned as they are good." Such was the position that Laynez established for himself that, when shortly afterwards he fell ill of a fever, it was agreed that the Council either should not meet or should only transact matters of trifling importance on the days on which he was not able to be present.

Charles V. called on the Protestants to send their theologians to the Council and to state their case. The Protestants were not very keen on coming. Not unnaturally they remembered what had happened to John Huss and Jerome of Prague at Constance. They therefore demanded for themselves a more ample safe conduct, and, from the Council, a declaration of independence of the Pope. Julius III. was urgent that the first demand should be fully granted; the second was of course inadmissible.

The Protestant envoys who had been commissioned to demand these general conditions appeared in January, 1552. They retired to fetch their theologians, but before the theologians could come the whole situation had been altered. Maurice of Saxony, the Protestant leader, had supported Charles in the campaign of Muhlberg against his own cousin, John Frederick, and, as a reward for his fidelity, had received the electoral dignity which John Frederick had forfeited. Now, having got all that he could out of the Emperor, he thought that the time had come to turn against him. Charles was at Innsbruck. Maurice boasted that he would " run the fox to earth," and one night, as Charles was sitting down to supper, news was brought that Maurice with his army was on the way to kidnap him. There was just time for flight, and Charles, racked with gout, was able to make his miserable escape to Villach in Carinthia, where he had to borrow the expenses of living from Cosmo de Medici. Trent was no longer a safe place for the Fathers, and the Council had no alternative but to adjourn itself on March 8th, " having," as one of its members said with much sense, " no mind to argue points of doctrine with soldiers in arms."

While the Council was in session, St. Ignatius was engaged in an unpleasant controversy between the Archbishop and the members of the Society at Alcala. The Spanish bishops, as has been said, had at both meetings of the Council shown themselves vigorous supporters of what they claimed as their privileges against the central disciplinary powers of the Pope. The Jesuits had strongly supported the Papal claims. Whether for this reason or for some other the Archbishop of Toledo, Juan Siliceo, persuaded himself that the privileged status of the Jesuits at Alcala was a menace to regular ecclesiastical jurisdiction. Siliceo's Erasmian predecessor, Fonseca, had, it will be remembered, befriended St. Ignatius after the judgment of the Alcala Inquisition a quarter of a century before. But Siliceo seems to have been one of those who have no patience with that with which they are unfamiliar. We know little of the incident save through the minute of which Polanco wrote at St. Ignatius' dictation, and the Archbishop's motives are obscure. It seems possible that some admirers of the Jesuits, more enthusiastic than discreet, had been so far exaggerating the Jesuit teaching of the desirability of frequent communions as to advise people to communicate twice in one day. Anyhow, Siliceo suddenly suspended the Jesuits from the sacerdotal functions which they exercised in virtue of special powers granted to them from Rome. In spite of the remonstrances of the Grand Vicar, the Archbishop was unrelenting, and appeals had to be made both to the Royal Council of Castille and to St. Ignatius, who carried the matter up to Julius III. Julius III. wrote to Siliceo in support of the Jesuits, " this community . . . so much loved, esteemed and cherished at this time in all Christendom," but Siliceo would pay no attention to the Pope, and only at last yielded before the threat of open rupture with the Crown. He yielded then with a bad grace and without apologies. The story is an interesting little example of that perversion of 16th-century Spanish Catholicism by an evil nationalistic pride, without an understanding of which the history of the times and the policies of subsequent Popes—in especial of Paul IV. and Sixtus V.—is quite unintelligible.

St. Ignatius imposed upon his subordinates the very sensible
policy of not pushing home their triumph to the humiliation of
the Archbishop.   It was throughout life his teaching that the
greatest of disasters for the Church came from her divisions in
the face of the enemy, and that therefore it did more harm than
good for the Society to attempt to carry on work in face of the
ill-will of the regular ecclesiastical authorities, however un-
justified that ill-will might be.   He comforted his subordinates
by promising them that Siliceo would be succeeded by an
Archbishop whose favour would exceed the hostility of his
predecessor.   This proved so.   Siliceo soon died, and one,
Gaspar Quiroga, a friend and admirer of St. Ignatius, was
appointed in his place.

Irritating as the troubles of the Society in Spain must have
been, at least they did not reveal any differences within the
Society itself.   Its members stood firm and united in face of
Siliceo's attacks.   More disturbing to St. Ignatius must have
been the problems with which in a few months he found himself
faced in Portugal.   As will be remembered, from the first
establishment of the Society in Portugal, its provincial had been
Simon Rodriguez.   He was a pious man, and the work that he
had done in that country had been marvellously successful and
in many ways for the good.   Yet there was a danger in the
very magnetism of Rodriguez' personality.   He was one of
those who can make others work for them, but only by
attaching their assistants to them by strong ties of personal
enthusiasm.   This was not in itself reprehensible, but within
such a Society as that of Jesus, where all was to be done solely
for the greater glory of God, there was danger in such a strong,
special, personal influence.

Nor is there any denying that some very extravagant things
were done in Portugal under Rodriguez' rule.   Students were
as eccentric as their masters.   Two of them brought a skull into
a class and set it down on the desk before them in order that
they might mortify themselves by gazing at it during the lecture.
As they had done this without permission, Rodriguez not
unnaturally determined that they should be punished, but the

punishment that he ordered them was to go home to the mother of one of the students, to tell her the whole story on their knees, and to beg forgiveness.   This they did, and on their return found that Rodriguez had locked them out of the college. After sitting on the doorstep for some time, they were at last admitted within owing to the intercession of the rector, and even then as a further punishment Rodriguez sent them to Coventry.   None of the other students were to speak to them until further notice.

In the hope of mollifying Rodriguez, one of the offenders a few days later entered the refectory at dinner-time, barefooted, bareheaded, with his hands tied and with a cord which passed round his neck and tied his tongue between two sticks.   At supper his companion in ill-doing, not to be beaten in eccentricity of penance, came in, stripped to the waist and with a rope round his neck.   Rodriguez sent them both back for having acted without permission.

As extravagant was the behaviour of a young musician whom Rodriguez had refused for the novitiate.   In order to prove the sincerity of his desire to abandon all for the love of God, he walked through the town, dressed in a death's head and inviting all the street-urchins to kick him and throw stones at him. His eccentricity moved Rodriguez.   He obtained permission to enter the novitiate, where he was allowed at his own request to perform the most menial of tasks, carting heavy logs and burning his fingers with the cooking.   Another student went out half-naked and tied himself to a pillar in a public square, whence he cried out, " O Lord Jesus, Who for our sins wast tied to a pillar in Pilate's house, forgive the sins of this city." Many others were guilty of many other eccentricities.

To every man his own mortification, and one must not forget that what would be ridiculous in the 20th century was not necessarily ridiculous in the 16th.   Yet it is certain that public eccentricity, whose purpose is to move spectators to repentance, is more likely in fact merely to excite their curiosity and to satisfy an appetite similar to that which would take them to the circus or to performing animals.   St. Ignatius was right to be suspicious of a régime which encouraged such public eccentricities.

St. Ignatius became concerned at the reports of what was going on, and asked King John III. to allow Rodriguez to come to Rome so that they might talk over the situation. John said that Rodriguez could not be spared. In 1552 St. Ignatius made up his mind that the wisest plan was to remove him from the Provincialship. One Mirone was installed in his place. There was no kind of disgrace in this, for it is the rule of the Society that the superior posts are only held for limited periods. As a matter of fact, the Constitutions prescribed a change in the Provincialship every three years, and Rodriguez had already been left on for twelve. Nor did Rodriguez at the first protest. Soon, however, a change came over him. Mirone, whether it was that he thought it his duty to react against the policy of Rodriguez or whether he was by nature a wooden fool and knew no better, attempted to rule in his province in a silly, petty, interfering way. No one was ever less of the mere rule-worshipper than St. Ignatius. A rational freedom was as necessary as a rational discipline if men were to give of their best to the service of God. "Preserve always your liberty of mind and see that you lose it not by anyone's authority, nor by any event whatever," was the advice which he put at the head of his Spiritual Exercises. He knew enough of human nature to know well how absurd and impossible it was for the Superior to attempt to regulate and interfere with every detail of the subordinate's life.

Rigid as was his insistence on the duty of obedience to positive commands when they were given, he was yet very reluctant to give them if it could be avoided. "Do your duty," was all the instruction that he would normally give to those whom he appointed to be Superiors, and he expected them in their turn to be as wise and sparing in their exercise of authority over their subordinates. He once ordered a minister to employ all the novices on the building of a wall. There was one clearly unfitted for the work, whom nevertheless the minister, in fancied obedience to St. Ignatius' command, compelled to take a hand. St. Ignatius was very angry. "When I give you an order, do I deprive you of your charity and discretion?" he asked. Manares records that when he was appointed Rector of the college at Loretto, and asked St. Ignatius for instructions, Ignatius answered, "Oliviero, do as you think best and as God inspires you. See, and adapt the rules to the place as you best can." Manares asked who should be appointed to which offices. "Cut according to your cloth; only inform me of all your arrangements," said St. Ignatius. "It is my wish that in future you act thus, without scruple, and do what you judge to be expedient under new circumstances, notwithstanding the letter of the rule," he told another Father.

So now he wrote to Mirone. "It is better not to give minute directions. For in that case, if anything went wrong you would be placed in a position unsuitable to your authority, and those who are nearest the work can often judge how best to do it."

The effect of Mirone's conduct on Rodriguez can easily be guessed and understood. He saw those whom he had attracted by sympathy to the Society now repelled from it by Mirone's stupidity. He appealed to King John III. to know if the change in the Provincialship had been made with his assent. John said that it had. He then replied to St. Ignatius' command that he should go either to Aragon or Brazil by saying that his health would not permit him to go to either. He went instead to the college at Coimbra and took up his residence there. However, when Torrez, the Rector of Salamanca, who had been appointed by St. Ignatius to settle the dispute, commanded him to go to Aragon he obeyed, but from his new residence besieged St. Ignatius with requests that he be allowed to return to Portugal. St. Ignatius at first wrote most kindly, agreeing to the request, but later he learnt that a friend of Rodriguez, Father Gomez, had been intriguing with King John on behalf of Rodriguez against the Superiors of the Society. St. Ignatius replied by giving to the Provincial complete powers to settle what was to be done with Rodriguez, and by imposing on Rodriguez a duty of complete submission. Soon after he summoned him to Rome, thinking that to be the only safe solution of the problem.   It was his design to summon St. Francis Xavier back from the East, and he might perhaps have been called in to compose the difficulty, but, if such was the design, it was fruitless, for unfortunately St. Francis was dead before the letter of recall reached him.

Though Rodriguez was in disgrace, yet St. Ignatius never failed in courtesy towards him.   The letter summoning him to Rome is proof of this.

"Master Simon Rodriguez, beloved son in Our Lord,— After I had received, read and considered your letters of February 10th, and of March 23rd and 26th, and April 12th and many more, which I received from where you are, and because I feel and acknowledge that it is desirable for the greater peace and spiritual comfort in the Lord of those of our Society who remain in Portugal, and also that we may consult on the common subjects which concern the whole community, and which cannot be discussed except in conversation, I have resolved in Our Lord to give you a little bodily trouble by a journey to Rome.   And so, as it is a matter of importance, I command you this in the power of obedience on behalf of Christ Our Lord, whether by water or land, as you find it more easy ; and this must be as soon as possible ; therefore in eight days from the receiving this, set out on your journey and do not delay.   I pray God that He may lead and accompany you.

"Son Simon, trust to me that your soul and mine when you come here will find comfort in Our Lord ; and all that we both wish for the greater glory of Our Lord will be happily accomplished.   Meanwhile hold fast to what we see with much piety ; and, if yours is not very great, yet God Our Lord will give you more, if you strive to accomplish this journey.   Remember that when I had yet no authority over your actions you did what I desired of you, and went to Portugal with all readiness, though you had the quartan ague at that time, and you got well ; then how much more now when you have not such a serious illness ?

" Son, Master Simon, set out immediately and doubt not that health of body and soul will refresh us here to the greater honour of God. Only have confidence in me and you will remain satisfied in Our Lord."

Rodriguez was not the only member of the Society to fall into disciplinary difficulties. After the adjournment of Trent Laynez returned to Italy. He was the man who had dominated Europe. He had been the spokesman of the Pope. Kings, Cardinals and Emperor had been his audience. In 1552 he was appointed to succeed Brouet as Provincial of Italy. He protested that he had not yet learnt the virtue of obedience sufficiently to command others. St. Ignatius insisted, but it was soon proved that Laynez had correctly diagnosed his own fault. He began to quarrel with St. Ignatius' policy of collecting at Rome all the Society's most eminent scholars. St. Ignatius instructed Polanco, his secretary, to write to Laynez.

" This dictatorial way of writing which becomes no one towards a superior he does not approve ; rather he bids me tell you you should consider your own charge, and if you fulfil it as you ought, you do no small thing ; but you had better take no other burden upon you ; whereas you give him counsel respecting his own business which he only desires to receive when he asks it of you, and less now than before you entered on your own charge, for, in conducting it, you have not given him a great opinion of your fitness to rule. Consider these faults before God Our Lord, and pray thereupon three days, and after that write whether you recognise these faults or mistakes, and decide the penalty which you think you have incurred and send this in writing ; but you are to accomplish none till you have received our Father's answer."

This to a man who had been Papal theologian at Trent, and who was to succeed St. Ignatius as General of the Society. Yet Laynez accepted the rebuke and wrote back to St. Ignatius only to ask him never to spare such salutary reprimands whenever they might be necessary. " I wish," he wrote, " and pray you by the mercies of Our Lord Jesus Christ, that to punish my sins and conquer my untamed passions, which are their source, you withdraw me from all command, preaching and study, leaving me no book but my breviary; that you make me come to Rome, begging all the way, and there employ me till I die, in the lowest services of the house. Or if I am not fit for that, command me to pass the rest of my days in teaching the first elements of grammar, taking no notice of me, and regarding me always as the outcast of the world." St. Ignatius relented, and instead set him the more useful penance of composing a manual of theology in answer to the Lutherans.

One cannot but compare the treatment meted out to Rodriguez with that meted out to Laynez, and to reflect how high must have been the standard of obedience in the Society if these were the worst acts of insubordination of which its members were guilty. Yet why did Laynez, whose fault was surely the lesser of the two, receive the harsher treatment? One cannot be certain of the answer, but I think that it was a compliment to Laynez that he was called on to bear the heavier burden. It was always St. Ignatius' policy to be most severe with those whom he most loved—Codace, Ribadaneira, Polanco, Nadal, Laynez himself. " Oh Lord, what harm have I done to the Society," Laynez once asked with groanings, " that El Santo treats me with such severity?" Laynez was called to bear this heavier burden because St. Ignatius knew that he would be able to bear it. So undivided was his love of Christ that St. Ignatius knew well that a harsh word would not turn him from His service. Of Rodriguez he could not be so sure. Yet I think, too, that he had great sympathy with Rodriguez, for the root of all Rodriguez' fault had been a too great affection for those for whom he worked. And St. Ignatius, though he preached that the love of the creature should be entirely swallowed up in the love of the Creator, yet knew how few there were who were capable of that perfect immolation. Laynez' fault had been a fault of cold judgment, Rodriguez of hot emotion. It was St. Ignatius' way to be more tender with the latter than with the former.

CHAPTER XV

THE GROWING SOCIETY

THERE were during these years other quarrels than those with Laynez and Rodriguez. The most important was the determined fight of the Sorbonne, the Parlement of Paris, and others against the attempt of the Duc de Guise and King Henry II. to establish the Jesuits in Paris—a fight chiefly notable perhaps because it saw the first appearance of the famous and bogus *Monita Secreta*, or secret instructions, supposedly issued to all Jesuit Superiors in contradiction of the innocuous rules that were advertised before the world.

Then there was in 1552 the determined attack on the Society of the heretical party of Cologne, a legacy of the folly of Hermann of Wied. Again and again, too, St. Ignatius was engaged in hard fights to prevent preferments and titles being forced upon members of the Society. First there was the attempt to make St. Francis Borgia a Cardinal in 1550—an attempt which caused him for the first time to publish to the world his membership of the Society. Then there was the attempt of the Duke of Bavaria to make Peter Canisius a canon, and that of Ferdinand, King of the Romans, to make him Bishop of Vienna. All these St. Ignatius resisted, as he was afterwards to resist the attempt to force a Cardinal's hat upon Laynez. On the other hand, when King John III. of Portugal asked for a Jesuit confessor, St. Ignatius insisted that the request be granted. For here was a question not of the acceptance of rank, but of the conferment of spiritual services, and it was the business of Jesuits to labour for the salvation of souls, wherever they might be found—even in king's palaces.

St. Ignatius, as has been said and shown again and again, was

one of those who though occupied day after day with decisions
of high policy of the greatest moment, was yet always able to
find the time to preserve and strengthen personal friendship.
Public life was never permitted to crowd out private life, and
these very years, the years of the quarrels in Spain and Portugal
and France, were the years of one of the most attractive and
fruitful of St. Ignatius' friendships, the friendship with St. Philip
Neri, a friendship the intimacy of which is commemorated by
the charmingly absurd tale, worthy of Charles Lamb, that the
reason why the Jesuits wear no buttons on their cassocks is that
St. Philip pulled them all off, one by one, when buttonholing
St. Ignatius. St. Philip Neri had lived in Rome ever since
1533, when he was eighteen years old. His friendship with
St. Ignatius began, it seems, in 1544 and continued unbroken.
Many of St. Philip's disciples found their vocation in the Society
of Jesus, so much so that the joke which in a more modern day
Pius IX. made about Pusey and the Catholic Church—that he
was like the church-bell which is for ever ringing others inside
but itself remains outside—was first made about St. Philip and
the Society of Jesus. Yet both Philip and Ignatius quite agreed
that Philip's own vocation lay elsewhere. In 1551 he was at
last ordained priest, and he lived in Rome, surrounded by those
companions who much later, in 1575, were formally recognised
as the Congregation of the Oratory.

To those who complain that the Catholicism of the Counter-
Reformation was a grim and dour and joyless business, it is
sufficient to answer with the example of Philip Neri. He, to
whom the Italians have given the lovely title of the *Amabile
Santo*, was in outward behaviour a very different man from
Ignatius. He had the Franciscan spirit in him. St. Ignatius
walked the streets a great captain, full of high and grave thoughts,
a Christian stoic, imperturbable before the accidents of pain or
misfortune. Zurbaran might have painted him. St. Philip,
God's fool, would go down the street with a hop and a skip and
a jump and a laugh for every passer-by. When they asked to
see his library, he showed them a single jest-book. Yet the
two, who differed so much in these little things, were drawn

together by their great love of souls, and their friendship, once formed, continued unbroken until the end of St. Ignatius' life.

These same years were the years during which the Jesuit schools throughout the Continent were growing up and the famous Jesuit system of education was developing. It would be quite impossible to attempt a list of those who in these years owed a first early training to the Jesuits, and who afterwards played remarkable parts in the life of Church or State. Yet one cannot refrain from noting that in these very years, when the busy policy of St. Ignatius was re-making Europe, one of the poorest of the scholars at the Jesuit school at Medina del Campo was a' young John de Yepes, whom to-day the altars of the Church honour as St. John of the Cross, one of the first of all masters of the mystical life. At about the same time there set forth every morning to the Jesuit college at Naples, lighted on the way by the torches of his parents' servants, a little boy of seven, Torquato Tasso, who in later years was to tell again in undying verse the story of mediæval Christendom's attempt to win back the Holy Land to Christ.

In 1558 was founded the Roman college to which parents, even non-Catholic parents, sent their children from every country of Europe. For it was always St. Ignatius' order that non-Catholic children should be received in the Jesuit colleges, provided that the parents requested it, and, indeed, the Jesuits in Prague at about this time got into some trouble with a certain sort of Catholics because of their insistence on giving free education to Hussite children. The Roman college in its early years was not without its difficulties. Polanco, who was in charge of the building, reported that funds were running out. "Though I am not a prophet nor the son of a prophet," answered St. Ignatius, to whom it was a matter of conscience not to allow himself to be disturbed by financial anxieties, "I am persuaded that the Lord will not abandon us. Do you keep on the college six months longer, and I will take care of it afterwards." And, as it happened, that very night, two large donations came in from people who knew nothing of the

---

Society's difficulties, and during the six months sufficient gifts were received to free them of embarrassments.

There were other difficulties—one in particular of an unforeseen but most intelligible nature. From the most unmixedly high motives, St. Ignatius had laid it down that the Jesuits were to take no fees for any instruction that they might give. The result, of course, was that parents sent their children to the Jesuit schools, and other poor schoolmasters who were dependent upon their pupils for their living were deprived of occupation. The grievance of these schoolmasters was intelligible, and it was the schoolmasters, fearing loss of occupation, who first kept the Jesuits out of the Spanish Netherlands altogether during St. Ignatius' lifetime, and after his death prevailed upon King Philip that they should only be admitted under grudging and harsh conditions.

Yet the method which some of the Roman pedagogues chose for the airing of their grievances was not to be commended. Some schoolmasters one day forced their way into the Roman college and attacked with a great fury a Jesuit who was attempting to teach a class, to the very great delight, doubtless, of the pupils, who saw this unexpectedly delicious division among the ranks of their natural enemy, but hardly to the greater glory of religion and sound learning. St. Ignatius at once saw that with the increase of Jesuit schools, such collisions were bound from time to time to occur. He also saw that the Jesuits were not likely to be so exceptionally favoured above all other schoolmasters as to escape occasional disputes with unreasonable parents. He therefore sent round to all rectors of colleges the following most sensible letter.

"This very week, two boys being missed from their fathers' houses, the mothers came to our chapel during the Mass, and called out and made an astonishing scandal, and also in the college, and at the house of some of the Cardinals, as we heard from some of them, saying that we had made the college on purpose to steal away people's sons, and that we kept theirs, etc.; and in fact neither of these (boys) had

entered either our college or our house.   I thought it right
to mention these things, as a warning that your reverences
may be the better prepared for similar accidents. . . .

"Let them take care also that none of the auditors of the
schools admit (any children) without the assent of the parents,
because the harm done by the disturbance and alienation of
minds would be greater than the benefit in receiving them,
having regard to the universal good ; and there will be no
lack of ways to aid the laudable desires of those who wish to
enter, sending them to other places, or as God may instruct
you."

It is perhaps a large part of the success of the Jesuits that they
have never forgotten that the rights of the parent are primary.
They have never made any attempt to capture the young,
whether as pupils or as novices, contrary to the will of the
parents.   When Adrian Adriani, the Rector of the Jesuit
college at Louvain, received a pupil contrary to the wish of his
father, St. Ignatius vigorously took the father's side and bade
Adriani ask his pardon.   Again a certain Octavius Cæsar in
1553 entered the novitiate in Sicily without his father's consent.
His father does not seem to have objected violently, for he
subsequently gave his consent, nor is it certain whether Octavius
Cæsar was of age or not.   St. Ignatius, with the agreement of
Julius III., does not seem to have thought that there was here
sufficient cause to warrant returning him to the world.   Yet he
took the opportunity of the incident to make clear his general
policy.   In a circular to all rectors of colleges, he laid it down
that "no youth who may still be under the care of parents or
guardians be admitted into our company, either in any college
or by sending them elsewhere, without the will and consent of
those who have charge of them ; and much less ought they to
persuade or exhort such scholars to enter our religion."   As to
the general policy of Jesuits' bringing pressure to bear on their
pupils to enter the novitiate, he was clear and firm.   "Though
it be in itself a thing permitted and praiseworthy," he wrote,
"to help those who have arrived at years of discretion, and

exhort them to a state of perfection, that is, to religion, yet for
our schools to exhort in this way, or receive any, we consider
not advisable." On no point has St. Ignatius made his mind
more clear to his followers than on that of the wrongfulness of
any attempt to bring uninvited pressure to bear on young boys
in order to persuade them to enter the novitiate. Indeed, if it
was found that an intending novice had any friendship with a
member of the Society, St. Ignatius would only admit him after
he had proved the sincerity of his desire by an especially long
period of consideration.

*　　*　　*　　*　　*

It has frequently been observed, and is certainly true, that
when people lose the proportion of true religion, they attach a
religious and uncritical value to some other activity in which
they themselves happen to be engaged. The artist thinks that
the whole world was made for art, the politician for government, the don for scholarship. Through this loss of balance,
there came in with the Renaissance, and remains with us still,
an uncritical worship of specialised learning, which is thought
by some to make a man a god. For wherever there has been
revolt from religion, there the intellect is underrated, and,
wherever that happens, there, unless it be among a quite barbarous
people, learning is overrated. The specialist's attack on the
Faith is one which it is peculiarly difficult for the Catholic to
meet, for the very balance and proportion of Catholic philosophy makes the individual Catholic disinclined to that last
ounce of effort which is required if a man is going to be an
authority of the first order on his subject. The effort of acquir-
ing very great learning is so large that only those who are not
quite sane will undertake it. For it is the whole problem of life
that happiness is the end of man, and the most important things
are not the most amusing. St. Thomas is a much more important writer than Mr. Wodehouse, but Mr. Wodehouse is a
much more amusing writer than St. Thomas, and it is not to be
expected that, once they have been taught the fundamental
truths, any save peculiar people will bother themselves very
much further with serious reading and writing. For the normal

person the world is so full of many interesting things that he is not willing to devote himself entirely to minute specialisation. A man with a sane philosophy will not spend all his time reading and writing about it.

The result is that, though the Catholics are usually the superior of their opponents in the breadth and sanity and proportion of their philosophy of life, on each particular point their opponents are apt to have a specialist more learned than any whom they can themselves produce. It is useless to expect Catholics to be deceived by the pseudo-mystical promises of a richer happiness and a superior being that can only be enjoyed through the possession of learning and education, for it is their Catholicism itself which saves them from falling victims to such talk and prevents them from the giving to themselves of those airs which are to so many men the main reward of very great learning.

In plain truth, knowing is not such fun as all that—and yet the Church must have her scholars and philosophers, for it is necessary that she should repel attacks wherever they are delivered. How, then, are champions to be procured, ready to give a specialist's answer to the specialist's attack? It was the task of St. Ignatius' Society, more than anyone else, to provide such champions, to provide those who for the greater glory of God were ready to undertake those tedious labours of scholarship, the rewards of which do not themselves repay the fatigues which they entail. It is, more than anything else, Jesuit education, of which Lord Bacon said, " There is no training beyond that," which has during three hundred and fifty years repelled the attacks of the specialist and saved Catholics from that tiresome worship of literacy and learning which is so large an enemy to happiness throughout the non-Catholic parts of Europe. Other Orders have rendered great services to the cause of Catholic sanity, but they all flourished first in the days before printing, when this especial menace did not threaten us. The Jesuit, the only large Order which has come into being since the printing machine, has been reserved for this especial work.

As to the Jesuit system of education, it was at the first less original than has sometimes been supposed. St. Ignatius was no great believer in systems or in rules. The famous *Ratio Studiorum*, in which were embodied the lessons of the Jesuits' first experiences, did not appear until some years after St. Ignatius' death. He was always very willing that his Society should adopt and follow whatever customs might be in fashion at any particular time or in any particular country. The Jesuits adopted the educational habits of the world around them, their education differing from that of their neighbours only perhaps in the greater emphasis which the Jesuits laid on the subordination of the merely intellectual to the religious training and in the severity of their condemnation of all dishonesty, of lies, whether those of private advantage or those of patriotism and *esprit de corps* ; insisting always on what Montesquieu, none too warm a friend, finely calls in speaking of their work in Paraguay, " *ce sentiment exquis pour tout ce qu'ils appellent honneur.*" Indeed, one is tempted to the paradox that the great superiority of Jesuits over other schoolmasters has arisen from the fact that the Jesuits alone have never believed in Education —have never believed in it, that is to say, as an end and a religion with capital letter and bated breath. They have never made the mistake of worshipping the means to the neglect of the end.

It was an age when even Protestants were only just beginning to discover a deep hostility to the stage and when Popes and Cardinals still found their highest recreation at the comedy. There was therefore nothing surprising to the taste of the day in the large part in education (indeed, as one cannot sometimes help feeling, the too large part) which they assigned to acting.

Of St. Ignatius' own reflections on education the most interesting are perhaps those which he airs in a letter to an unknown Cardinal, wirtten some time after 1551, and in which he discusses the anti-Catholic nature of what is known as a classical education. To-day educationalists debate the rival merits of classical and scientific educations, but from the Christian point of view it is not possible to take very seriously the extreme claims either of the one or the other. It is a very useful thing to know something about Greece and Rome, and it is a very useful thing to know something about physical science, but a Christian can hardly agree that either a system of education which teaches people nothing of the life of the last two thousand years, or one which deals entirely with inductive truth, has any claim to be called a complete system. The dangers of the scientific education have come to us but recently, those of the classics have been with us since the Renaissance and have played a powerful part in creating in the minds of England and of Europe a contempt for Christian truth.

A Shrewsbury master, who was killed in the war, left behind him as testament a not ignoble piece of prose in which he paid his tribute to those things which he had loved here on earth— among others " to the Greek tongue because it is the perfect tongue, and the Latin because it has fought and conquered the centuries." It is true enough, but it is not true of the Latin of the classical education ; Cicero has not fought the centuries, nor has Ovid conquered them. It is the Latin of

" Lauda, Sion, salvatorem "

or of

*" Pangue, lingua, gloriosi
Corporis mysterium,"*

which has fought and conquered the centuries. Does the classical schoolmaster tell his pupils much about this Latin ? He does not. He gets as far as Tacitus, where he finds a vague hint that there were some people called " Christians " coming up into prominence—and then he drops the subject like hot plates. The enemies of religion know little of their own business when they sneer at a classical education.

St. Ignatius did not at all condemn the study of the classics. He patronised them. Indeed, it is often said—and perhaps with truth—that classical education owes its survival to the Jesuits. Yet from the first St. Ignatius recognised its great dangers. Perhaps a lack of sympathy with much that was good in the Renaissance helped him to his discovery ; mere prudery may have played its part. Yet his discovery was fortunate for

Europe, which escaped thereby that curse which was so harmful to the English pubic schools of the 18th and 19th centuries—a curriculum exclusively classical, uncorrected by the balance of any real religious apologetics.

In 1553, the year in which St. Ignatius made his last trip out of Rome—to Alirto, in order to attempt to reconcile Ascanio and Giovanna Colonna—he was busily engaged in the organisation of the Jesuit mission to Corsica. The story of it is interesting, as showing the incredible degradations to which religion had fallen in that island. The Jesuits whom St. Ignatius sent reported that the clergy differed neither in clothes nor in lives from the laity. Some of them knew neither how to say Mass nor how to give absolution. The peasantry had forgotten how to make the sign of the Cross.

The mission of the Jesuits aroused the deepest hostility of the Grand Vicar because of the censure which their reports implied upon his conduct. He wrote to Rome complaints of their arrogance and presumption, so circumstantial as to deceive even such a man as Cardinal Cervini, soon to succeed Julius III. under the title of Marcellus II. St. Ignatius agreed to send a certain Sebastian Romé to the island, who, dressed in lay clothes and not making himself known to his fellow Jesuits, was to investigate all that was going on. Romé went and, returning, brought with him letters from the Governor, from the Provincial of the Franciscans—the only Order established there—from magistrates and from private persons, all bearing testimony in favour of the Jesuits. Cervini was convinced and offered an apology to St. Ignatius.

The campaign of Juan de Vega had by no means freed the Mediterranean from the menace of the Mahommedan. The Sultan had taken up Dragut's quarrel, and Henry II. of France, preferring the satisfaction of his private spite against the Hapsburgs to the larger interests of Christendom, made an alliance with the Mahommedan. More and more daring became the corsair raids upon the coasts of Spain and Italy. Even one of the Jesuit Fathers, a Frenchman called Godan, had fallen a victim to the pirates, when on a voyage from Gandia to Italy and been taken off to Algiers, where, in spite of many efforts to rescue him, he died in captivity. St. Ignatius threw himself into the project for uniting the princes of Christendom in crusade against the infidel. It was even his own ambition to go to Africa as a missionary. As Nadal warned him, the time was not yet ripe. In default of crusades the next best thing, it was thought, was to establish colleges wherever possible throughout the Eastern world. It was proposed to establish one at Jerusalem, one at Cyprus and one at Constantinople. The Pope approved, and Rodriguez was to be in charge of the mission. With what success they could have hoped to meet in face of the triumphant intolerance of the 16th-century Turk it is hard to see. Nor was it ever tested, for Rodriguez fell ill at Venice and the project languished with him.

CHAPTER XVI

PAUL IV. AND THE DEATH OF IGNATIUS

WHILE the question of the Eastern mission was still under debate, the Papacy had twice changed hands. On March 23rd, 1555, Julius died. An indolent Conservative, he was not a good man, and his pontificate, though redeemed by some reforms, had not on the whole been a fortunate one for the Church. Yet the Jesuits had no personal reason to complain of him. His treatment of them had, on the whole, been the most creditable episode of his career. Only once had they quarrelled with him —when Julius resented Charles V.'s attempt to enforce the Tridentine decrees concerning the residence of bishops and persuaded himself that the Jesuits were the supporters of Charles' policy.

Julius' old colleague of Trent, Cervini, was elected to succeed him as Marcellus II. The hopes of all were high. Here again was a Pope worthy of his great office. He promised neutrality in political squabbles. He drew up schemes of reform. He received St. Ignatius with kindness, begged that every member of the Society should be made personally known to him. " You are soldiers ready for battle and I will make use of you," he said. The highest of hopes were raised. Whether or not they would have been disappointed, we cannot say. For on the twenty-second day of his pontificate Marcellus was struck down with apoplexy and died.

> " *Nimium vobis Romana propago*
> *Visa potens, superi, propria haec si dona fuissent,*"

his contemporaries quoted, applying the words which fifteen hundred years before Virgil had used of that other Marcellus, the son of Octavia.

There succeeded one whom we have already met as Provincial of the Theatines, the fiery Cardinal Caraffa, who took the title of Paul IV. St. Ignatius was sitting by the window in his room when they brought him the news. " A visible change came over his countenance," records Gonzales. " All his bones shook in his body." As zealous for reform as Marcellus, Paul did not possess Marcellus' talent for combining zeal with tact, and his reign was to be a stormy one in the history of the Jesuits, in the history of England, in the history of Spain and in the history of his own nephews and of many others besides.

Many worse men than Paul Caraffa have sat upon the Papal throne, but few, I think, have sat there whose rule has brought more of disaster to the Church and to Christendom. When he was elected most men were willing confidently to predict the nature of his reign. An old man of seventy-nine, a reformer of austere and vigorous fanaticism, he was expected to push forward with great energy and with perhaps a certain lack of tact the policies of reform of discipline and morals which had been inaugurated under Paul III. Nephews, it was expected, would be ruthlessly banished from Rome ; heterodox speculators need look for no mercy. The days of art-loving Popes or of political Popes were gone, and there opened before the Church a prospect of austere, reformed and perhaps uncomfortably puritanical life.

The event was almost incredibly different. The Caraffas were an ancient family of Naples, and to a Caraffa the rule of the Spanish Hapsburgs in Naples was the rule of an impudent interloper. His hatred of the Hapsburgs was fed by Charles V.'s opposition to his election, and it was soon evident, to every one's surprise, that he was going to allow his whole policy as Pope to be subordinated to his extravagant family pride.

Wiser Popes than Paul—Paul III. before him, for instance, and Sixtus V. after him—saw a danger to Christian unity in the unchecked predominance of the Hapsburg family. As an Italian citizen, too, Paul was entitled to think, if he wished to do so, that the presence of the Spaniard in Italy was not for Italy's benefit. But to carry his hatred to the extreme lengths to which he did carry it, to call in an army of German Protestants to drive pious Alva from the Peninsula, to fail, to heap revenues and preferments on his scoundrelly nephew, provided only that he said an Amen to Paul's almost lunatic diatribes, to accuse of heresy such men as Morone and Pole for reasons that were at least strongly suspected of being political and personal—these were iniquities in contrast with which the more intelligible vices of an Alexander Borgia are easily pardonable. Indeed, it is hardly possible to speak with patience of Paul unless one is able to accept the hypothesis that he was not wholly sane.

Before the end Paul repented of his policy, and his last years were years of that rigid reform with which it had been expected that his whole pontificate would be filled. His nephews were banished and politics forgotten, but before the change came he had succeeded in throwing many difficulties in the way of those who were working for the good of the Church—in that, among others, of St. Ignatius. On his first accession Paul had treated St. Ignatius more kindly, and had spoken of the Jesuits more favourably, than had been expected from the memories of the coolness between Paul and St. Ignatius over the question of the union between the Jesuits and the Theatines. But by 1556 we find St. Ignatius kept waiting for fourteen hours in the Papal ante-room and Paul sending troops to search the Gesù on a preposterous charge that the Jesuits had concealed arms there. Paul withdrew the subscription which his predecessors had given to the Jesuits' German college. After St. Ignatius' death Paul's relations with Laynez, his successor, were even less friendly than were those with the saint himself.

St. Ignatius was firmly insistent that, whatever Paul might do, no Jesuit must give scandal by speaking against him. When Ribadaneira was setting out for Belgium, St. Ignatius commanded him on his obedience to speak only of Paul's virtuous actions. When Ribadaneira said that this might be difficult, St. Ignatius answered, " Then you must say nothing at all, and speak only of Pope Marcellus who showed us so much affection." And St. Ignatius, on one occasion, even allowed himself the charitable falsehood that no Pope had done so much for the Society as Paul IV.

Paul was rude to St. Ignatius simply, no doubt, because he was a rude man. But he probably took some special pleasure in offensiveness because St. Ignatius was a Spaniard, as were so many of his followers. It is perfectly true that no one could have taken more trouble than St. Ignatius had taken to prevent the Society from being captured for Spanish political purposes, but Paul, who knew what he liked and knew what he did not like, was not in the habit of dwelling upon extenuating circumstances. To his mind a Spaniard was a thing to be rude to, and he knew a Spaniard when he saw it.

Indeed, under Paul's violent and eccentric policy, the poor Jesuits suffered the buffets of both sides. While Paul treated them with a lack of cordiality because they were Spaniards, the Government of the Spanish Netherlands excluded them from their country on the ground that they were especially vowed to the service of the Pope. The same disastrous suspicion of Paul IV. was responsible for their exclusion from England, in spite of the statesmanlike advice of Ruy Gomez, who urged " that the wisest thing they could do would be to summon the new Order to the help of religion in England and Ireland." There the effects of the blunder were quite irreparable, for before Paul was dead Elizabeth was established on the English throne and everything was lost.

The result of Paul's withdrawal of his subscription was that the German college had to be closed down and its inmates dispersed among the other colleges. The financial condition of all the Roman houses of the Society grew desperate, but St. Ignatius was confident in his faith that God would provide for their necessities. " It would be miraculous indeed if God had failed to support those who trust in Him," he answered to those who argued that to expect such help was to expect a miracle. " The more hopeless matters are, the more we ought to trust in God," he said, and refused to make any special appeal for alms. At the Gesu they were once so reduced that, when the dinner-bell rang, there was not a morsel of food in the house. At that very moment they received a gift of supplies sufficient for all. At another time, when they were in straits, a mysterious gift of flour and wine was found left at the door. No one knew whence it had come.

There were hardships to be suffered on the way, yet none seem to have complained except one German who had been expelled and who tried to revenge himself by going about everywhere and saying that the food was insufficient and the discipline severe. And it was St. Ignatius' faith that a generous God would provide not only for the necessities but even for the feasts of His servants. " O Father," said Guido Roilezio, Rector of the German college, to St. Ignatius one Christmastide, " we have barely bread, for the baker says he will not let us have any more." " Away with you," said St. Ignatius, " be of good heart. God will assist you. Master Guido, do you provide some kids and other things for the young men and leave the care of all to God." The next day there arrived a gift of five hundred ducats to be divided equally between the Roman and German colleges.

The position of the General of the Jesuits, tied as he was by his special oath of obedience to the Pope, was not enviable when there sat upon the throne a Pope who took no trouble to make himself easy to deal with. It may well be that Paul's tiresomeness played its part in bringing St. Ignatius to that grave which he was now approaching. St. Ignatius was not the man to be easily touched by a little lack of consideration. Yet these first years of Paul's pontificate were the years during which St. Ignatius was working hard to close up the Society's quarrel with the Sorbonne. It cannot, I think, be denied that Paul could have made that work less onerous had he been willing to be more helpful.

In the early days, whenever the Society was attacked, it had, as has been shown, been St. Ignatius' policy always to obtain a certificate of innocence from the regular authorities. When the Sorbonne issued its attack on the Society many of the Fathers were for insisting on an investigation into the charges. St. Ignatius refused. All the accusations which the Sorbonne made had already been officially proved to be false, and the man who was willing to repeat a calumny which had been refuted once would be equally willing to repeat one which had been refuted twice. There was nothing for it but to wait for the opportunity of time.

The Guises were always the Jesuits' friends, and the visit of the Cardinal of Lorraine and four of the leading theologians of Paris to Rome in 1555 gave St. Ignatius his opportunity. A conference was arranged between the Frenchmen on the one side and Laynez, Polanco and two other Jesuits on the other. All the charges that had been made against the Society were considered and answered. All the theologians admitted themselves to have been misinformed and declared the charges false. As a result permission was given for the establishment in France of two colleges of the Society, both of which prospered exceedingly.

After the conclusion of the quarrel with the Sorbonne the Society could congratulate itself that, with the one exception of England, it had established itself in every important penetrable quarter of the globe. There is nothing that can be compared with the rapidity of its progress save, perhaps, the rapidity of the rise of the Empires of Alexander and Napoleon. It was but fifteen years since Paul III. had sanctioned their existence. Already a hundred priests had gone out from the Roman college to evangelise Europe ; two hundred novices were in training there to carry on their work. Three colleges were flourishing in Germany, two in France, seventeen in Portugal, fifteen in Spain. Twenty-eight members of the Order were at work in the mission field in Brazil, a hundred in the East Indies. The savages of Corsica had begged that the Jesuit Fathers might be established in their midst in order to confirm them in their reformation. In Italy there were three provinces of the Society. From Poland, from Bohemia, from Hungary, Silesia, Transylvania, requests came in for Jesuit priests. The great Canisius, the most outstanding save Francis Borgia alone among what I may call the second generation of the Jesuits, was Provincial in Germany. Nor had a sterner and more awful test of success left the new Society untried or found it wanting. News came in from India that on the far-off pearl coast by the Straits of Manaar the Badages had put to death Father Antonio Criminali, and the Society had given in a martyr's blood its first tremendous witness to the love of God.

There was only one among the Catholic countries of Europe in which the Jesuits had not been allowed to establish their colleges, the Spanish Netherlands.   There the influence of de Croy, the Bishop of Cambrai, and of Viglius Zwicken, the President of the Council, was able to keep them out.   These two men played on the argument that, while Paul IV., Spain's enemy, was Pope, it was mad danger to allow into their midst a Society so especially vowed to the Pope's service.   Ribadaneira was sent to Brussels to plead for permission and to bring to the notice of the authorities the strict obligation of the Jesuits to take no part in politics and to treat as their own any country in which they happened to be stationed.   In the end he was successful, but not until the time of St. Ignatius' death.

There was only one among the major activities of the Church with which Fathers of the Society were not connected—the Inquisition.   There were some who were anxious to see even such activities put under Jesuit control.   King John III. of Portugal approached Mirone, the Portuguese Provincial of the Society, and asked him to accept the office of Grand Inquisitor. St. Ignatius, after some hesitation, refused his permission on the ground that "all conspicuous offices and places, such as commonly lead to bishoprics," are contrary "to the object of the Society."

Few will be found to quarrel with the comment of Genelli on this story—" whereupon they cannot but congratulate themselves."   Still it would be dishonest to pretend that St. Ignatius' refusal in any way implied a disapproval of the principle of an Inquisition.   On the contrary, he had supported Caraffa, as he then was, in the establishment of the Roman Inquisition in 1542, and it will be remembered that he had strongly approved of the establishment of a Portuguese Inquisition.   We have already considered how far it was perhaps true that the motives of the Portuguese Inquisition, professedly religious, were in reality largely economic, and how far it is probable that St. Ignatius was imperfectly informed on the true motive behind the demand. It is not necessary to reopen these questions. It is, however, important to dwell a little on the attitude of St. Ignatius to Inquisitions in general.

To the general reader the word " Inquisition " at once calls up visions of stakes, burnings, *auto-da-fés*. Whether or not St. Ignatius would have approved of *auto-da-fés* I do not know, but there is no doubt that he would have admitted, as every man who at all cares to tell the truth must admit, that occasions do arise upon which the ultimate remedy must be used and temporal punishments called in for the suppression of religious opinions that are either blasphemous or harmful to the community. Yet it was not in the question of the temporal punishments that he was at all interested, nor is there any reason to think that he advocated any especial severity of punishment. The Jesuits, who can point to such examples as those of Father Spee and Père Adam, have played an honourable part in the world's history in the mitigation of the violence of religious persecutions. Indeed, St. Ignatius' only dealings with the Spanish Inquisition, other than those in which he appeared as defendant, were when he pleaded for the pardon of some relapsed Moriscos.

To him an Inquisition was simply a court of inquiry. If the voice of the Church was the voice of God, then the most important thing in the world was to discover what was the Church's teaching. If some speculation was in the air, it was at any time of the first importance (and especially so in the 16th century) that there should be in existence a regular machinery which could pronounce with authority as to whether that speculation was or was not compatible with the Church's teaching. Such a machinery was a necessary protection for all the faithful. It was a necessary protection for the speculator himself, anxious, as he should be, to know whether his teaching was or was not permissible. For such assistance and guidance St. Ignatius himself had often appealed to the Inquisition. His experience, it is, true, had taught him that many Inquisitors were dull-minded and unimaginative people, and the Inquisition's methods most imperfect. But we do not embrace anarchy because some magistrates are fools and the law an ass.

The strain of responsibility was telling upon St. Ignatius, and those around him, though they refused to accept his resignation of the Generalship, yet urged him to take a coadjutor. St. Ignatius was at first unwilling—probably for the very sensible reason that, if he was to have responsibility at all, it was less wearisome to exercise it alone than to share it with another. However, at last, when he was compelled to keep to his bed, he was induced in the autumn of 1554 to agree with his friends' suggestion. Nadal was elected by thirty-one or thirty-two votes out of thirty-four. But the arrangement did not work very well. Nadal complained that not sufficient time was given to prayer in the colleges, and suggested the allotting to it of an extra hour a day, as was indeed afterwards done during the generalship of Acquaviva. But St. Ignatius, who hated innovations, was not well pleased, and after a few months, when he was able to rise again from his bed, he packed Nadal off to Spain.

Yet his recovery was no real recovery. The end was drawing on. Throughout all his life at Rome there is a surprising unanimity of evidence that his body was surrounded with a mysterious and, as his followers believed, a holy light. Nicholas Lannoy even claimed to have seen a bright flame playing upon his head, as he stood at the altar saying Mass. I do not know how much truth there is in these tales. On the one hand, there is no particular reason why God should not have clothed His servant in a robe of light; on the other hand, the sceptic can plausibly argue that some chance trick of the sun might easily suggest such a thing to the imagination, and that, once the tale had been put about, others would be sure to imagine themselves, too, to have seen the phenomenon. St. Ignatius himself was always very definite in his refusal to lay claim to the possession of any miraculous powers, and I am more than content to say of him as was said of St. Bernard, " He himself was the first and greatest of all his miracles." Yet, though I set no store by the opinion, it seems to me, on the whole, probable that St. Ignatius was truly clothed, at any rate on occasions, in a heavenly light.

The last of these professedly supernatural incidents took place about this time. His doctor, Alessandro Petronio, lay seriously ill. St. Ignatius went to visit him, tiptoed softly into the sick room, stayed a minute and then left without speaking. " What was that bright light which has filled the room ? " Petronio asked his wife. She told him that it was St. Ignatius, and from that moment the doctor began to mend.

The saint could cure the physician, but the physician could not cure the saint. As the summer of 1556 drew on St. Ignatius got weaker and weaker. It was clear, both to himself and to others, that the end was at hand. The functions of the General-ship he transferred to Polanco, Nadal and one Christopher Madrid, and he himself went to a country house near the convent of Sta. Balbina. There the fever took him and he grew worse instead of better. After two or three days he caused himself to be carried back to Rome, and there it was that he died on July 31st.

The end came, as it so often does, when it was least expected. I quote from Stewart Rose the circular letter which Polanco sent out to all the provincials a week afterwards.

" The Peace of Christ. I announce hereby to your reverence and to all the brethren who are under you that it has pleased God to call to Himself our blessed Father, Master Ignatius, early on Friday, the last of July. On the eve of St. Peter's Chains those chains were broken which bound him in the flesh and he was set in the liberty of the elect.

" God has heard at last the longings of His holy servant. For, though he bore his pilgrimage and the trials it brought upon'him with great patience and fortitude, yet he desired for many years past to see and praise his Creator and Lord in the heavenly country, Whose Divine Providence has left him to us hitherto, that his work in this small Society, which had begun through him, might better progress by his example, wisdom, prudence and prayers.

"Since your reverence will wish to hear something more of the dead Father, now in glory, you shall know that it was very easy, and it was almost an hour before we perceived that he had ceased to live. We had many sick in the house, and among them Father Master Laynez and Juan de Mendoza and some more, who were dangerously ill. Our Father also had a trifling illness and suffered four or five days from a fever, but very slightly; it was even doubtful if there were still any fever or not, though he was then, as at former times, extremely weak. In this condition he sent for me on Wednesday and desired me to tell Dr. Torres to attend him as he did the other patients; for, as we had not thought his indisposition considerable, the others were taken more care of than himself. Torres therefore watched him as well as another famous physician who is a friend of ours; Master Alessandro visited him every day. The next day (Thursday) he asked for me about two o'clock (i.e., 4 p.m.) and when he had sent the attendant out of the room he said it was time now that I should go to the Vatican, to inform His Holiness that he was near his end and had no longer any hope of temporal life; that he asked the blessing of His Holiness for himself and Master Laynez, who was also in danger, and that if God Our Lord granted them the mercy of being taken into heaven, they would there pray for His Holiness, as they had done daily on earth. I answered him, 'Father, the physicians see no danger in this illness, and I myself hope that God will preserve your reverence yet some years for His service. Do you find yourself as ill as the other?' He answered me, 'So ill that nothing remains for me but to give up my soul.' Then I expressed the hope I really had that he would live longer, but also said I would do what he desired, and asked him if it might wait till Friday, because I wanted to send letters that evening to Spain, by Genoa, and the post went on Thursday. He answered, 'I had rather it were done to-day, or the sooner the better; but do what you think best; I leave it entirely to you.' In order to learn from the judgment of the physicians if he was in danger, I that evening begged the principal of them, Master Alessandro, to tell me candidly if our Father were in danger, because he had charged me to announce this to the Pope. He answered me, ' To-day I can say nothing about his danger ; that must be to-morrow.'

" Under these circumstances, and as the Father had left it to me, I thought it best in human prudence to wait till the Friday and then obtain the opinion of the physician. On that same day, Thursday, at one in the evening (*i.e.*, 8 p.m.) Doctor Madrid and I were at the supper of our Father, who ate as well as he usually did, and conversed with us, so that I went to my room, not thinking of any danger from this illness. In the morning at sunrise we found our Father was dying, and immediately I went to the Vatican. The Pope showed sincere sympathy and gave him the fullest benediction that he could.

" And so he gave up his soul most peacefully to its Creator in the presence of Father Doctor Madrid and of Master Andreas Frusius, before the second hour after sunrise.

" When our Father was dead, we proceeded to embalm him as well as we could . . . and this caused greater wonder and edification ; for his stomach and abdomen were empty and shrivelled up, whence the physicians judged his abstinence to have been great in former times, and his fortitude, since in so much weakness he went about his laborious duties with such constant serenity. When they examined the liver, they found three small stones, which testified how true was what the good old man, Diego d'Eguia, said, that certainly our Father for a long time past was kept in life by a miracle. I, at least, cannot guess how, with a liver so diseased, he could have lived in a natural way, if God Our Lord had not provided for this organic disease and kept him in life while he was necessary to our Society.

" We deferred the interment of his holy remains till Saturday after vespers. The concourse of the pious and their devotion was very great, though he remained in the room where he had died ; some kissed his hand, some his feet or touched his body with their chaplets, along with our own

Fathers. We did all we could to keep off those who wanted to carry off a piece of his cap or clothes. Some painters made likenesses of him which he had never permitted during his lifetime, though many had asked leave. In the large chapel, on the Gospel side, in our own church, we made a little grave, in which his body, placed in a sarcophagus, after we had said the office as was customary, was deposited and a great stone placed on it, which can be removed whenever it is necessary. There he will remain, in some measure as waiting until another destination shall seem proper for him.

" The Doctor Olave went to the Pope to announce the decease, and his Holiness showed him much favour, expressing his liking for the Society which he had entertained through all its stages of progress. Some of the most influential Cardinals did the same, as well as many other friends who offered themselves liberally to the Society. Praised be God Our Lord, for He is our strength and hope. We have all offered the sacrifice three days for our Father, though some of us were impelled by a pious wish to ask his prayers rather than pray for him to God Our Lord. Nevertheless all that reason counsels should be done everywhere, both with regard to the three days' Masses and to the prayers of our brethren who are not priests. He had left thirteen provinces."

Laynez, of course, did not die. He survived to be St. Ignatius' successor in the Generalship.

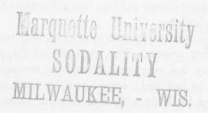

CHAPTER XVII

THE MEANING OF IGNATIUS

It would be easy to churn out a few thousand words in paraphrase of the Spiritual Exercises. I do not choose to do so. It would be easy, too, to examine again in detail the Constitutions of the Society and the record of St. Ignatius as a ruler of men, but, important as such an examination would be, I have not thoroughly attempted it in this book. Many others, more learned than I, have trod that path, and my fear was that, had I attempted to retread it, the reader's attention would have been distracted from the essential story on which I wish him to concentrate, and in the contemplation of Ignatius, the master of men, the features of Ignatius, the lover of God, would have been quite forgotten, as they have been only too frequently forgotten by the casual reading of the world. For the story on which I wish the reader to concentrate is the story of St. Ignatius' love affair.

I might have borrowed from the mystical theologians a more high-sounding description, but I have purposely chosen what will to some seem a vulgar phrase, seem perhaps to reek horribly of the novelette, because I wish for a common phrase, a phrase so simple that none can escape its meaning. And the first truth about St. Ignatius is that he was in love with God. Not until that first truth is understood can any of the further truths about him be properly comprehended.

The Ignatius of Manresa we cannot perhaps ever hope wholly to know. " It is a dangerous thing, it is too high a privilege," says Newman, " for sinners like ourselves to know the best and innermost thoughts of God's servants." But if you want a picture which proves how exact is the language which speaks of Ignatius as a lover, how close the parallel between his love

for God and our loves of the world, remember always that
wonderful story of him on the school-bench in Barcelona, his
mind straying off from the dull Latin in mystical day-dream,
as the wits of schoolboys wander to the beloved in the distractions of first love.

That he founded the Society, that he was almost the rebuilder
of Europe—these in the life of such a man were but secondary
things. None must misunderstand me when I say that they
were in a certain sense hardly more than unimportant accidents.
As Ferdinand made himself the " patient log-man " of Miranda,
so was St. Ignatius the " patient log-man " of God. God might
have set him to some petty, menial task. He would have been
glad, had it been so, for to such men as he public reputation is
a wearisome thing. " If he had only had his own desires to
follow," he said, " he would have cared nothing that men took
him for a lunatic, would have gone about with soleless shoes,
have shown uncovered the sores on his leg, have hung the
beggar's horn around his neck ; but all such things were of no
use for the saving of souls." The task which God, his Lover,
imposed upon him was the task of working in the world for the
salvation of souls. That task for his love's sake he accepted.

" The energy of the saints has left everywhere its dents upon
the world," finely writes Francis Thompson in *Health and Holiness*. " When these men, reviled for impotence, have turned
their half-disdainful hands to tasks approved by the multitude,
they have borne away the palm from the world in its own prized
exercises." Of no man is this more true than of St. Ignatius, to
the boys of Manresa " Father Sack," to Rome the confidant of
Popes, the adviser of Kings. Let us admire his greatness as an
organiser and as a ruler of men, but let us remember how small
he thought those gifts, how small indeed they were in comparison
with his greatness as a lover—*sicut palea*, like chaff, as St.
Thomas said of that knowledge to which philosophy had led
him, when he compared it with the knowledge of mystical
experience. " There is only one sorrow," M. Maritain quotes
a character in Léon Bloy's *La Femme Pauvre* as saying, " the
sorrow of not being a saint." " There is another, too," comes

the answer, " not to be sorrowful at not wishing to be a saint."
Both Ignatius Loyola and Thomas Aquinas would have agreed.

It is an accident of the Faith if it brings to us the joys of this
world. It is not of this world nor is its business with this world.
Its business is with holiness. Its business is not merely to teach
men to be good, but to teach them to live consciously in the
company of God. Every year on the mysterious feast of the
Body of Christ the Church bids us dare to pray that one day
we may come to share the very table of God.

> " *Tuos ibi commensales,*
> *Cohaeredes et sodales*
> *Fac sanctorum civium,*"

and as comfort and as proof that it is possible to come to this
tremendous comradeship God sends to us the saints—those
great men and women who, even when in this world, are not of
it, and to whom the comradeship of God is already the only
true reality. The world hardly knows what to make of these,
its strange master-spirits. Only the very foolish try to laugh
them away as fools. Only the very heroic are brave enough to
strive honestly to follow in their footsteps. And most men
abandon the attempt to understand and turn to other things with
a shrug and an " I daresay that there's something in it."

> "So the All-Great were the All-Loving, too.
> The madman saith Hé said so—it is strange."

Meanwhile, let us go and play billiards.

*   *   *   *   *

Those who look upon history as a record of predictable
evolution, and the actors in it as creatures of their inevitable
circumstances, may be able to explain away the statesmen and
the soldiers and the diplomats, but they cannot explain away the
saints. It is the promise of God that the gates of Hell shall not
prevail against His Church. " Though doomed to death," she
is, as Dryden puts it in his fine paradox, " yet fated not to die."
And it is, it seems, the design of His Providence that whenever,
as has happened again and again, that destruction seems at last
to be at hand, God raises up a saint through whom she is saved.

The saint comes from beyond this world, and none can foresee the moment or the manner of his coming. In the crumbling days of the Roman power none could have foretold how Rome was to survive her own death through the genius of St. Benedict. When the evil horrors of the East threatened the very heart of Christendom, who guessed that St. Dominic would come to save us? When anarchy made foul the whole face of France, would not anyone have been thought a madman who predicted that the deliverance would come in arms from a peasant girl of Domrémy? And so, too, in the corruptions and confusions of the 16th century, none guessed, or could have guessed, that salvation was to come not from Pope or Emperor or reformer, but from a lame Spanish gentleman, a little dwarf, from out the high mountains where Charlemagne had fought and Roland died. These things cannot be known nor understood, for our world is interlocked with another world that is not ours and the workings of which are not revealed to us.

When the disciples argued among themselves as to who was the greatest in the Kingdom of Heaven, Our Lord gave to them no encouragement in their foolish competition. God sends His especial servants each to his especial work. There is no precedence nor order of merit among them. I will not attempt the stupidity of comparing St. Ignatius with any of his fellow-saints. It is enough to record that, if it be the purpose of Man to love God with all his heart and to serve Him with all his mind, then there has not yet been among men a greater than Ignatius of Loyola. And we who live out our petty, passing days of laughter and sorrow, failure and success, should turn again and again, as to a magic spring, to that great soul, whom God sent to us as a reminder of the awful permanence of the eternal things.

St. Ignatius, pray for us that we may pray with you. " *Suscipe, Domine, universam meam libertatem. Accipe memoriam, intellectum atque voluntatem omnem. Quidquid habeo, vel possideo, mihi largitus es ; id tibi totum restituo, ac tuae prorsus voluntati trado gubernandum. Amorem tui solum, cum gratia tua, mihi dones, et dives sum satis, nec aliud quidquam ultra posco.*"